Joseph Reed

NUMBER 595
COLUMBIA STUDIES IN THE SOCIAL SCIENCES
EDITED BY THE FACULTY OF POLITICAL SCIENCE
OF COLUMBIA UNIVERSITY

JOSEPH REED

PORTRAIT BY CHARLES WILLSON PEALE

Independence National Historical Park Collection

Joseph Reed

A MODERATE IN THE AMERICAN REVOLUTION

by JOHN F. ROCHE

COLUMBIA UNIVERSITY PRESS

NEW YORK, 1957

The Columbia Studies in the Social Sciences (formerly the Studies in History, Economics, and Public Law) is a series edited by the Faculty of Political Science of Columbia University and published by Columbia University Press for the purpose of making available scholarly studies produced within the Faculty.

LIBRARY OF CONGRESS CATALOG CARD NUMBER: 57-7187

COPYRIGHT © 1954 COLUMBIA UNIVERSITY PRESS, NEW YORK
FIRST PUBLISHED IN BOOK FORM 1957

PUBLISHED IN GREAT BRITAIN, CANADA, INDIA, AND PAKISTAN
BY THE OXFORD UNIVERSITY PRESS
LONDON, TORONTO, BOMBAY, AND KARACHI

MANUFACTURED IN THE UNITED STATES OF AMERICA

To My Father

Preface

THE career of Joseph Reed illuminates the critical problem of the moderate man caught up in the turbulence of revolution. Reed was twenty-two when the Revolutionary era of American history opened in 1763, and his death in 1785 came only fourteen months after ratification of the Peace of Paris marked the victorious termination of the War of Independence. His mature life, then, is identical in time with the vibrant years when a new nation was born.

For many Americans of this era the separation from Great Britain worked no violent wrenching of treasured ties. Concentration on the great work of developing an American future weakened the sense of vital identification with an old link—perhaps several generations in the past now—to the mother country. Then, too, when that link was snapped and independence was proclaimed, the domestic impact was relatively slight. For most Americans there was no violent alteration in internal political mores or balance of interests, no abrupt economic or social reorientation.

Joseph Reed was not among this fortunate group for whom the Revolution, the sufferings of the actual war apart, was an almost benign change. America's union with Britain was, for him, a deeply treasured one. He had studied law at the venerable Inns of Court in London, he married an English girl there, he had seriously contemplated taking up permanent residence in England. Thus, in the angry years preceding Lexington, while he called upon his English friends to acknowledge the just claims of the colonists he also counseled moderation and patience upon his fellow Americans. Then came the time for decision—and for service: service as Washington's secretary, as adjutant general of the Continental Army, as member of the Continental Congress. The esteemed tie with Britain was resolutely broken.

In his adopted state of Pennsylvania, the Revolution produced
an internal upheaval toward political and economic democracy
far more radical than in any other part of America. Amid the
bitter partisanships thereby engendered, calls for moderation were
rare and somewhat suspect. But Reed believed that the success of
both the War for Independence and necessary democratic changes
at home required harmony between the Pennsylvania factions,
and he offered himself as a mediator between them.

Though his career aptly illustrates the dilemma of the man who
would preserve stability amid rapid change, though he was a supporting actor in most of the great scenes of the Revolution and
a central figure in more than a few of them, Reed has not hitherto
been the subject of special study and analysis. With only one
major exception all the works on him have been unfortunate
prolongations of a political controversy, the Cadwalader-Reed
controversy, in which he was involved in the last two years of his
life. The scurrility and bitterness of these writings have hidden
Reed's solid contributions and have undoubtedly confused and
repelled the would-be investigator of his career.

The exception noted above is the two-volume *Life and Correspondence of Joseph Reed* published by Reed's grandson, William
B. Reed, in 1847. The title, authorship, and date indicate both
the merits and shortcomings of this work. The carefully preserved manuscripts of Joseph Reed on which the volumes were
based gave them an authenticity and value which continue to
render them important and convenient tools for today's student
of the Revolution. More than three-fourths of each volume is
composed of the texts of letters written by Reed or written to
him. Yet the work cannot be considered as a publication of the
Reed manuscripts, for many papers in this collection, some of
major importance, do not appear in the volumes, and in other
cases only excerpts are given. It should also be mentioned that
the transcription from the manuscripts does not display a high
degree of accuracy.

The present study, though also based primarily upon these
same Reed manuscripts (now in the collection of the New-York

Historical Society), is not intended as an attempt toward an edition of this source material. Rather, it seeks to perform the service which William B. Reed essayed but sketchily and with understandable preconceptions, a critical narrative of Reed's life and an estimate of his contributions in the Revolutionary era. An effort has also been made to give some picture of Reed's early years and professional career, topics almost entirely neglected by his grandson biographer.

I am indebted to many individuals and to the staffs of many institutions for assistance in preparing this book. It has grown out of doctoral research carried on under the direction of Professor Richard B. Morris of Columbia University. I am deeply grateful to him for introducing me to the career of Joseph Reed, for his invaluable counsel, and for his warm interest in this study. My obligations to many others at Columbia are heavy, particularly to Professor Dumas Malone and to the staffs of the Butler and Law School libraries. At the New-York Historical Society, Mr. Wayne Andrews and Mr. Wilmer R. Leech of the manuscripts division were most generous in assisting me, and to Miss Catherine H. Miller of the same division at the Historical Society of Pennsylvania I must express a particular appreciation too.

For special service and assistance from which I profited greatly I also wish to thank Mr. Edward B. Morrison, manuscripts division, New York Public Library; Dr. Guy S. Klett, Research Historian, Presbyterian Historical Society; Miss Edna Huntington, Librarian, Long Island Historical Society; Mr. Alexander Clark, manuscripts division, Princeton University Library; Miss Maude Greene, librarian of the New Jersey Historical Society; Dr. Clifford K. Shipton of the American Antiquarian Society; Dr. Kenneth Boyce of the Morgan Library; Mr. Edwin Wolf, 2d, Library Company of Philadelphia; and Mr. Roger H. McDonough, Division of Archives and History, New York State Library.

Mr. Henry Hope Reed has shown a keen interest in this biography of his great-great-grandfather. He materially aided the research by turning over to the New-York Historical Society for addition to the Reed manuscripts there a collection of nearly one

hundred letters to or from Joseph Reed which were in his possession. Another descendant of Joseph Reed, Mrs. Arthur N. Starin
of Philadelphia, provided valuable genealogical information.

Finally, I express my indebtedness to my father, Michael J.
Roche, for his encouragement and many valuable suggestions and
for his assistance in editing the manuscript.

JOHN F. ROCHE

Fordham University, New York
September, 1956

Contents

Joseph Reed

CHAPTER I

The Student

ON October 20, 1763, the British transport ship *Dragon* cast off from its dock in Philadelphia, moved out into the current of the Delaware, and dropped down the river toward the sea, bound for London.[1] Those Philadelphians who saw the ship off returned to their homes and shops and spoke to their families and friends of seeing merchants, royal officials, and returning army officers depart for England. It is doubtful whether any on the Philadelphia dock took notice of young Joseph Reed, another of the *Dragon*'s passengers. Yet the name of this twenty-two-year-old Jerseyite, bound for advanced law studies at London's Middle Temple, was to be written in much larger letters in the history of Pennsylvania and of its capital than those of his fellow passengers.

There were few portents of the linking of Joseph Reed and Pennsylvania history in 1763. It is true that even at this time the young lawyer was not entirely unknown in Philadelphia. He and his brother Bowes had been among the first students enrolled in the Philadelphia Academy, and their father, Andrew, was a well-known figure in the bustling mercantile life of the city during a four-year residence there in the early 1750's. But this sojourn had been only a temporary uprooting from Trenton, New Jersey, the home of the Reed family for decades.

The first member of the Reed family in America had not made his way directly to that quiet town. Young Joseph Reed's grandfather, also a Joseph, left his home in Carrickfergus on Belfast Lough in 1671 and crossed the Atlantic to Massachusetts in the ship *Arabella*. He lived successively in Lynn and in Salem, and may have been the "Joseph Read, malster" who appears on the Salem County tax list of 1683.[2] The time of his removal from Massachusetts to New Jersey cannot be ascertained, but as to motive, it is to be suspected that Reed, staunch Presbyterian as he was, found the cultural climate of New Jersey much more congenial than that of the Bay Colony.

Reed did not, apparently, attain any great prominence in Trenton. He built up a small mercantile business and did attain the title of "Esquire," but upon his death in 1737 the administration of his estate was granted to his principal creditors, merchants Matthew Clarkson and Anthony Duane of New York City.[3] Reed's widow, Anne, lived until 1744, long enough to see the birth of a grandson named for her husband.[4]

Before their deaths, Joseph and Anne had seen the stock of their sons Thomas, Joseph, and Andrew rise in the little community. In 1734, Trenton's first post office was established at their house, with Andrew as postmaster. The latter was empowered to receive letters and deliver them in Trenton and the countryside near the town. In keeping with the practice of most colonial postmasters, he supplemented his official income by selling subscriptions to the offerings of New York and Philadelphia publishers, among them the sermons of George Whitefield.[5] In 1736, Andrew was one of the Presbyterian congregation who issued the call to the Reverend David Cowell to become their pastor.[6]

In 1739, Andrew's wife, Sarah Pearson, died, leaving two daughters, Elizabeth and Sarah. Eighteen months later Andrew married again. His second wife was Theodosia Bowes, daughter of Francis Bowes, a well-to-do counselor and landowner of Hunterdon County.[7] Theodosia was to bear Andrew six children, only four of whom were to survive childhood. Of these, Joseph was the first-born.

Joseph Reed was born at Trenton on August 27, 1741.[8] The town at that time boasted some one hundred houses, built, as the traveler Peter Kalm observed, partly of stone, generally two stories in height with the side rather than the front of the house on the street, and with a garden and well along the opposite side. On King Street stood the Hunterdon County Court House and the jail, built about 1730. The Quaker meetinghouse and the Presbyterian church were outstanding landmarks, as was the Stacy Mill, nucleus of the growing industries of the town. Primarily a market town, Trenton drew additional importance by virtue of its position on the main route from New York to Philadelphia.[9]

Young Joseph was to spend the first nine years of his life in Trenton in the company of his half-sisters, Elizabeth and Sarah, and two sisters and two brothers, Ann, Mary, John, and Bowes, who came after him to swell the Reed family. Theodosia was a good mother, described by her sister Rachel as a "pattern of Duty and love to all that she had any connection with." [10] For her and their children, Andrew Reed was a diligent provider. Some twenty years later his daughter Sarah's husband, Charles Pettit, was to remark that Andrew's "vigorous days have been spent in a toilsome application to Business, in which he accumulated a Sufficient Stock to carry him comfortably thro' Life and give his Children a handsome setting out in the world." [11]

The business to which Joseph's father was applying himself so assiduously was of considerable complexity and extent by the mid '40's. He followed his father's lead in building up a mercantile business and apparently speculated in West New Jersey land as well. Then, in 1743, he joined with his father-in-law, Francis Bowes, and another partner, Joseph Peace, in buying the Black's Creek or Bordentown Iron Forge in Burlington County. Reed sold his shares several years later, but his interest in the iron industry by no means ended. In 1752 he handled part of the sale of a quarter interest in the Mount Holly Iron Works and was undoubtedly a shareholder himself. In 1764 he and Charles Pettit bought a number of the properties of the Kingwood Forge at Pittstown in Hunterdon County.[12]

Meanwhile, Andrew Reed's part in the public affairs of Trenton in the years immediately following Joseph's birth became an increasingly prominent one. In 1744 he was chosen loan officer of Hunterdon County in an election whose informality irked Governor Lewis Morris.[13] When King George II granted a charter in 1745 incorporating Trenton as a free borough town, Reed was named in the charter as one of the burgesses and as treasurer of the borough.[14]

Despite this progress in Trenton, Andrew decided, sometime in 1750, to move to Philadelphia. Perhaps it was the greater commercial opportunities which beckoned him there. However, since one of his first acts after getting settled in the Quaker City was to enter Joseph and Bowes in the Academy of Philadelphia, it may be that the desire to provide for the proper education of his sons was a motive of more than minor importance.

The Philadelphia Academy, from which the College of Philadelphia and then the University of Pennsylvania were to develop, opened its doors on January 7, 1751. The trustees, of whom Benjamin Franklin was the leading figure, had purchased the "New Building" in Fourth Street below Arch in 1750. Alterations were made in the building, books and equipment were purchased, and teachers were recruited from Philadelphia and its environs. Finally, on December 11, 1750, the trustees gave notice of the opening date on the first Monday of January next. The announcement stated that the youths would be taught "the Latin, Greek, English, French and German Languages together with History, Geography, Chronology, Logic and Rhetoric; also Writing, Arithmetic, Merchants Accounts, Geometry, Algebra, Surveying, Gauging, Navigation, Astronomy, mechanical Philosophy, etc." [15] The exceptionally broad curriculum owed much to Franklin's insistence upon adding courses in science and the modern languages to the traditional program of classical languages, religion, and rhetoric.[16]

Joseph and Bowes were entered in the Academy by their father early in its first year, 1751, and continued to attend there until the family moved back to Trenton in 1753.[17] Joseph was probably enrolled in the Latin School, presided over by Francis Alison, the rector of the Academy. Doubtless he wrestled with his mathematics under the watchful eye of Theophilus Grew and, in his English classes, felt the bite of the sarcastic tongue of the forceful and able David Dove. The Academy boasted one hundred and forty-five pupils in its first year and a teaching staff of three assistants in addition to Masters Alison, Grew, and Dove.[18]

The family's sojourn in Philadelphia was terminated tragically by the death of Joseph's mother on March 19, 1753. The children were sent back to Trenton soon after her burial, their father joining them a short time later, after he had tied up the loose ends of his business affairs in Philadelphia.[19] Though Joseph was only twelve years old at this time, his father, pleased by the aptitude for serious study shown by the boy at the Academy, decided to send him on to college immediately. The institution he selected was the College of New Jersey at Newark, now in its sixth year. A Presbyterian school and the closest college to Trenton at the time, it was a natural choice.[20]

The president of the College of New Jersey in 1753 was the scholarly and gracious Reverend Aaron Burr, father of the future vice president of the United States. The burden of nursing the college through its infancy had been thrust upon Burr when the first president, Jonathan Dickinson, died only three months after the school was opened at Elizabeth in 1747. The student body of eight was thereupon moved to Burr's parsonage in Newark, and in 1748 he was officially named as Dickinson's successor.[21] For nine years the only college edifice was Burr's own house, and the college library was Burr's collection of the classics and works on religion. Classes probably were held in his parlor. A fortunate few among the student body resided in spare rooms in the president's home; the rest roomed in the homes of neighbors.[22]

When Joseph Reed entered the college on September 26, 1753,[23] the original student body of eight had expanded to about forty and President Burr now required the assistance of two tutors, Jonathan Badger and Alexander Gordon. No room being available in the Burr home, Joseph was obliged to live with the family of a neighbor, Colonel Baldwin. The charge for lodging and meals there averaged a little over nine shillings a week. Tuition charges amounted to only three pounds a year, making expenses at New Jersey lower than those at any other colonial college.[24]

Though no letters from Reed written during his college days have survived, his account with the Reverend Mr. Burr, the college records, and the letters of other students which have been preserved give much information on this important period in his early life. The close ties of the institution to the Presbyterian Church were borne out in its program and regulations. Every morning and evening the students met with the president for prayers and scripture readings. Attendance at some Divine Service on Sunday (not necessarily at the Presbyterian church) was obligatory and offenders were liable to a fine of four pence. Students who frequented taverns or kept company with persons of ill repute were liable to be expelled, as were those who played with cards or dice. A student caught leaving Newark without official permission incurred a heavy fine of five shillings.[25]

Joseph's freshman course of study was heavily weighted along the traditional lines of classical languages. The entrance requirements emphasized with reason the ability to translate Virgil, Cicero, and the Gospels in Greek, for Latin and Greek together with mathematics constituted the heart of the first year's program. The language studies were based upon the works of Xenophon, Cicero, Virgil, and Tully, and included an introduction to Hebrew as well. Reed's account with Burr gives evidence of other elements in the freshman curriculum; in March, 1754, he was charged for a scale and divider, and in April for a copy of Watt's *Logic*. Rhetoric, geography, and astronomy also appeared, though quite irregularly, in the program of studies.[26]

The boy's non-academic accounts with the president during his first year reveal an advance of eleven shillings for a journey home, occasioned perhaps by home sickness, an entry for having shoes made and mended, and payment of six shillings to the barber for "one-half year Sheaving," which, in the case of a twelve-year-old, must have meant hair cutting. Joseph was apparently hard on his clothes or else was becoming clothes conscious, for his bill with Mr. Riggs, a tailor, came to almost seven pounds.[27]

When Joseph became a sophomore in the fall of 1754 his course of study, though still revolving about classical reading, shifted more emphasis to science. Astronomy now became a major part of the curriculum, as did natural philosophy. Mathematics continued to hold its important place in the program.[28] Reed also took up the study of French late in his sophomore year. In June, 1755, he purchased a grammar and paid for a French text. In August he was charged a little over one pound for "French Schooling," indicating that instruction in this language was outside the regular course of study.[29]

Undoubtedly the most absorbing interest of all at the college in 1754 and 1755, from the president down to the youngest freshman, was the progress being made toward the erection of a spacious college building at Princeton. As early as 1748 the trustees, with Governor Belcher in the lead, had discussed obtaining a permanent site for the school. No definite action was taken, however, until 1751 when the trustees voted to move the college to New Brunswick if the people of that town would raise one thousand pounds for the college, grant it ten acres of cleared land for a campus, and also turn over two hundred acres of woodland not more than three miles from the town. Informed of this action, the inhabitants of Princeton, anxious for the trade and prestige the college would bring to their town, made a counter offer. A stalemate resulted which lasted more than a year. Finally, in the fall of 1752, New Brunswick having failed to comply with the above conditions, the board voted to move the college to Princeton when that town met the specified terms, thanks in particular to the efforts of Nathaniel FitzRandolph, a Quaker.[30]

In July, 1754, land was broken at Princeton for the college edifice, Nassau Hall.[31] Planned by Robert Smith and Dr. William Shippen of Philadelphia, the building was to measure one hundred and seventy-seven by fifty-four feet. Lecture rooms, a library room, a prayer hall, a dining room, living quarters for the faculty, and rooms for the accommodation of one hundred and forty-seven students (with three to a room) were all provided for under the one roof. By the late summer of 1756, the end of Reed's junior year, the building was ready for occupancy.[32]

The last commencement at Newark was held in September. Shortly thereafter President Burr took leave of his congregation and accompanied by four tutors and some seventy students set out for the new home of the college. The formal opening of the new school year at Princeton was held on November 13.[33]

Joseph Reed, at fifteen years of age, was now a senior in the college. He studied ethics, natural science, the classics as always, and could, at his option, pursue studies in mathematics and even navigation.[34] He was becoming quite the young gentleman, as account items for the rental of horses, for the making of green breeches and a vest, and for the mending of his wig testify.[35] The living quarters in the wings of Nassau Hall were plain but comfortable. The college provided a bed and mattress, a table and chairs. The students supplied their own linens, blankets, and rugs.[36] The Reed family must have been pleased to have Joseph so much closer to home, and Andrew was undoubtedly impressed by the savings in traveling and boarding expenses, for it has been estimated that charges for board in private homes (as at Newark) ran about 30 percent above those for equivalent services in college halls.[37]

Joseph Reed was graduated from the College of New Jersey with the degree of Bachelor of Arts on October 28, 1757. But the occasion was not a festive one. Only four days before commencement, the first at Princeton, the beloved president, Reverend Aaron Burr, had died. Presiding in his place was William Smith, one of the trustees, as twenty-two candidates received their bachelor's degrees and four candidates their master's degrees. The thirty shilling diploma fee from each of the graduates was turned over to Mrs. Burr, and on the following day the trustees voted to invite her father, the Reverend Jonathan Edwards, to succeed her husband as president of the college.[38]

Reed's connections with the College of New Jersey and with the little town of Princeton were not severed by the end of his undergraduate work at the college. For the next three years he was considered to be "in residence" as he carried on the reading and self-directed study which brought him, at the age of nineteen, his Master of Arts degree on September 24, 1760.[39] Actually, Reed really was residing in Princeton during these years. Having decided upon law as a career and quite evidently having displayed real ability in college, he was accepted as a clerk in the office of the town's most distinguished citizen and one of the province's outstanding attorneys, Richard Stockton.

Stockton himself was an alumnus of the College of New Jersey, a member of its first graduating class in 1748. He studied law under David Ogden, obtained his license as an attorney in 1754, and began practicing in Princeton that same year. He attained the rank of Counselor in 1758.[40]

Reed probably entered Stockton's Princeton office early in 1758. Personal letters or papers dealing with his five years of clerkship are apparently non-existent. It is likely, however, that his experiences differed but little from those of all the budding lawyers in the colonies, for clerkship was, at that time, the only means of preparing for a legal career. The clerk usually paid a sum to the mentor at the outset, promised to serve a certain number of years (usually five), and agreed to be faithful, obedient, and discreet, to abjure marriage, and to avoid all manner of company and places which might injure his master's reputation. In return the attorney promised to instruct the clerk in the law and usually paid the latter a miserably small salary. Room and board at the master's house were customarily provided for the clerk.[41]

The lot of the law clerk was not an easy one. The duties were difficult and exacting, and more often than not the attorney was most grudging in providing the tutelage and direction he had promised. But even a moderately well-equipped law office would have copies of *Coke on Littleton,* Finch's *On Law,* and Wood's *Institutes of the Laws of England.* It was from these treatises rather than from formal instruction that most of the neophyte attorneys acquired a proficiency in their field.[42]

Reed reached the end of this rather grueling period in 1763. On May 14 of that year William Franklin, governor of New Jersey, issued a certificate which proclaimed that he,

being well assured of the Integrity, Learning and ability of Joseph Reed Gent: Have thought fit to constitute and appoint him Attorney at Law, hereby authorizing him to appear in all his Majesty's Courts of Record within the Province of New Jersey, and there to practice as an Attorney at Law according to the Laws and Customs of Great Britain and the Laws and Customs of this Province of New Jersey.[43]

It was undoubtedly William Franklin who convinced Reed that he should round off his legal education by study in England at the venerable Inns of Court. Franklin himself had enrolled in the Middle Temple in 1757 when he had accompanied his illustrious father, Benjamin Franklin, to England.[44] Stockton also, judging by the sentiments expressed in the letters he sent to Joseph in England, urged this step. Reed was highly receptive to the idea. Whatever opposition was encountered at home was worn down and overcome in the summer of 1763. And thus it was that on that October day, Joseph Reed, carrying a letter in which the governor recommended him "as a friend of mine, and a person of merit," [45] stood on the deck of the *Dragon* and watched the spires of Philadelphia disappear from sight as the ship headed down the Delaware, bound for London.

CHAPTER II

England: Law and Love

WHEN Joseph Reed left America for England's Inns of Court, he was following a tradition which had become well established by 1763. For aspiring colonial attorneys who could meet the very considerable expenses involved, attendance at those venerable institutions brought prestige, knowledge, and "address" which promised a successful career back in Charleston, Philadelphia, or New York. Edmund Randolph, William Byrd II, Charles Carroll, John Dickinson, James Alexander, and Thomas Hutchinson, to name but a few, had preceded Reed to either the Inner or Middle Temple in the shadow of Westminster.[1]

Actually, the eighteenth century was a period of retrogression for the Inns. The old forms persisted, but little of the substance of instruction, guidance, and screening of candidates remained. A contemporary critic complained that the requirements for a call to the bar consisted solely of paying the necessary fees at the Inn and producing "a certificate of having dined a certain number of times in the hall of the inn."[2] This was substantially correct: to be credited with a term's attendance (there were four terms in the year) one's presence "at the time when Grace after dinner is said" for merely three days of the term sufficed.[3] Consequently, the student was left in the main to his own resources. Those who were conscientious supplemented their self-directed reading and study by attending the courts or by paying a fee to obtain a desk and some firsthand experience in the office of an established attorney or solicitor.[4] The unsatisfactory nature of the training at the Middle Temple was to be a contributing factor in the brevity of Reed's attendance there.

These disappointments were in the unforeseeable future as the *Dragon* plowed through the long swells of the North Atlantic. The unfamiliar world of ship and sea was exciting to one with as quick and inquisitive a mind as young Reed. Whatever pleasures the voyage brought were forgotten, however, in the terror of a nearly fatal gale on the last leg of the journey. While making its way through the English Channel the transport was caught in the great storm which struck England on the night of December 1. The *Dragon* managed to ride through to safety, but several packet ships were not as fortunate.[5]   To the sophisticated traveler the arrival in London would have been an anticlimax after this narrow escape. But to one who regarded Philadelphia as a great city, the size, the noise, and the confusion of London were overwhelming and stimulating.[6]

On December 16 Reed was formally enrolled at the Middle Temple. A sheet preserved among his papers records the payment of an entrance fee of six pounds, fourteen shillings, and six pence. Other fees were involved in the matriculation process: fees for meals, for the rental of a furnished room in the Garden Court buildings of the Temple, for the services of a laundress who also made the bed, and for a porter who kept one's shoes cleaned and one's cloak brushed. There is no evidence that Reed made any arrangements for working in an attorney's office, but this record of disbursements does reveal that he made provision, by paying the respective doorkeepers about a shilling each, for gaining entry to the House of Lords, the Court of King's Bench, and the Court of Common Pleas "for cases." [7]

Reed was determined to show his family and friends in America that his mind was on serious study, that he would not be "captivated with the Amusements and Pleasures of such a Place as this." [8]   All evidence indicates that his actions fitted his words. Acquaintances of Andrew Reed in England wrote to tell him of Joseph's praiseworthy conduct, and young Reed's former mentor, Richard Stockton, also received word of Joseph's "application." [9]

During his fifteen months at the Middle Temple, Reed had the company of five fellow Americans. Nicholas Waln of Philadelphia entered on the same day as Joseph and hence may have crossed with him in the *Dragon*. In 1764 William Hamilton of Philadelphia, Charles C. Pinckney of Charleston, and John Matthews, also of South Carolina, enrolled. They were joined early in 1765 by another man destined to distinguish himself in South Carolina, Thomas Hayward.[10]

An even closer personal link to home was provided for Reed during his attendance at the Temple by the presence in London of his distant cousin and fellow graduate of the Class of 1757 at Princeton, Stephen Sayre. Sayre, five years Reed's senior, was a native of Southampton, New York. He had followed up his undergraduate studies by obtaining two master's degrees in 1760, one from the College of New Jersey, the other from Harvard.[11] He failed to settle upon a career, however, giving early indications of that "impetuous and rash nature which often involved him in difficulties and which prevented him all his life from any solid accomplishment."[12] In 1762 he was employed by the Penn family and Pennsylvanians interested in the lands of the Wyoming Valley to gather information on the claims put forward by a Connecticut group known as the Susquehanna Company to that same area. In May, 1762, Sayre visited Connecticut, gathered important data there, and then sailed for England where his findings were utilized by the Penns in a hearing before the Board of Trade.[13] Sayre was still in England when Reed arrived late in 1763, and in fact not until 1793 was he once again to take up residence in America. By the time Reed reached London, Sayre, the possessor of a very charming manner, was already quite the young man about town and was diligently in pursuit of a wife with a fortune.[14] After Reed left the Middle Temple and returned to America, he and Sayre remained in contact with one another thanks to connections which will be described below.

It is not apparent that Reed formed firm friendships with any of his fellow Americans at the Temple. With his friends in Trenton and Philadelphia, however, he maintained close ties through the medium of an extensive correspondence. Joseph was very faithful in writing to his father: Andrew acknowledged the receipt of twelve letters between April 5 and June 20, 1764, grudgingly admitting that "I can not charge you with any neglect."[15] The elder Reed, however, failed to reciprocate in kind. Among the letters Joseph received in London there are only three from his father. The most faithful correspondent, and a most excellent one, was Charles Pettit, Joseph's brother-in-law and now partner with his father in the mercantile firm of Reed and Pettit. His long letters contained a wealth of detail on family news and business and political affairs in Philadelphia and Trenton, sprinkled with words of encouragement for the young student and occasional words of advice proffered with affection and understanding. Other correspondents with whom Reed exchanged more than an occasional letter were his brother Bowes, Richard Stockton, Daniel Coxe, Jr., and Isaac Allen of Trenton, Moore Furman of Philadelphia, former business partner of Joseph's father, and Abraham Hunt, a leading Trenton merchant related to the Reeds by marriage.

All at home were anxious to obtain the latest news as to the government's political and commercial policy. Reed made it a point to attend debates on American affairs in the House of Commons and did his best to supply his friends with the latest information.[16] Pettit, for example, asked Reed for news as to Parliament's action respecting trade in molasses, for he and Andrew Reed had begun to operate a distillery in April, 1764, and held high hopes for substantial profits if the molasses trade were not "too much cramped." [17] In addition to supplying this information Reed sent copies of the Parliamentary resolves of March, 1764, to John Cox, supplied Richard Stockton with details of the Grenville acts and of the state of the bar in England, and sent Governor William Franklin an estimate of the character of Frederick Smyth, newly appointed chief justice for New Jersey.[18]

In addition to acting as a channel of news for his family and friends in America, Reed carried out with apparent good grace many petty commissions for them,[19] and performed that inescapable duty of the American in England, namely, visiting the English friends and relatives of American acquaintances. Governor Franklin sent a gracious note expressing his gratitude for a task which Joseph had performed for him; John Coxe, Jr. appointed Reed his agent for the purchase of lands in America held by English owners, and his father and brother-in-law made him their agent in settling the affairs of a privateer, the *Britannia,* in which

they owned shares.[20]   Pettit also asked Reed to be on the alert
for opportunities to buy American lands.   In this respect Joseph
wrote back that bargains were becoming rare, as "People here begin to know more of their land Values than previously and many
conceive a very extravagent one of it." [21]

The letters from home bearing these requests also brought interesting expressions of a common theme: Parliament's postwar
political and economic program meant stagnation and ruin for
the American colonies.   Charles Pettit wrote that unless the terms
of the Grenville acts were relaxed or a new market found for
American produce, "our navigation must be reduced to about
one Half its present standard and our Imports from Great Britain
must immediately abate."   In that event, Pettit continued,
America would build up its own manufacturing industry and the
British would then see "tho' too late, that they have destroyed the
usefullness of the Colonies to Great Britain." [22]   In a similar vein
Moore Furman cried:

Commerce where art thou fled, Thou that so lately seemed to thrive
on Our happy Shores, at Once to quit us and leave us in almost total
Eclipse?   What can our mother, as she is pleased to stile herself, think
will be the Consequence, first to us, and then to herself? [23]

Stockton wrote that America must be represented in the House of
Commons "or else we shall be fleeced to some purpose." [24]   Young
John Coxe of Trenton was more belligerent.   Calling the Parliamentary acts "very arbitrary and oppressive in our present
infant State," he declared that higher imposts brought smuggling
rather than increased revenue, and remarked darkly that smuggling "ever produces murmering and discontent, and generally
ends in Rebellion." [25]

Unfortunately, Reed's replies to these observations have all
been lost, with the sole exception of his letter of June 11, 1764,
written to Stockton.   In this letter Reed praised the efforts of
Richard Jackson, agent for Pennsylvania, to moderate the ministerial plans, and castigated Henry Ellis, governor of Georgia from
1757 to 1760, for "an extravagent proposal of raising £500,000
per annum from the colonies."   Reed went on to blame "the ex-

aggerated accounts the officers from America have given of its opulence and of our manners of living" for the "very high false idea of our capacity to bear a part in the national expenses. The unpopularity of the present ministry prevents their attempting to raise any new imposition here." [26]

While Reed continued to maintain his ties with home and a high interest in developments there, he made new connections in England as well. Favored by a letter of recommendation from Governor Franklin, he became friendly with Richard Jackson, member of Parliament and colonial agent for Connecticut and Pennsylvania. Thomas Ruston, a fellow alumnus of the college of New Jersey now studying medicine at Edinburgh, tried to lure Reed to Scotland, but reluctantly had to admit that there would be little profit in studying law there since Scotland's legal system was so different from that of England and of the American colonies.[27] Reed became known in the society of Bath as well as in that of London.[28] Of all the new contacts the young law student made, however, none was nearly so important as that with Dennys DeBerdt and his family.

When Reed met Dennys DeBerdt shortly after his arrival in London in December, 1763, that worthy gentleman was then nearly seventy years old. Descended from a Flemish family which had fled to England seeking religious toleration, Dennys, by 1763, had become a leader among the London exporting merchants engaged in trade with the American colonies.[29] One of DeBerdt's American customers was the firm of Reed and Pettit. When Joseph left America for England, therefore, he carried letters from his father introducing him to the London merchant, and it was to the care of DeBerdt that letters from America were addressed to Reed in London.

Dennys and his wife Martha received the young student very cordially. For Reed, as for other Americans in London before him,[30] the DeBerdt home on Artillery Court in northeast London became a second home. Before long he became a regular Sunday dinner guest [31] and during the summer a frequent weekend guest at the DeBerdt country home at Enfield, a quiet country town some nine miles from London. With Dennis DeBerdt, the merchant's only son, Reed attended the London theatres.[32] But a much closer attachment between the DeBerdt family and the young American was in the making. Within a few months of Joseph's arrival in London, a romance had blossomed between him and DeBerdt's only daughter, Esther.

When they first met in December, 1763, Esther, at seventeen, was five years Joseph's junior.[33] A portrait painted later in her short life shows her to be, in the words of her grandson biographer, "slight of frame, with light hair, and fair complexion, and an air of sprightly intelligence and refinement." [34] The serious young law student quickly recognized in the deeply religious and genteel young woman a kindred spirit.

The path of the young lovers was not to be a smooth one, however. When Reed wrote a formal letter of proposal in September, 1764, he met with a rebuff, not indeed from Esther, but from Mr. DeBerdt, who evidently felt that a colonial without an independent fortune, a man who would be largely dependent upon his earnings as a lawyer, was not an ideal husband for his daughter.[35] DeBerdt forbade Esther to see or correspond with Joseph in an attempt to bring the matter to a close, but all to no avail. Aided by John Macpherson, a doughty sea captain of Philadelphia who had business dealings with Mr. DeBerdt and was often at the latter's home, the pair continued to carry on a correspondence and soon became secretly engaged. The family impasse was thus described in one of these letters from Esther to Joseph:

My Parents have not the least suspicion of our Correspondence; my Father seems very well satisfied that you have given it [Reed's proposal] up as [a] thing impossible and the other day he said, Mr. Reed must see I have treated him with a great deal of tenderness, yet at the same time taken care of my Daughter . . . . Mamma is often saying you have intirely forgot it, tho' in her own mind I believe she does not think it . . . and I am often telling her I fancy otherwise.

In the same letter Esther mentioned the visits to her home of a wealthy merchant whom her father regarded favorably as a possible son-in-law, though as yet there had been no proposal forthcoming from him. Esther's own sentiments were vigorously stated: " I can assure you my cold water is ready, but if he gives me no Opportunity I can't fling it on." [36]

First Mrs. DeBerdt and then Mr. DeBerdt came to realize that their injunctions had not crippled the romance between Reed and their daughter. Esther's mother apparently prevailed upon her husband to relax his stand so that he, while continuing to oppose a formal engagement until such time as Reed should settle permanently in England, permitted Joseph and Esther to see each other freely again.[37] He apparently had little realization of their deep attachment, however, until he witnessed his daughter's grief when Reed took leave of her to return to America in February, 1765. "My Father," Esther wrote Reed, "was a good deal Affected at our Parting, and my Brother said he did not think it [the romance] was gone so far. I strove hard to stiffle those Tears, but it was impossible." [38]

Reed's departure for America and the long-standing imminence of this move was in many ways a more serious obstacle to the romance than the opposition of Esther's parents. When Joseph left home in October, 1763, his father was not well, and throughout the period of his stay in England he continued to receive disquieting news concerning Andrew's health and stability. As early as June, 1764, his brother Bowes was entreating Joseph to return, exclaiming that their father's conduct was so erratic and his disposition so ill-natured that "I think I can't possibly live with him without he alters very soon." [39] Matters between Joseph's father and brother came to such a pass that, despite the efforts of Charles Pettit to act as peacemaker, Bowes was banished from the Reed home and the mention of his name was barred from conversation there.[40]

Pettit was equally unsuccessful in curbing his father-in-law's rashness in the conduct of their partnership. The elder Reed quarreled with almost everyone he came into contact with, drank to excess, antagonized customers, and, in the face of the gathering business depression, made no move toward economizing.[41] Pettit and Reed began to fall upon bleak days, and with this development Joseph's days abroad became numbered.[42] By the early autumn of 1764, Reed was making plans for a return to America

in the spring of the following year. His departure was speeded
when Pettit wrote from Philadelphia on December 20 that the
firm of Reed and Pettit was on the brink of ruin and that he had
decided to liquidate the business while a chance remained of paying all the debts and saving something for Andrew Reed.[43]

Apparently Joseph was a good deal more upset about leaving
Esther than he was by the curtailment of his studies at the Middle
Temple. Judging by the replies of Daniel Coxe to two letters
from Reed, the latter had expressed some disappointment at the
benefits to be gained from the costly sojourn in London. Coxe
wrote that from Reed's description "a good collection of Books
well perus'd and considered in America will answer the same and
nearly indeed the advantages of attending Westminster Hall,"
and in another letter remarked, again paraphrasing the sentiments Reed had expressed to him, that an American attending
the Inns of Court would find "the addition to his Stock of Knowledge cannot be equal to the Expense attending the Tryal of it." [44]

But parting with Esther was another matter. Even if her parents had consented, she could not bear to leave them to go to
America. She had hoped that Joseph might stay in England, and
when that became impossible the romance nearly floundered.[45]
It was only when Reed promised that he would return to England
as soon as possible from America that an informal engagement
became possible.[46] It was with this plan, that of returning to
England and taking up his permanent residence there, that Reed
left the Middle Temple and took leave of the DeBerdts in February, 1765. He sailed for home on the *Britannia* early in March.[47]
The projected return was to be delayed five long years. During
this period Reed's determination to return to England remained
constant, however, and the efforts of the DeBerdts to make that
step possible were equally unswerving.

CHAPTER III

The Colonial Counselor

SADDENED by his separation from Esther and troubled by
reports of family difficulties at Trenton, Reed could hardly
have enjoyed his crossing on the *Britannia*. Yet the fascinating
Captain Macpherson undoubtedly kept gloom at a respectful distance from his young friend as the ship plowed westward. The
voyage took almost two months, but finally port was made at
Philadelphia and Reed reached his home in Trenton early in
May, 1765. He found the situation of his family most disheartening. Reed and Pettit, the mercantile firm headed by his father
and brother-in-law, was bankrupt. A combination of unwise
ventures in insurance by Pettit over the past several years coupled
now with a severe province-wide depression had produced its fall.[1]

To Andrew Reed, no longer a young man and troubled by ill
health, this blow was a crushing one. Weary and dispirited, he
seized upon his eldest son's return to abdicate his family responsibilities. Upon Joseph he now cast the entire burden of maintaining the Trenton household and caring for the younger children, Bowes, John, and Mary. As for himself, after constituting
Joseph his lawful attorney, he left Trenton in July and took up
residence in the country some twelve miles away at Amwell,
probably with his bachelor brother.[2]

Joseph, approaching his twenty-fourth birthday, now faced the
task of supporting his two brothers and his sister as well as himself. That was not to be all: no less than five other dependents
were soon added to his household. For Charles Pettit found himself unable to obtain any employment after his partnership collapsed. First Sarah Pettit, Joseph's half-sister, and her three children moved in with Reed. Then, in the fall, Pettit did too after
a fruitless trip to Nova Scotia in search of an advantageous land
grant.[3] Fortunately, the Reed home on King (now Warren)
Street, a two-story brick house, had ample accommodations for

all.[4] It remained to be seen whether Reed's legal practice would provide an income sufficient for all.

Reed, it will be recalled, had been admitted to the New Jersey bar in 1763 before he went to England. The period of study at the Middle Temple, brief as it had been, now helped him attract a large clientele quickly. Reed made his first appearance in court at the May term of the Hunterdon County Court of Common Pleas held in the courthouse only a few steps down King Street from his home.[5] During the summer he extended his practice beyond the Trenton area. When the supreme court of the province held its September term he appeared before it for clients from Burlington, Middlesex, and Somerset counties as well as from Hunterdon. Within another year, despite the setback of a virtual cessation of legal business in late 1765 and early 1766 caused by the Stamp Act crisis, he could boast a clientele drawn from ten of New Jersey's thirteen counties.[6] By mid-1766 Reed had built up not only a widespread practice but a volume of business which, in his home county at least, was matched by only four of the sixteen other attorneys then apearing before the court.[7]

Only very rarely did Reed appear in a criminal case. The great bulk of his practice at this time and in his subsequent legal career in Pennsylvania was civil in nature. But in all court appearances Reed placed great emphasis upon the value of a vigorous, dynamic approach.[8] Nevertheless, closely reasoned argumentation rather than histrionics was the quality in Reed's work which most impressed his colleagues. William Rawle, a fellow member of the Philadelphia bar, wrote of Reed after the Revolution:

His mind was perspicacious, his perception quick, his penetration great, his industry unremitted. . . . His manner of speaking was not, I think, pleasing; his reasoning, however, was well conducted and seldom failed to bear upon the proper points of controversy. When he had the conclusion of a cause he was formidable. I have heard an old practitioner say that there was no one at the bar whom he so little liked to be behind him as Joseph Reed.[9]

Tangible evidence of the high esteem for Reed within the legal circle was his selection as counsel by Chief Justice Smyth in 1769 when the latter was personally involved in a dispute with an associate justice of the supreme court.[10]   Another indication of Reed's standing was his appearance in October, 1769, before the assembly of the province together with two other members of the bar as a committee to defend their profession against critics who charged that lawyers were overcharging for their services and were deliberately lengthening lawsuits.   Reed and his veteran confreres, James Kinsey and Samuel Allinson, presented a very able rebuttal.   They denied that the attorneys were in any way responsible for the large number of financial failures and pointed out that their bills of cost were regulated by law and had to be filed with the courts.   On the other hand, they pointed out, the sheriff's fees were not regulated and were often the real basis for complaints against the cost of a suit.   The three attorneys neatly turned the tables on one of their most outspoken critics in the assembly, Samuel Tucker, by charging him with having exacted exorbitant fees in three particular cases while sheriff of Hunterdon County, charges later sustained by the assembly after an investigation.[11]

Since none of Reed's account books have been preserved, it is not possible to document in detail the income from his profession.   But in April, 1767, that is, after two years of practice in New Jersey, he wrote Esther DeBerdt that he was garnering £1,000 a year and added that his business was "increasing beyond my ability to go through it, though my two brothers and a young gentleman who is serving a clerkship with me, assist me." [12]

For Reed, gratifying as his success at the bar was and invaluable though it was in saving his family's situation, a great problem persisted.   Absence from Esther had not altered his determination to return to England and marry her, and her attachment to him, despite advances by several suitors in England, had also remained fast.   But Esther could not contemplate leaving her elderly parents and moving to America after her marriage: this she had made clear when Reed courted her and she had persisted in this viewpoint.[13]   Reed was willing enough to reside in England, but he had to wrestle with two vexing questions.   First, how could he leave New Jersey and abandon a lucrative practice when his brothers, his sister, and even the Pettit family continued to depend upon him for their livelihood?   Secondly, even if the first problem were solved, how would he support himself and Esther in England? He could not practice in the courts there until he had completed at least another year's residence at the Middle Temple.

The effort to find a solution to this two-sided dilemma involved Reed and the DeBerdts in many plans and schemes between 1765 and 1769. First Reed suggested that he would give up the law if Esther's father would make him a partner in his mercantile firm. But DeBerdt had just made Stephen Sayre, Reed's distant cousin and Princeton classmate, a partner, and there was no room for still another.[14] Then Sayre himself became the central figure in a second plan, a grandiose scheme for speculation in lands in America, but this too never got beyond the talking stage.[15]

Ultimately, political office was to prevail as the means which made Reed's return to England possible. Yet here again there was, at first, only dashed hopes or almost hopeless delays. A case in point was the plan which would have seen Reed brought to London in 1766 as secretary to William Legge, the second earl of Dartmouth, when that nobleman, president of the Board of Trade in the Rockingham ministry, obtained an anticipated appointment as secretary of state for the American colonies. DeBerdt was on fairly intimate terms with Dartmouth and had gained the earl's ear concerning a place for his prospective son-in-law. Dartmouth was quite impressed when shown reports Reed had sent DeBerdt on the Stamp Act crisis in the colonies. In one of these, dated October 5, 1765, Reed warned that "the whole Country is ripe for Insurrection, Riot and Confusion, and should some resolute Fellow blow the Trumpet of Sedition (for such I suppose it would be call'd on your side the Atlantick) thousands would join him." [16] But the Rockingham ministry fell before Dartmouth got his appointment and another opportunity for Reed had failed to materialize. Nevertheless, the ground for the highly significant Reed-Dartmouth correspondence of 1773-75, to be described later, was prepared by these stillborn plans for a more intimate connection between the two men.[17]

Before the year 1766 was out a new opportunity for official placement had arisen for Reed and this time, happily, it was seized successfully. In November Maurice Morgann [18] was appointed secretary of the province of New Jersey by George III. This was a lucrative post, for it included, among others, the offices of clerk of the council, clerk of the supreme court, surrogate, and keeper and registrar of records of the colony. But Morgann had no intention of going to New Jersey to perform in person the duties of these departments. The practice, rather, was for the secretary to appoint a deputy, usually an inhabitant of the province, and charge this deputy a flat sum called "rent" for the privilege of collecting the fees and salaries connected with the offices.

When the news of Morgann's appointment reached New Jersey, Reed at once invoked DeBerdt's influence toward securing the deputyship. But the incumbent deputy, Charles Read of Burlington, a justice of the supreme court, had held that office since 1744 and now waged a spirited battle of bids by proxy to retain his post. The issue remained in doubt throughout the winter of 1766-67. But DeBerdt worked most assiduously in Reed's behalf, and finally his daughter was able to send word on April 11 to her fiance that he had won the appointment from Morgann.[19] The latter signed the formal commission for Reed in June, at which time DeBerdt, acting for Reed, deposited a bond guaranteeing performance of the duties of the office and payment to Morgann of an annual "rent" of £250.[20] Charles Read attempted to retain his grip on the subsidiary offices surrounding that of deputy secretary, but after a heated contest which reached up to the governor and council for adjudication Joseph Reed prevailed and took up his duties in the fall of 1767.[21]

As deputy secretary Reed had to serve personally as clerk of the council and maintain offices in the two capitals of New Jersey, Burlington and Perth Amboy. The position as clerk brought him an annual salary of £30 and, of greater importance, gave him experience which was to be invaluable when he became George Washington's secretary and adjutant in the Revolution. Direction of the two offices brought an immediate advantage to Reed, for it enabled him to provide employment for Pettit and Bowes Reed (and possibly John Reed too), which ended their dependence on him for room and board.

Pettit was put in charge of the Burlington office with Bowes as his assistant. Rather than pay his brother-in-law a salary, Reed permitted the latter to retain all the revenues of the office, revenues comprised of fees collected for drawing up licenses and township patents, registering deeds and wills, issuing commissions to judges, sheriffs, military officers, etc. Since this income was quite adequate to the support of his family, Pettit was able to establish his own home in Burlington and, by early 1768, bring there his wife and three children (and Bowes Reed too) from Reed's household in Trenton. "I will not harrass you with acknowledgements," Pettit wrote Reed, "tho' my Heart swells with them." [22]

These arrangements left Reed without any very appreciable net revenue from his deputyship, probably no more than £100 a year.[23] But he was left free to pursue his legal practice with scant interference and, what was more important, he had ended a family situation of utter dependence upon him. When, in October, 1769, Reed prevailed upon Maurice Morgann to transfer the deputyship from himself to Pettit,[24] he could regard as complete the leveling of the first obstacle which had blocked his return to England.

By 1769 a solution to Reed's second problem, that of supporting himself and his expected bride in England until he had qualified for the bar there, had also been worked out. Reed, it had been agreed, would come to England as assistant to Esther DeBerdt's father in the latter's capacity as London agent of the Massachusetts house of representatives. For this assistance DeBerdt had promised Reed half the agency salary of £300 per year.[25]

DeBerdt's official connection with Massachusetts dated back to 1765 when he had been selected to present for the Bay Colony the petitions of the Stamp Act Congress. His yeoman service toward bringing about the repeal of the obnoxious measure led the legislature to designate him as permanent London agent for the province. But Governor Bernard and the council refused to approve this choice and an impasse resulted: the house retained DeBerdt as their agent, the council hired its own spokesman in London, William Bollan.[26]

In 1769 disquieting reports reached DeBerdt that his age (he was then seventy-five) and state of health (he had been seriously ill in 1766-67) were being used in Boston to deprecate his effectiveness.[27] Hiring an assistant with Reed's youth, energy, and ability, DeBerdt reasoned, would go far toward spiking these attacks. The arrangements were made. Reed visited Boston in the summer of 1769 to bolster DeBerdt's standing and to make himself known to the Massachusetts leaders. He made a good impression: Sam Adams wrote to DeBerdt of Reed's "good sense, agreeable conversation and polite behaviour," and James Otis wrote in a complimentary vein too.[28]

Reed returned to Trenton late in September, succeeded in transfering the deputy secretaryship to Pettit as was mentioned above, and then made ready to depart for England. Then a suddenly fatal turn in his father's health delayed again his reunion with Esther. Andrew Reed became seriously ill in November and died on December 16. Writing to DeBerdt the day before, Reed had predicted that recovery could not be expected and commented that his father regarded "the approach of death with a firmness and serenity which show it to be . . . an enemy he is prepared to meet. . . . I have the approbation of my own heart that I have neglected nothing in my power to support and comfort his declining years." [29]

Reed's departure for England was thus set back until early 1770. But finally he boarded the brig *James* in Delaware Bay on March 16 and got under way. After a swift but stormy passage, Reed landed at Newry in Ireland on April 17 [30] and soon was in Dublin. While awaiting a packet ship for the trip across the Irish Sea to England, he received, through London newspapers, catastrophic news. Dennys DeBerdt, the patron upon whose aid he was counting so heavily in taking up a new life in England, had died on April 11. Reed dashed off a letter to Pettit and then rushed on to London.[31]

There Reed again found himself catapulted into the position of chief support for a distracted family. He was appalled to find the financial affairs of the DeBerdt firm in utter confusion, a confusion for which he placed heavy responsibility upon the deceased merchant's partners, Stephen Sayre and Thomas Burkitt. At first

Reed hoped several thousand pounds might be salvaged for the family, but after several weeks of negotiation with creditors this hope evaporated and destitution faced the DeBerdts.[32]

The abrupt reversal of all Reed's expectations did not delay his marriage with Esther. The wedding took place in London at St. Luke's Church on May 31.[33] Now it was all the more necessary that Reed do some serious stock-taking. With Mr. DeBerdt dead he had no patron in London. He lacked the prestige to be given DeBerdt's Massachusetts agency appointment (Benjamin Franklin received the post). He could not practice law before the English bar. Reed concluded that he must return to America with Esther. Subsequently it was decided that Mrs. DeBerdt would accompany her daughter and son-in-law, while young Dennis, Esther's brother, would remain in England and seek employment in London.[34]

The three passengers left London aboard the *Pennsylvania Packet* on September 3 and docked in Philadelphia October 26.[35] Reed, his bride, and Mrs. DeBerdt were guests at the Pettit home in Burlington for the first two weeks after their arrival, for Reed had leased his house in Trenton when he sailed for England in the spring. The latter had more than the lack of a home in New Jersey to worry about. He had given up the deputy secretary's post to Pettit and he had recommended his law clients to other attorneys. Rather than attempt a difficult picking up of old threads, Reed decided to make a fresh start in an area offering greater professional opportunities than western New Jersey: he decided to settle in Philadelphia. By mid-December it was done. He, Esther, and Mrs. DeBerdt were comfortably settled in the Quaker City in a house rented from a Mr. Tilghman.[36]

Esther Reed found Philadelphia somewhat disappointing. She thought the plan of the city "remarkably good," but she described most of the houses as "low and in general paltry." Of her new friends and neighbors Esther confided to her brother that she found their conversation singularly confined to personal gossip. Their lighthearted attitude toward obligations to English creditors appalled her. She described her women companions as "pretty but no beauties; they all stoop, like country girls." [37]

For some two years Mrs. Reed treasured the hope of a return

to England and permanent residence there. The birth of her first child, Martha ("Patty"), in May, 1771, at first stimulated this desire, concerned as the young mother was by the inadequate provisions for the education of girls in America. But the arrival of two more children within the next three years (Joseph, Jr. in July, 1772, and Esther in July, 1774) served as a serious obstacle to a change of hearth. Also, the poor health of little Martha made an ocean voyage for the family a practical impossibility. Reed, in fact, several times despaired of the child's life in 1772 and 1773, but, though an invalid, Martha lived until 1821, long surviving both her parents.[38] By 1773, therefore, Esther was reconciled to permanent residence in America, for, as she wrote her brother in England, "everything, while his life and abilities last, is promising here and there is no prospect for him there." [39]

Reed's abilities and the good fortune that some illustrious members of the Philadelphia bar resigned their practice just as Reed commenced his in the city [40] produced indeed a promising situation which the young attorney capitalized upon with immediate success. As he had in New Jersey, Reed practiced not only in the local county court but followed the supreme court on circuit in other counties of Pennsylvania too.[41] His volume of business mounted rapidly. As early as 1772 he employed two law clerks in his office, one of whom, Gunning Bedford of Delaware, later served as a delegate to the Constitutional Convention of 1787 and was named to the Federal bench in 1789 by President Washington.[42] Reed's law office was noted for its fine law library, valued at £150 in 1774. He supplemented these volumes with his own notes on Pennsylvania decisions, notes compiled with such care that they were used after his death in the publication of the Pennsylvania *Reports* by A. J. Dallas.[43] By the eve of the Revolution Reed had won a prominence which led a distinguished visitor from Massachusetts, John Adams, to comment that he was at the head of his profession in Philadelphia.[44]

Reed's professional success brought him moderate wealth as well as acclaim. In an estimate he made of his financial situation in July, 1774, Reed listed debts totaling £1,008 and credits of £7,335. The credit notations reveal a very comfortable mode of living: household furniture worth £300, a wine cellar whose contents were valued at £70, a library of non-legal titles worth £40, and ownership of four horses and three carriages. Reed also had two Negro slaves: Jack, whom he had owned before his marriage, and Cyrus, purchased for £90 in 1774.[45]

Reed's balance sheet shows that most of his wealth was invested in land. To a purchase of land in Orange County, New York, made in 1768 while he was still living in New Jersey, Reed added extensive holdings in Pennsylvania and New Jersey after establishing himself in Philadelphia. Some lands he owned outright, in other cases he shared ownership with partners such as Pettit, Robert Morris, and Thomas Willing.[46] The most valuable of Reed's landed investments was in shares of the West Jersey Society, a company with large tracts in New Jersey and Pennsylvania. In August, 1772, Reed authorized his brother-in-law in England, Dennis DeBerdt, to buy as much as £500 worth of society shares for him from English stockholders. DeBerdt made an initial purchase of forty shares in November at £5.15 each, and another purchase of twenty-five shares the following year at a slightly higher price. In his 1774 estimate Reed valued the shares at £20. In 1773, anticipating this rise in value, he had attempted to form a syndicate to purchase all the society's lands for £10,000. But the English stockholders refused to consider any such sale and Reed had to content himself with his sixty-five shares and with an appointment as an attorney for the society in America.[47]

Reed more than repaid DeBerdt for the latter's services as his proxy in the West Jersey Society. Young DeBerdt had slowly worked up a business as purchasing agent and consignee for Americans doing business in London. Many of his first customers were solicited for him in Philadelphia by Reed. The latter pledged himself as guarantor for Dennis's obligations, collected unpaid balances due the old DeBerdt firm, and secured settlement for the DeBerdt estate of the father's salary from Massachusetts.[48] The grateful Londoner wrote his sister that what Reed did for him "has been more like a Father than an absent Brother-in-law." [49]

Reed also strove to gain an appointment for DeBerdt as a

colonial agent. In 1775 Benjamin Franklin resigned as New Jersey's representative in London and Reed succeeded in having DeBerdt named to fill the vacancy. When Reed sent these tidings to the latter, he advised him to keep his expense account low and urged that DeBerdt "keep up a goodly Jealousy of the Intentions of all Ministers but infusing as little as possible into your Constituents; they now have quite enough." [50]   But the Revolution was already under way at this time, and with the Declaration of Independence DeBerdt's career as colonial agent came to a quick conclusion.

In addition to these family relationships with DeBerdt and with Charles Pettit (who was unquestionably his closest friend), Reed was forging new contacts in Philadelphia. He joined the Second Presbyterian Church, Arch and Third streets, in 1771, and quickly was given positions of responsibility and leadership by the congregation: trustee in 1771, president of the corporation in 1773, vice president in 1775.[51]   He was honored by election to the American Philosophical Society.[52]   He played a leading role in Philadelphia among the alumni of the College of New Jersey active in their alma mater's behalf.[53]

These early years in Philadelphia, then, were happy, promising years for Reed. Writing to Pettit in January, 1775, he surveyed the family's good fortune:

When we look back and see how happily in various Respects the Situation of our Family has mended and what a different appearance it makes from all those who have been sunk so low, there is much more reason to rejoice than complain. I profess I am sometimes surprised at it myself, and am not Infidel enough to doubt there is a particular Providence which directs the Affairs not only of Men but Families.[54]

Unhappily, the cheerful scene of Reed's private affairs was in direct contrast to the growing tenseness of the political arena. To the darkening cloud of war between Britain and her colonies and to Reed's role in the patriot movement in Philadelphia we must now turn our attention.

CHAPTER IV

The Patriot Who Would Be Peacemaker

THE first two years of Reed's residence in Philadelphia coincided with the calmest period in the relations between Britain and the thirteen colonies since the Treaty of Paris in 1763. Early 1770 had indeed been hectic, marked as it was by the riot on New York City's Golden Hill in January and by the "Boston Massacre" in March. But on April 12, the day before the ship carrying Reed to England for his marriage came within sight of the Irish coast, George III assented to the conciliatory measure which his new chief minister, Lord North, had pushed through Parliament: repeal of all the Townshend duties except that on tea. This gesture, while it settled nothing in so far as determining where, in the last analysis, the power to legislate for the colonists was lodged, did produce an immediate relaxation in the tensions which had crackled across the Atlantic. By the time Reed returned to America in the fall of 1770 with his bride and her mother, the colonial non-importation agreements were being rapidly abandoned, despite the retention of the tea duty. On September 20, six days before Reed's ship reached Philadelphia from London, the merchants of the Quaker City, following the example of their brethren in New York City, voted over the heated protests of such patriot leaders as Charles Thomson to end the boycott on all imports except the dutied tea.[1] Only Virginia, as 1770 drew to its close, held to the sinking cause of non-importation. Thus, although the tea tax rankled (and incidentally made Philadelphia a great smuggling center for tea on which no tax had been paid),[2] the outlook for 1771 was hopefully calm.

Most moderate Americans, and Reed may be counted among them, were pleased by the more tranquil course of events throughout 1771 and into 1772. An event which seemed to augur even more cordial imperial relations was the resignation of Lord Hills-borough as Secretary of State for the American Colonies and the appointment, on August 14, 1772, of Lord Dartmouth to succeed him. Hillsborough was generally regarded in America as un-friendly to its interests, while his successor, remembered grate-fully for his work as a member of the Rockingham ministry which had repealed the Stamp Act, was highly respected by the colonists. They received the news of his appointment with enthusiasm, be-lieving it heralded a change of policy toward the colonies.[3] Such anticipation not only exaggerated Dartmouth's influence, but indicated a misapprehension as to his political outlook. Amiable and pious, but lacking both imagination and administrative abil-ity, he had an undeserved reputation for conciliatory ideas. Actu-ally, he was most firm in his belief that Parliamentary supremacy over the colonies was a cornerstone of the British constitution.[4] In 1771 he had deserted the Whig party and moved under the Tory banner of his half-brother, Lord North. After intraparty strife led to Hillsborough's resignation from North's cabinet, Dartmouth was rewarded with the vacant secretaryship, but he exercised little real influence from that office.[5]

Dartmouth's appointment, nevertheless, was of considerable interest to Joseph Reed. It will be recalled that when Dartmouth had previously sought the colonial post in 1766 and 1768, plans were afoot to obtain an appointment for Reed as his secretary. Reed had also been in contact with the Earl since 1768 concern-ing purchases of land in America. The news received from her brother of Dartmouth's new office brought Esther Reed briefly rekindled hope of a return to her beloved England,[6] but Reed himself does not appear to have ever considered renewing his old application. Yet Dartmouth's appointment did affect him di-rectly. For, at Dennis DeBerdt's urging, he soon began a corre-spondence with the new secretary remarkable for its reflective view of the relations between Britain and the American colonies on the eve of the Revolution.

Reed's purpose in embarking upon this correspondence, which was to total twelve letters from him between December, 1773, and February, 1775, was clearly communicated to DeBerdt early in

1773 when the enterprise was first being discussed by the brothers-in-law:

I have often had thoughts of making his Lordship a tender of my services in pointing out some things which would be of mutual advantage to both countries, and tend to make his administration honourable and useful. But the difficulty of introducing it in a proper manner and free from any suspicion of interested views has hitherto prevented it. The intelligence from this country has generally flowed through such corrupt channels as would expose any Minister to danger and difficulty. I think I could procure his Lordship one or two correspondents in other Provinces, who would, if it was agreeable, render him any services in that way, and who have nothing to ask from him but his cheerful acceptance of their honest and disinterested endeavours to serve both the Mother Country and the Colonies.[7]

DeBerdt saw Dartmouth several times in the spring months of 1773 and on August 14 wrote him about Reed's suggestion.[8] Later that month Dartmouth replied to DeBerdt as follows:

I have no doubt that Mr. Reed is very capable of suggesting Matters that may be very useful to me in my present situation. I shall be very much obliged to him for any Information he may think fit to send me and he may depend upon it that whatsoever he may communicate to me in Confidence I shall take care to make no improper use of.[9]

Dennis sent a copy of this letter to Reed and urged that he act upon it. DeBerdt did not know that a letter from Reed to him was already on its way enclosing a brief note to Dartmouth concerning land purchases.[10] It was not until after receiving DeBerdt's August letter with the favorable report of Dartmouth's attitude, however, that Reed set about explaining and defending the colonial attitude to the minister.

The dozen letters penned in this endeavor were sent by Reed unsealed through the hands of Dennis DeBerdt, whom Reed empowered to hold or deliver them on the basis of his on-the-spot judgment as to their propriety.[11] None of DeBerdt's letters to Reed indicate that any of the letters went undelivered. The former, however, did warn Reed against including too much personal opinion in his letters. This was done not for fear of the reception afforded Reed's opinions by Dartmouth but for fear of the consequences on Reed's side of the Atlantic should his views be cited as the basis upon which unpopular ministerial action was cast.[12]   Reed acknowledged the need of caution, but asserted his determination to continue to send information to Dartmouth which "if it does not tell him what he wishes yet it tells him what he ought to know." [13]

As Reed took up this correspondence, imperial relations once more bore a threatening aspect.   The calm of 1771 had been rent by the *Gaspée* incident in June, 1772, and by the new flare-up later that year between the royal governor of Massachusetts and the house of representatives, a development which the patriot circle used to secure the reestablishment of committees of correspondence for the coordination of opposition policy not only within Massachusetts but with patriot groups in the other provinces as well.   In Pennsylvania no formal action was taken toward the appointment of such a committee.   But Reed, who was well known in Massachusetts thanks to his visit there in 1769 and through his link with the late Dennys DeBerdt, became an important center of communication between the patriots of Boston and Philadelphia.   It was to Reed's home, for example, that Josiah Quincy came in 1773, acting in Philadelphia, as in the other colonial centers he visited, as unofficial good-will ambassador of the Massachusetts circle.   The visit inaugurated a close friendship between Reed and Quincy which was cut tragically short by the latter's death in April, 1775.[14]   Reed wrote Thomas Cushing, speaker of the Massachusetts house of representatives, that Quincy's visit had had an admirable effect in tightening the bonds between Pennsylvania and Massachusetts and suggested that much could be done by men of Quincy's character and ability traveling through the colonies to "cement" them in the common cause.   In the same letter Reed praised the stand of the Massachusetts legislature in their struggle with Governor Hutchinson, applauded Virginia's patriotic action in establishing a committee for intercolonial correspondence (March 12, 1773), and expressed the hope that "some sparks of the sacred fire [of American liberty] will in time warm the intermediate provinces." [15]

These connections between Boston and Philadelphia became of

prime importance when the opposition brewed by the North ministry's Tea Act of May, 1773, was manifested in forthright action in each of these cities in December of that year. The Tea Act not only retained the Townshend duty on tea entering the American colonies but—and this was the new source of grievance—attempted to save the East India Company from bankruptcy by special privileges of direct sale and duty drawbacks which gave it a potential monopoly of the trade in tea in the colonies. The *Pennsylvania Gazette* of September 29, 1773, carried an ominous report that the company intended to send 600 chests of tea to Philadelphia and sell them at public auction from its own warehouses. Thus not only the law-abiding colonial merchant, whose selling price was swollen by full payment of duties and by middlemen's commissions, but even the tea smuggler was faced with being undersold by the company's direct invasion of the American market. The chorus of opposition and protest was in full voice by the fall of 1773, and it was this new clamor which Reed sought to explain and defend in the first of his reportorial letters to Lord Dartmouth in December.

The first open defiance to the Tea Act came from the normally conservative mercantile community of Philadelphia. On October 18 they sponsored a public meeting at the State House (Independence Hall) and launched a campaign denouncing the tea tax as tending to introduce arbitrary government through the circumvention of colonial assemblies. All Pennsylvanians were called upon to refrain from assistance toward landing, unloading, storing, or marketing the expected tea shipment. A twelve-man committee was chosen to persuade those Philadelphians who had been named agents by the East India Company to resign their appointments.[16] Such was the weight of opinion on this issue in the city that all the consignees, over a period of two months, fell into line. In describing these developments to Dartmouth, Reed remarked that not even the opposition to the Stamp Act was as unanimous as that to the Tea Act, for the latter was condemned not only by those who saw in it a point of constitutional liberty but by powerful merchants who "dread a monopoly whose extent may destroy one-third of their business." [17]

Even as Reed composed this letter, the ship *Polly,* bearing the East India Company's tea, was nearing Philadelphia. On Christmas day it was as far up the Delaware River as Chester, fifteen miles south of the city. Messengers from Chester brought news of its appearance into Philadelphia the same evening. The next morning a committee which had grown from that formed at the protest meeting in October [18] met to perfect their plans to confront the master of the *Polly,* Captain Ayers, inform him of the city's determination not to permit the landing of the tea, and demand his return, with his cargo, to England. At 2 o'clock that afternoon, December 26, the ship appeared off Gloucester Point, some three miles below Philadelphia. Three members of the committee hailed Captain Ayers and requested that he proceed no further but come ashore for a conference. The latter complied with this request and accompanied the men into the city.

Except for the taunts of some boys in the streets, Ayers was treated with grave courtesy in Philadelphia. But his hosts left no doubts in his mind as to the disastrous consequences which would follow a refusal on his part to turn back for England. Any such obstinacy, Reed predicted to Dartmouth, might well prove fatal to himself and to his vessel.[19] At 10 o'clock on December 27, the morning after his arrival, Ayers was the "guest" at a gathering of several thousand hastily summoned Philadelphians in the State House Square. Fully convinced by this show of strength of the hopelessness of resistance, he gave his promise not to land the tea and to set sail for the return voyage by the following day at the latest. Actually, thanks to the cooperation the captain received in securing provisions for the eastward crossing, the *Polly* weighed anchor from Gloucester Point within a few hours of the meeting's adjournment. Ayers himself remained in Philadelphia until the following day when he took a pilot boat to his ship.[20]

When Captain Ayers left Philadelphia he carried with him Reed's second letter to Lord Dartmouth, written the afternoon of the mass meeting, December 27. In describing the events of the past three days, Reed again emphasized the unanimity of the opposition to the Tea Act, stressed that this opposition not only included but indeed was conducted by "some of the principal inhabitants" of Philadelphia, expressed pride that the tea incident there had brought "no insults to individuals or injury to private property," yet forcibly asserted his opinion that "any farther attempt to enforce this act . . . must end in blood." In his previous letter Reed had predicted that the repeal of the Tea Act (and that of the tea duty) would restore harmony between the colonies and the Mother Country. Now he pointed out that the smuggling which had resulted from the duty on tea had deprived England of not less than £100,000 in profits in Pennsylvania alone.[21]

On one matter Reed could not in all honesty, and did not, report the presence of unified sentiments in Philadelphia. That was upon the reaction to the news of Boston's more violent solution to its tea crisis, the famous "tea party" of December 16, 1773. On December 24 a messenger from New York galloped into Philadelphia bearing dispatches describing that event and a letter from the Boston committee of correspondence addressed to two members of the Philadelphia tea committee asking advice and support. The news from Boston was circulated through the city at 5 o'clock that afternoon by a special edition of the *Pennsylvania Gazette*. Writing to DeBerdt that evening, Reed expressed his opinion that Governor Hutchinson of Massachusetts had, by his obstinacy, driven the Bostonians to destroy the tea.[22]

That this was a popular view was indicated on the following day, Christmas, when a nineteen-man committee, of whom Reed was one, drafted a reply to the letter from Boston. The Philadelphians began by explaining their own plan (as yet unexecuted) for sending the tea back untouched as "the most eligible and unexceptionable." Then the varying reactions of the committeemen to the act of destruction at Boston revealed themselves in the guarded tones which followed:

The different fate however which the tea has met with [at Boston] appears well justified by a strong necessity, created perhaps by those among you who have so long distinguished themselves as the inveterate enemies of American Liberties and who seek their own advantage in compelling you to any measures of violence.

The letter concluded with an assurance that Philadelphia would stand firmly against the landing of the tea destined for it.[23]

More vigorous approval of the Boston Tea Party was voiced by resolutions introduced and ratified, despite a previous committee decision against raising the subject, at the mass meeting of December 27 mentioned above.[24] Thus, when Reed wrote to Dartmouth that evening, he said that the action of the Bostonians was generally approved but admitted some difference of opinion on this matter.[25]

All America now strained for word from Britain which might reveal the government's reaction to the violence at Boston and to the more peaceable but equally successful interference with the marketing of the East India Company's tea at Philadelphia, New York, and Charleston. Would the ministry seize upon the disgust with which many Americans viewed the action in the former city and, by scrupulously just demands upon Boston, strike at the unity of intercolonial opposition? Or would it, by harsh treatment of the Bostonians, arouse sympathy for them even among those who disapproved of the tea's destruction? Lord North's ministry, with the overwhelming support of Parliament, chose the latter course and by so doing at once set in motion the events which led directly to the outbreak of the Revolution.

Lord Dartmouth, influenced undoubtedly to some degree by Reed's warnings in his two letters, vainly attempted to dissuade his colleagues from coercive action against Boston.[26] The latter could not be dissuaded, nor could Parliament, despite the oratory of Edmund Burke, Colonel Barré, George Johnstone, and others. The first of the "Coercive Acts," that closing the port of Boston effective June 1, was signed by the King on March 31. Reed, writing his third letter to Lord Dartmouth on April 4, knew nothing of this, of course, nor indeed of the temper revealed by Parliament. Hopefully he stated that he knew of "no cloud rising in our political hemisphere, unless our conduct respecting the tea should produce any." And, quickly passing from that subject, he devoted the bulk of the letter to an analysis of the need for reform in the postal system and in the admiralty courts in America.[27]

By the end of April some indications of the British government's program for the punishment of Boston had reached Reed. The *Pennsylvania Gazette* of April 22 carried the news that additional British warships had received sailing orders for America early in March, and the issue of May 4 reported that the Mother Country had decided upon a series of coercive measures to impress upon the colonists their duty to the empire. The extreme nature of these measures was finally revealed when the text of the Boston Port Act reached the city and was published in the *Gazette* on May 18. The next day, while the act's provisions were still being studied and interpreted, Paul Revere rode into Philadelphia bearing a circular letter from the Boston committee of correspondence requesting an immediate pledge of non-importation of British goods. With this letter were private letters from Boston patriot leaders to Reed and others in Philadelphia.[28]

Factional differences immediately sprang up in Philadelphia over the question of how the request from Massachusetts was to be treated. The more radical of the city's patriots, led by Charles Thomson, the "Sam Adams of Philadelphia" as John Adams subsequently described him,[29] wanted to hold mass meetings at once and rush through resolutions of non-importation to show their solidarity with the Bostonians. Conservatively minded merchants, particularly from among the Quakers, wished to limit the remonstrances against the Port Act to petitions from the assembly of Pennsylvania. In an attempt to decide on action which would meet with general approval, Reed, Thomson, and Thomas Mifflin called a meeting for the evening of May 20, the day after Revere's arrival. All three realized that there was little chance of agreement without the active participation of John Dickinson, the famous author of the *Letters from a Pennsylvania Farmer,* trusted by the Quakers and others for his moderation. Accordingly, the three visited Dickinson at his home during the day and were invited to dinner, during the course of which they obtained Dickinson's promise to attend the meeting that night. Reed and Mifflin left for the meeting, leaving Thomson to follow with Dickinson.

The Long Room of the City Tavern on Second Street near Walnut had been chosen as the meeting place. It was already jammed with over two hundred men when Reed and Mifflin arrived. It had been agreed at dinner that Reed would act as chairman and be the first speaker. With some difficulty he humored the impatient gathering until Thomson arrived with Dickinson. Then he opened the meeting with a speech delivered with moderation, but calling for spirited measures in making common cause with Boston. Thomson followed with a more vigorous address, but so intense was the excitement and heat in the closely packed room that he fainted while speaking. This event threw the meeting into confusion and it was with difficulty that Reed obtained sufficient order to permit Dickinson to speak. The latter, to keep the conservatives from bolting the meeting, spoke more moderately than either Reed or Thomson but did endorse Reed's suggestion that the governor be petitioned to call the assembly into session.[30]

After the speech-making, the meeting proceeded to name a nineteen-man committee, of which Reed, Dickinson, Mifflin, and Thomson were all members. The committee was authorized to (1) express to the Bostonians the sympathy with which Philadelphia viewed their sufferings in "the general cause," (2) write to committees of correspondence in the other colonies, (3) ask Governor John Penn to call the assembly into session, and (4) call, whenever necessary, a meeting of the inhabitants of Philadelphia.[31]

The meeting had succeeded in forming a unified front of opposition to the coercive program. But unity required that the mode of opposition should be on a lower key than Thomson or Mifflin or perhaps Reed desired. The committee of nineteen was eminently moderate in character, a fact clearly revealed by the cautious answer to the appeal from Boston which was written and sent off with Revere on May 21, the day after the meeting at the City Tavern. The letter described the resolutions adopted at the meeting but expressed hesitation as to offering advice to Boston in the present crisis until more time could be had for deliberation and for consulting more Philadelphians. It was promised that the suggestion contained in the circular letter as to non-importation would be given careful study. But, the reply went on, the convocation of an intercolonial congress was to be preferred as a first step, with economic boycott reserved as a last resort. The committee also pointedly remarked that if paying for the destroyed tea would settle the controversy and "leave us on the Footing of Constitutional Liberty for the future" it felt sure that Bostonians would do so, for after all what was important was not "the value of a tax but the indefeasible Right of giving and granting our own Money (a Right from which we can never recede)." [32]

On May 30 Reed wrote to Lord Dartmouth of these turbulent developments. He flatly informed the Earl that no greater mistake had ever been made than the coercive measures against Massachusetts if they were undertaken on the supposition that the other colonies would abandon the former to its fate. Reed predicted that all the provinces except Canada and the Floridas would soon send shiploads of provisions to Massachusetts for Boston's use. No one, he stated, had urged Boston to submit. Unless Parliament receded from its policy, therefore, "the most dreadful consequences will follow." [33]

The next day, June 1, was the date on which the closing of the port of Boston became effective. Business in Philadelphia came to a standstill and church bells tolled mournfully.[34] One week later a petition bearing the names of over eight hundred freeholders was presented to Governor John Penn begging that he call the assembly into session to consider the Boston Port Act, an act the petitioners denounced as one to compel Americans to acknowledge Parliament's right to tax them at will. In a curt reply Penn refused to grant the petition.[35]

Reed and the other patriot leaders in Philadelphia had been anxious to have the assembly meet in order that it might be persuaded to name delegates to represent Pennsylvania at the intercolonial congress which was clearly in the offing. The governor's refusal to summon that body led them to turn to other expedients. On June 10 a preliminary meeting, at which Reed was present, was held to prepare for a great mass meeting later in the month. It was readily agreed that the Boston Port Act should be soundly condemned, that measures should be undertaken to send relief to the people of Boston, and that the desirability of a Continental Congress be affirmed. How the province's delegation to this congress was to be chosen now that a session of the assembly was extremely unlikely occasioned some debate, in which Reed took an active part. Reed opposed Dickinson's suggestion that this be done by a provincial convention. He favored awaiting the next session of the assembly, even though that might be at a date uncomfortably close to the congress's convocation. Reed had no great confidence in the legislature, however. On the contrary, he felt that the assembly would refuse to act on the people's mandate in this matter and believed that such intransigence, by strikingly disclosing the lack of patriotism of many in whom the people had placed their trust, would be of incalculable value in achieving the unseating of "improper persons" at the next election.[36]

The meeting adopted neither Reed's nor Dickinson's plan. It merely deferred decision on this matter. But other plans for the mass meeting were pushed through. The Quakers and other conservatives present, extremely suspicious of the town meeting technique, succeeded in having Dickinson and the even more conservative Thomas Willing named as co-chairmen. It was agreed that Reed, Thomson, the Reverend William Smith, and several others would speak at the gathering, but, to guard against radicalism in these addresses, these orators were required to write out what they intended to say and submit their texts to the co-chairmen for possible revision.[37]

The next day, June 11, Reed wrote the fifth of his informative letters to Lord Dartmouth. Its purpose was clearly to convince the minister that the hostile reaction to the Boston Port Act was not limited to New England and that the agitation against it was not the work of turbulent lower-class elements but that, on the contrary, support for Boston came from every colony and from every rank of society. Reed told Dartmouth of the strong probability of a Continental Congress meeting in the near future and predicted correctly that this congress would attempt to perpetuate itself by fixing subsequent meeting dates, would draw up a statement of colonial rights, and would, should this statement be treated with "neglect or contempt, which in my humble opinion it will not deserve," propose economic boycott against Britain.

Correctly apprehending that the opposition in America was still

being painted in the colors of lower-class radicalism by many of
the Earl's correspondents, Reed tried to underscore the respecta-
bility of those who condemned the government's course of action
toward Massachusetts. Speaking of the meeting of the night before, he stated that it was comprised of "the most considerable
gentlemen of this city both in fortune and ability, as well in office
as out," and emphasized that it included "the principal persons
of all denominations." Nine-tenths of the inhabitants of Philadelphia, Reed stated, were determined to stand by Boston on the
broad ground of resistance to Parliamentary taxation. Before
the Americans would submit to the latter, Reed concluded vigorously, "all the dreadful consequences of civil war will ensue." [38]

On June 15 the *Pennsylvania Gazette* printed the texts of the
"Coercive Acts" with which Parliament had followed up the
Boston Port Act: the Massachusetts Government Act which virtually annulled that province's charter, and the Administration of
Justice Act which permitted trial for certain crimes committed in
Massachusetts to be held in Britain. Thus additional fuel had
been added to the flame of resistance when the great public meeting of protest was held in State House Square on June 18. Thanks
to the preparations made on the 10th, the meeting went off
smoothly. Reed, Thomson, Reverend Smith, Mifflin, Dickinson,
and three others spoke on the British government's measures and
on six previously prepared resolutions. These denounced the
Port Act as unconstitutional, called for a Continental Congress,
and named a forty-three-man committee of correspondence for
the city and county of Philadelphia. This committee, to which
Reed was elected, was authorized to correspond with committees
in the other counties of Pennsylvania and in other colonies in
order to raise subscriptions for the relief of the poor of Boston
and, more important politically, to decide upon and execute a
plan for the selection of Pennsylvania's delegates to the congress,
now definitely scheduled to open in their own city in September.[39]

John Dickinson, who was chairman of the Committee of Forty-
three, hoped that provision for the appointment of the province's
delegates could be made by persuading the speaker of the assembly, Joseph Galloway, to summon an unofficial meeting of that

body and by petitioning that meeting to name the delegation. The step proved unnecessary, however, for Governor Penn, citing Indian unrest as the reason, issued an official summons for the assembly to meet on July 18. Nevertheless, at a meeting of the committee held June 27 in Carpenter's Hall, it was decided to convene also a provincial convention of delegates from the counties of Pennsylvania. A circular letter addressed to leading patriots in each county urged that representatives be chosen to meet in Philadelphia on July 15 in order to frame recommendations for presentation to the assembly.[40]

The provincial convention opened as scheduled at Carpenter's Hall, Friday, July 15. Reed, Dickinson, Mifflin, and Thomson were among the thirty-four delegates representing the city and county of Philadelphia. Smaller delegations were present, some belatedly, from all the other counties of the province. Thomas Willing was elected chairman and Charles Thomson, secretary. Resolutions of protest against the Coercive Acts, pledges of Pennsylvania's support of economic boycott against Britain if the Continental Congress so recommended, and promises to adhere to even more rigorous methods if proposed by Congress were passed, the first unanimously, the second by "a great majority," the third "by a majority." The vote was by counties, a boon to the less populated inland rural areas.[41]

On the second day of the convention, July 16, a committee was appointed to prepare instructions to guide the assembly in selecting and in instructing the Pennsylvania delegation to the Continental Congress. Reed was one of the eleven members of this committee.[42] Writing to Pettit that evening he reported that there were some warm debates on "Modes and Expressions" but no vital difference of opinion or principle.[43] The committee made its first report, largely the work of John Dickinson, on Monday the 18th, the same day on which the assembly convened. The report was closely examined, recommitted to committee on Tuesday, and a revised draft read, amended slightly, and adopted on Wednesday. The last section of the resolution constituted Dickinson, Reed, and Thomson as a committee to write to the other colonies and inform them of the convention's decisions and recommendations.

The next day the entire membership of the provincial convention proceeded to the State House and there presented their recommendations to the assembly. The latter body, acting upon them the following day, July 22, agreed to appoint delegates to the Continental Congress but rejected the convention's suggestion that Dickinson, Thomas Willing, and James Wilson be selected together with four members of the legislature. Instead, all seven men named were drawn from the assembly's membership. Of these only one, Thomas Mifflin, had been conspicuously vigorous in the patriot cause to date. Dickinson, however, was subsequently made a delegate after winning an assembly seat in October. The instructions for this delegation drafted by the assembly were also conspicuously less vigorous than those recommended by the provincial convention. The latter had asked a sweeping renunciation by Britain of all powers of internal legislation, and plans for non-importation and non-exportation agreements on a permanent basis. The assembly did not echo these demands.[44] Nevertheless, the very fact that a provincial convention had met gave impetus to extralegal action and popular sovereignty in Pennsylvania.

During the course of the convention, Reed had written again to Dartmouth. Unfortunately, the text of the letter is not to be found among his papers, merely a note of July 18 as to its contents. This indicates that Reed "did not quite concur in the whole" of the resolves entered into by the convention, but is silent as to the identity of those points with which he disagreed.[45]

Another letter followed on July 25. Here Reed stated that he had participated in the protest movement in Philadelphia with reluctance and added that he would have publicly opposed some of the measures undertaken if only "I could be convinced that submission to the claims of Parliament did not virtually and necessarily imply a surrender both for myself and my children of the blessings of liberty." If opposition to the Parliamentary claim of taxing Americans at will was a crime, he continued, "I do not

pretend to acquit myself of it." Concerning the pending congress
he pleaded that nothing be done to prevent it from meeting (there
were rumors that General Gage had orders to disperse it) for, he
argued, only from such an assemblage could the true desires of
America be made known to the government.[46]

Reed could not know when he wrote these letters that Lord
Dartmouth's limited imagination had already snapped quite shut
against any thought of a retreat on the part of the ministry or
Parliament. As early as June, 1774, the Earl wrote General Gage
that he no longer had any confidence that tranquillity could be
restored except by such stern measures as the Massachusetts Government Act and the Administration of Justice Act. Then, in
July, he wrote his only reply to Reed's communications. Reed
called it Dartmouth's political creed and told Pettit that it was
"bad enough, God knows!" [47] Dartmouth began his letter by
thanking Reed for his "very candid" messages, proclaimed himself a real friend to America's constitutional rights, and then pro-
tested that there was never any intention on the government's
part to enslave the colonists. The threat to American liberties,
he said, came not from the Mother Country but from the violence
and misconduct of America herself. If the colonists resisted the
punitive measures aimed at "treasonable" opposition in Massachusetts, they would say in effect that "they will no longer be a
part of the British Empire." Clearly, if the dreadful consequences
of which Reed had warned him were to be avoided, it was requisite that America, not Parliament, recede from its position.[48]

Reed's reply, written on September 25, was spirited. He reiterated his old warning that Dartmouth was being misinformed
by ignorant men or men whose advice was based on their desire
for office or profit. It would be quite as fair, Reed claimed, to
judge George III from the writings of Junius as to accept the
representations of such men as accurate. Then, referring to Dartmouth's assertion that there was no intention to enslave the colonists, Reed stated that in his opinion the Declaratory Act of 1766
and the Coercive Acts "degrade us from the scale of freedom."
He continued, "A gentle tyranny is no more compatible with the
rights of an English subject than a violent one. . . . There cannot

be a divine right of doing wrong in Parliament any more than in the King; and all the principles of the [Glorious] Revolution show that there are certain cases wherein resistance is justifiable as to him." [49]

Reed had not yet received Dartmouth's discouraging letter when the first of the delegates to the first Continental Congress began, in mid-August of 1774, to arrive in Philadelphia. By the beginning of September nearly fifty were in town, and little else was talked of. Reed was particularly impressed by the fire of the Virginia delegates, terming the Massachusetts men "mere Milksops to them." [50]

Reed, it will be recalled, not being a member of the Pennsylvania assembly, had not been chosen a delegate from his province. But his high place among the patriot leaders of Philadelphia threw him into close contact with the Congress. The delegates were lavishly wined, dined, and entertained, and in this sphere Reed and his wife had a prominent role. Esther Reed was especially pleased to meet the Massachusetts delegates, men with whom her father had corresponded while agent for that province's house of representatives: Thomas Cushing, Sam Adams, and Richard Cary particularly. The last-named lived with the Reeds nearly a month during the course of the Congress, and his son also spent a week with them.[51]

The diary of another and more famous Massachusetts delegate, John Adams, reveals that Reed was indefatigable in showing the visitors the points of interest in the Quaker City. On August 30, the day after his arrival, Adams was taken on a tour of the Philadelphia Hospital by Reed and Dr. William Shippen; on September 8 Reed led the New Englander up the steeple of Christ Church for a view of the city and the river; two days later Adams "rambled in the evening with Jos. Reed"; and on the following day he, Thomas Cushing, and Reed strolled to the Moravian evening lecture where "we heard soft, sweet music." During his stay in Philadelphia, Adams dined at Reed's home at least twice and had Reed as a companion at dinners given by Miers Fisher, Thomas McKean, and John Dickinson. On October 27, the day before Adams left Philadelphia for Boston, he took the time to hear Reed argue a probate case before the supreme court of Pennsylvania.[52]   John Adams, then, had an opportunity to observe Reed quite closely and his diary comment on the latter's character is thus more than an off-hand impression.   He wrote: "This Mr. Reed is a very sensible and accomplished lawyer, of an amiable disposition, soft, tender, friendly, etc.; he is a friend to his country and to liberty." [53]

The presence of the delegates in Philadelphia gave Reed the opportunity to renew acquaintances with other than the Massachusetts representatives.   Alexander McDougall and Isaac Sears of New York, both of whom Reed had met previously in his visits to New York City, were among these.[54]   One new contact was Silas Deane, a delegate from Connecticut who dined at Reed's home.   He found the Philadelphian "polite and sensible" and described Esther Reed as being of "a most elegant figure and countenance . . . a Daughter of Liberty, zealously affected in a good Cause." [55]   Of far greater importance for Reed's subsequent career was his introduction to George Washington.   The latter dined at the Reed home on October 3.[56]   The acquaintance thus formed was to be strengthened when Washington returned to Philadelphia for the second Continental Congress the following May.

Through September and into October the work of the Congress went forward.   In the long letter of September 25 with which Reed, as mentioned above, answered the one he had received from Lord Dartmouth, considerable space was also devoted to the affairs of the Congress.   Reed reported that a declaration of American rights was being prepared, that the Quebec Bill was a new source of grievance, that the people were inflamed and "ripe for any plan the Congress shall advise, should it be war itself."   He admitted that the unanimity revealed in Congress's endorsement of the radical resolves of a convention in Suffolk County, Massachusetts, astonished him and revealed the absolute necessity of "healing measures," not force.   Should the British government turn to the latter expedient, a long bitter conflict would ensue bringing depopulation and destruction in the colonies and, perhaps, independence.   Reed predicted correctly that the Congress would propose an immediate non-importation agreement, a non-consumption agreement for a later date, and also for a future date, an embargo on exports to Britain. Should these measures fail to produce redress, Reed continued,

The Northern Colonies, I think, will try the last resort, while the middle and southern colonies either openly or secretly will assist them. I cannot dissemble with your lordship that it appears to me we are on the verge of a civil war not to be equalled in history for its importance and fatal consequences.[57]

In a letter written to Dennis DeBerdt at this same time Reed spoke with equally gloomy foreboding of the anarchy and confusion of civil war if hostilities should be initiated by the government. The resolution of the people, he said, would not have disgraced the ancient Romans in their best day: he hoped wisdom would blend with this to avoid extremes as long as possible. Reed stated that if Parliament would repeal the tea duty and the coercive acts against Massachusetts, the tea would be paid for and the crisis would be resolved. "Nothing else will save this country and indeed Britain too." [58]

Two days before the Congress adjourned Reed wrote again to Dartmouth, this his ninth letter. Again he described in vigorous terms the determined spirit of the colonists never to submit to a recognition of Parliament's authority to lay taxes upon them or interfere in their internal government. The economic measures recommended by the Congress would be, he predicted, faithfully carried out by Pennsylvania and the other provinces, though the loss of all trade be the result. Should this pressure fail, America was preparing, through the formation of military associations, to resort to arms. However, the Congress had strongly impressed upon the Massachusetts delegates that the inhabitants of that province must be restrained from any hostile action against General Gage's forces in Boston. Reed closed with the hope that Gage would not take the offensive and that bloodshed might thus be avoided.[59]

Reed's prediction that Pennsylvania would honor its pledge to carry out the Continental Association, the name given those measures designed by the Congress to bring economic pressure to bear on Britain, was speedily realized and in a manner which cast Reed into a prominent executive position. On November 12 elections were held for the city and county of Philadelphia to choose committees to carry out the non-importation agreement (due to go into effect on December 1) and the other measures of the Association. The very fact that new elections were held rather than permit the existing Committee of Forty-three (named the previous June) to supervise the boycott is indicative of the growing radicalism within Philadelphia. Of the new committee for the city, sixty-six in number, only seventeen had been members of the much more conservative older body. Reed, Dickinson, Thomson, and Mifflin were among those renamed, but such men as Thomas Wharton and the Reverend Dr. William Smith were dropped.[60] Moderation was not thrown completely to the winds, however. Reed, who made no secret of his hope that the crisis might yet be resolved peaceably, was named chairman of the city committee.[61] But the truly revolutionary nature of the new undertakings could hardly be disguised. The Congress, a body with absolutely no legislative powers, had drafted and recommended the Association. Extralegal committees such as the one which Reed now headed were then formed, usually on a county level, throughout America and set about enforcing the Association as if it were law, this even before the provincial legislatures had voiced their approval of the Congress's proceedings (the Pennsylvania assembly did so on December 10). These committees inspected incoming cargoes, promulgated regulations for storing or reshipping goods which fell within the ban, kept a close watch on individuals suspected of a lack of zeal for the patriot cause, and publicized infractions of the Association—in short, constituted themselves as a *de facto* government existing side by side with the lawful one.[62]

It is clear from letters he wrote that Reed thought his countrymen were moving away too rapidly at this time from lawful procedures of protest and remonstrance. Writing on December 24, 1774, he confided to Dennis DeBerdt his belief that there was ground for censure on both sides of the controversy, that in the colonies "too keen a resentment has taken place, which has given birth to doctrines and measures in which perhaps passion has mingled in our councils and disturbed the work of reason and judgment." Elsewhere in the letter he lamented that the coercive measures of the Mother Country had produced in America "a spirit of libertinism rather than of liberty." [63]

An open manifestation of these opinions followed shortly upon the dispatch of this letter. Reed consented to represent two Philadelphia merchants, Stacey Hepburn and John Duffield, in a civil action against seven inhabitants of Cumberland County, New Jersey, who, together with a number of unidentified persons on the evening of December 22, 1774, had burnt a quantity of tea consigned to the plaintiffs. The tea, which had apparently been smuggled in from Holland, was temporarily in storage at Greenwich, New Jersey, at the time. Reed, assisted by Charles Pettit, brought the case before the supreme court of New Jersey at its April, 1775, term. Complications caused by the fact that the plaintiffs were non-residents led the case to languish through 1775 and into 1776. With the Declaration of Independence the action was dropped entirely. The efforts of Chief Justice Frederick Smyth of New Jersey to obtain criminal indictments against the tea burners of Greenwich also failed.[64]

Despite these indications of qualms concerning the road the patriot movement was taking, Reed felt it obligatory that a united front be maintained by the colonists against Britain. He stated this belief succinctly in a letter to Charles Pettit:

Though I think the Congress proceeded on too high a scale, I know the designs of the Ministry and the temper of the people of England so well, that I am confident nothing but a union in any scheme would relieve us from the oppressions which were meditating, and which the present measures were only designed to introduce. While they [the Ministry] claim all, I can, with a safe conscience, deny all. Our mutual interests and necessities point out some middle line which I should be for adopting. We have left room enough to recede, and I doubt not shall be ready to do it whenever Great Britain shows that she is willing to recede on her part from those extravagent claims which annihilate all security for life, liberty and property.[65]

Meanwhile, the patriots in Philadelphia were steadily losing confidence in their province's legislature as an efficient vehicle for their resistance movement.[66] Consequently, on December 28, 1774, the committee of Philadelphia called for a second provincial convention to assemble in the capital on January 23, 1775. When the body met, its conservative elements were speedily forced to take a back seat thanks to a coalition of the moderates led by Reed and Dickinson, with more radical delegates led by Charles Thomson and western leaders. Reed was elected president of the convention, a tribute of recognition for his attachment to the patriot cause and, at the same time, for his moderation in seeking peaceful means of obtaining redress of grievances. The convention was in session from January 23 through January 28. A series of twenty-six resolutions were passed, all unanimously. They expressed approval of the actions of the Continental Congress, pledged faithful execution of the Association in Pennsylvania, and dwelt in detail upon plans to promote manufactures (including that of gunpowder) within the province to soften the adverse effects of non-importation from Britain. The convention constituted the Philadelphia committee a standing committee of correspondence empowered to call another convention when necessary.[67]

In his eleventh letter to Lord Dartmouth, written December 24, 1774, Reed had predicted that some attempt would probably be made to have the convention consider military preparations.[68] But the convention did not, aside from recommending the manufacture of gunpowder, debate any steps in this direction. Here the influence of the Quakers, who were strong advocates of passive resistance to Britain at this time, was undoubtedly a strong factor. But many other moderates, Reed among them, also opposed such action.[69]

With the adjournment of the provincial convention of January, 1775, the patriots of Philadelphia settled back into relative quiescence to await the second Continental Congress scheduled to convene on May 10. Reed's Philadelphia Committee of Sixty-six, the "Committee of Observation, Inspection, and Correspondence" to give it its formal title, remained active of course and in fact assumed new duties when, on March 1, that portion of the Association calling for non-consumption of British products went into effect. The late winter and early spring was a period of watchful waiting, all America again looking for some indication as to how the Mother Country had received the petitions of the first Continental Congress.

Reed himself was rather optimistic during the early months of 1775. On January 31 he wrote to Pettit and, basing his opinion on November dispatches from England and perhaps on an October letter from Dennis DeBerdt which reported that Dartmouth had expressed approval of the Congress, maintained that "the tide is certainly turning towards America; all the accounts agree that the Ministry are disposed to relax the articles of the Boston Port Bill and the act for the administration of Justice." [70] This optimism is also reflected in Reed's letter of February 10 to Lord Dartmouth. Reed stated that the old affection of the colonists for the Mother Country had not vanished and that, particularly in Pennsylvania, there was a great desire for a reconciliation upon any terms which would validate the distinction between an English colonist and a colonist of an arbitrary nation. He did not fail to remind Dartmouth, however, that "this country will be deluged with blood before it will submit to any other taxation than by their own Assemblies." But Reed believed the colonists would submit to "all acts of Parliament of general superintendence and control of trade" if that body would renounce taxation powers over the colonists, repeal the Boston acts, ease trade restrictions somewhat, and make some changes in the British officialdom in America, particularly, as to the last point, requiring "a courteous and civil demeanour in all officers instead of that haughty supercilious deportment they too generally assume." [71]

This was the last in the series of twelve letters written by Reed to Lord Dartmouth. The letters failed, in the last analysis, to convince their recipient of the depth of conviction and the breadth of popular support which lay behind the disturbances in America. Yet Reed was not unjustified in feeling some satisfaction, as he wrote Pettit, for "having done my Country some service by removing some aspersions and Prejudices." [72] The ministry's decision to receive the petitions sent to the Crown, Commons, and Lords by the first Continental Congress, for example, owed something to Reed's advice to Dartmouth, if Dennis De-Berdt's opinion is to be valued. Dartmouth himself delivered the petitions addressed to his royal master.[73]

Reed's task in these letters had been a most difficult one. First he had attempted to dissuade the ministry from a program of violent coercion by emphasizing the unity and resolute nature of the colonial opposition. Secondly, he had to try to convince the ministry that old loyalties were yet strong enough for a favorable and grateful response should the government proffer a sincere offer of redress of grievances and a reconciliation. The second task was the more difficult one, particularly because of Reed's leading role in the resistance movement in Philadelphia. He could not have hoped to succeed in this task of persuasion if he had adopted the ranting tone of the militant revolutionary. This realization and, more important, his own deep convictions led him to shun such an approach. Yet, his moderation exposed him to charges that in Philadelphia he assumed the role of the patriot but in his letters to Dartmouth posed as a defender of the empire. Such charges, interestingly enough, did gain circulation after hostilities had begun, but in London, not Philadelphia. Dennis DeBerdt wrote to Esther Reed in June, 1775, that rumor had it there that Reed had been paid for his communications to the minister. He feared that this falsehood would be transmitted to Philadelphia.[74] Both Mrs. Reed and Charles Pettit became somewhat apprehensive on this score, the more so since Reed was away with the Continental Army besieging Boston. But the fears of both were soon quieted, for as Pettit wrote to Reed, not a "lisp" of the fabrication appeared anywhere in Philadelphia.[75]

It was left to a nineteenth-century American historian of the nationalist school, George Bancroft, to take up the London rumors and, by quoting Reed out of context, assert that the latter, disloyal to America, made assiduous attempts to convince the ministry of the importance of having him on their side.[76] The full quotation which Bancroft diluted, taken from a letter to Dennis DeBerdt with which Reed's last letter to Dartmouth was enclosed, reveals that Reed had said his activities in Philadelphia might lead the Earl to consider him as a "factious, turbulent person, unworthy his further notice . . . or as a person who acts uprightly on mistaken principles and has some weight and influence . . . whom, upon the whole, the Government might wish to be on their side." In the next sentence, which Bancroft did *not* quote, Reed went on to say, "But my opinion of the system of Colony Administration must be wholly changed before I can think of supporting any measure of the British Government founded upon it." [77]

Reed himself, conscious of the honest and disinterested motives which had prompted the entire correspondence, was not greatly distressed by the news from his wife and brothers-in-law as to the London rumors. His reply to Charles Pettit's message informing him that the reports had not gained currency in Philadelphia is notable for its clarity and candor:

I should not be desirous of disclosing my letters to Lord Dartmouth, but I have no reason to be afraid of doing so if necessary. I only communicated to him transactions earlier than he found them in newspapers. I gave no opinions but what led to a renunciation of the present system. I avowed my own principles that the right of taxation was incompatible with my idea of our rights derived under the British Constitution, and cautioned him against trusting to letters and advices from this country of men holding or seeking office. In my first letter I absolutely disclaimed all office or reward for myself. The general sentiments I am sure would be approved; some may fault particular expressions. . . . I have not wrote to him since the beginning of last February, though he has through Mr. DeBerdt solicited it strongly . . . .[78] With common candour my friends need have no fear for me.[79]

These unpleasantries were all in the future, however, as early 1775 saw winter give way to spring and Reed anxiously awaited news from England. A letter from DeBerdt brought the good news of a petition by the merchants of London bewailing the fatal effects of a stoppage of trade with America. Dennis also reported, however, that steps were afoot to prevent the meeting of the second Continental Congress.[80]

The drastic move which *had* been decided upon, the dispatch of orders to General Gage to accept a test of force by arresting

the principal patriot leaders in Massachusetts, was evidently unknown to DeBerdt. In his letter of February 10 to Lord Dartmouth, Reed had posited his prediction of subsiding bitterness
upon the absence of "some new severity . . . some common misfortune, or a severe punishment of any particular colony." [81] But
as this letter was beginning its ocean crossing, Dartmouth's orders
to Gage were also on their way. The latter constituted, of course,
exactly that "new severity" against which Reed had warned.
General Gage, as is well known, acted promptly upon receiving
the dispatches on April 14.[82]   On the afternoon of April 24 a
breathless rider from Trenton galloped up to the City Tavern in
Philadelphia with the news of Lexington and Concord. The dispatches he bore had originated at Watertown, Massachusetts, on
the morning of the skirmish and had come via New Haven, New
York City, New Brunswick, and Princeton.[83]   The latest wind
from the north had brought the stirring news that the patriots of
New England were already in the field.

CHAPTER V

1775: General Washington's Confidant

THE clamorous news of that spring afternoon and the excitement which gripped Philadelphia in its train sounded a death knell for the tenacious hope that Britain and America might be honorably reconciled without bloodshed. This hope Joseph Reed had treasured fondly. It was with deep pain, not with exultation, that he heard of the hostilities at Lexington and Concord. He realized that these distant events could not be treated as an isolated incident if American liberties, so dependent upon intercolonial unity, were to be successfully defended. He realized that a general war must now ensue. Eminently sober for his thirty-four years, Reed could not but view this dark prospect with an anxious heart. This anxiety sprang from the full realization that remonstrance had failed and that the war must be vigorously sustained, rather than from doubts as to whether or not Pennsylvania would be involved in the conflict. Reed knew that it must be, and his actions testified to this conviction.

Action was what was demanded now, and Reed and other patriot leaders of Philadelphia spent hectic hours after receiving the fateful news mapping out their plans. The first step was a call for a great mass meeting of the city's inhabitants at State House Square on the afternoon of the next day, April 25. By the appointed hour, 3 P.M., some 8,000 men were assembled. The speeches they listened to, though eloquent, were superfluous, for the martial mood of the inhabitants was unmistakable. This spirit received expression in a resolution that the patriots of Philadelphia "associate together for the Purpose of defending with arms their Property, Liberty and Lives." [1]

With this resolution was born the revolutionary militia of Pennsylvania, the "Military Association," belated counterpart of

New England's Minute Men organization. The network of
county committees of inspection and correspondence already in
existence provided a convenient nucleus for the enlistment and
direction of the association throughout the province. In Philadelphia itself the organization took form rapidly. On April 29
the associators of the city held a meeting at the State House yard
at which it was decided that each of the city's ten wards should
raise one or more companies and select officers. On May 1 these
decisions were implemented. Meetings were held by the associators in each ward, companies were formed, and officers selected.[2]
The companies were subsequently linked into battalions. On this
latter level Reed accepted the first of many military offices which
were to be his during the course of the Revolution. He became
the lieutenant colonel, the second in command, of the second battalion of the militia of the city of Philadelphia.[3] The battalion's
colonel and commanding officer was Daniel Roberdeau, one of
the most fiery of the city's patriots, while its majors were John
Bayard and Reed's close friend, John Cox.[4]

To his friends in Massachusetts Reed sent encouraging reports
of the feverish activity in Philadelphia and heartening pledges
of support. From Charlestown, Richard Cary wrote back that
Reed's letter of April 28 was "like a cordial." Joseph Warren
wrote to Reed on May 15 thanking the latter for his expressions
of support and for a bill of exchange which Reed had enclosed
as a contribution for relief work in Boston.[5]

In Philadelphia, meanwhile, the assembly was striving desper-
ately to solve a vexing dilemma. To maintain popular support
it must put itself at the head of the movement to gird the province for war. Yet its members realized all too well that a civil
war, even if it remained short of a war for independence, would
inevitably bring to a focus the resentments over the restrictions
on the franchise and the unrepresentative character of the legislature. The dilemma was never resolved. After the mass meeting in Philadelphia on April 25, the legislature voted to enlist
4,300 men for Pennsylvania's defense. Further pressure from the
patriot groups led it to allot some £7,000 to the Philadelphia
committee of inspection and correspondence. But a petition re-

ceived on May 4 asking that £50,000 be voted for military expenditures was not acted upon. Nine days later the assembly adjourned until June 19. During the critical weeks of May and early June, Reed's Philadelphia committee and the military associations were the powers in the province.[6]

Added impetus to the patriot movement in Pennsylvania was supplied by the convocation of the second Continental Congress in Philadelphia on May 10. Once more Pennsylvania's delegation had been chosen from the membership of the assembly. But again, as during the meeting of the first Continental Congress the previous fall, Reed was in close contact with the delegates. Again the hospitality of his home was opened to them. Three of Virginia's representatives, Washington, Richard Henry Lee, and Benjamin Harrison, had supper there the night they arrived in Philadelphia and stayed into the early morning hours discussing plans for the defense of the Delaware River against British warships.[7] In addition to hospitality on this individual basis, there were now military reviews in Congress's honor as well. Reed's battalion and the other associators of the city drilled and paraded on June 8 and again on June 20.[8] John Adams, for one, was suitably impressed. Describing the review of the 8th in a letter to his wife, he spoke approvingly of the fine appearance of the "full two thousand men . . . all in uniform, going through the manual exercise and the manoeuvres with remarkable dexterity. All this has been accomplished since the 19th of April; so sudden a formation of an army never took place any where." [9]

Two days after watching the parade of June 8, Adams proposed that Congress assume the direction and support of the patriot army besieging Boston as a Continental Army. Approval of this significant step was quickly followed by a resolution to raise troops in Pennsylvania, Maryland, and Virginia to march to join the forces in Massachusetts. Plans were made to govern the Continental Army and to raise money to support it. Then, on Thursday, June 15, George Washington was named commander in chief of the new army, an office he accepted the following day.

Washington dined at Reed's home the following Monday evening.[10] The Virginian's imminent departure for Massachusetts to assume his command and his crying need for men of ability to aid him in the gigantic task he faced must have been topics of conversation. It is probable that Washington used this opportunity for his first attempts to enlist Reed as a member of his staff, either by a direct request or by dwelling upon his need for competent aides. In either case, Reed, quick of perception as he was, could not have been in doubt as to the general's desire to number him among his military "family." But he did not commit himself immediately. The interval between the dinner at his home and Washington's departure date, June 23, was one of indecisive inner debate. The only resolve Reed fastened upon was that he would accompany the general part of the way to Cambridge, to New York City at least. En route, perhaps, he could reach a decision.

It was on such a basis that Reed bid his wife farewell on the morning of the 23rd and set out northward with the commander in chief's party.[11] The departure, despite steady rain, was a gala one, members of Congress, patriot leaders of Philadelphia, and officers of the militia riding out from the city with Washington. Then these well-wishers were left behind. A troop of the Philadelphia Light Horse, smartly uniformed with brown coats, peaked helmets, and high boots, remained with the little party, however, as escort and guard for Washington and his distinguished companions. These were Major General Charles Lee and his aide, Samuel Griffin, Major General Philip Schuyler, until his appointment a delegate in Congress from New York, Reed, and Reed's compatriot from Philadelphia, Thomas Mifflin, already selected by Washington as an aide.[12]

The first night's stop was probably made at Reed's birthplace, Trenton. That after the second day's ride, June 24, was made at New Brunswick. The next morning, Sunday, an early start was made for Newark, which was reached about 9 A.M. There Washington consulted members of the provincial congress of New York who brought word that the royal governor, William Tryon, was expected to reach New York City from England that same afternoon. To avoid an incident it was decided that Washington and his party should enter the city from the north by crossing the Hudson from Hoboken rather than use the customary Philadelphia–New York route, the ferry from Paulus Hook to the Battery.[13] While these plans were being formulated, Reed had the pleasure of a brief reunion with his brother-in-law, Charles Pettit, who had come up from Perth Amboy to Newark to meet him. Pettit's subsequent letters to Reed reveal that at the time of this meeting the latter had not yet decided to accept a position on Washington's staff, or, if he had, and this surmise seems quite unlikely in view of their closeness, he did not reveal this to Pettit. The latter, when Reed departed with Washington's party, fully expected that his brother-in-law would accompany the general only as far as New York City and that he would thus see him on his return trip to Philadelphia "in the course of a Week." [14]

The little cavalcade reached New York without incident late that afternoon. There was a dinner at the home of Colonel Leonard Lispenard and then a parade into the city led by New York militia, a parade marked by the noisy and enthusiastic welcome accorded Washington by the city's inhabitants. The next day, Monday, June 26, was a crowded one. Washington drafted instructions for Schuyler, who was now to part company with the commander in chief and assume his command in New York, made some purchases, received an address from members of the provincial congress, and briefly replied to the address. The answer, which Douglas Freeman believed was probably written by Reed or Mifflin for Washington, contained the celebrated line: "When we assumed the soldier, we did not lay aside the citizen." [15]

Sometime that day, or perhaps sometime the night before, Washington had accomplished another important bit of business —he had persuaded Reed to accompany him to Cambridge and enter his military "family" as his confidential secretary. Reed's decision must have been reached suddenly. Elias Boudinot, an old friend of Reed's college and clerkship days,[16] had accompanied Washington's party from Jersey to New York City on the 25th and had taken his leave of Reed convinced that his friend would go no farther with the general. Indeed, Reed had promised to visit him at Elizabeth on his way back to Philadelphia. When Boudinot later learned that Reed had continued on with the commander in chief, he wrote to him and mentioned that this step indicated "a great change in your determinations after you left me at New York." [17]

Reed's decision, indeed, occasioned universal surprise. That even Mrs. Reed was nonplused by his new engagement is evident from her letter to her brother, Dennis DeBerdt, of July 22:

> An event has taken place which I little thought of and which I assure you my dear Mr. Reed as little suspected when he went from home; that is, his appointment as Secretary to the General. . . . I confess it is a trial I never thought I should have experienced, and therefore am the less prepared to bear it.[18]

Charles Pettit, awaiting Reed's expected visit at his Perth Amboy home, could not believe the reports he received as to Reed's action until these were confirmed by Bowes Reed. Then he wrote to Joseph and confessed that "it was with no small degree of surprise I heard you had accepted a post in the Army." [19] Another letter from a close friend, John Cox, indicates that no one in Philadelphia had any notion that Reed would accompany Washington farther than New York.[20]

Reed's action had been so sudden, in fact, that the first reaction of many of his friends was unfavorable. He had, of course, made absolutely no provision within his family or professional circle for an absence which was to stretch from a projected two weeks to over four months in duration. Pettit's sincere solicitude for Reed's family caused him misgivings over the latter's step. In the first letter he wrote to Reed at Cambridge, though asserting that he did not mean even to insinuate that Reed was accountable to him for his conduct, he conveyed his doubts as to its wisdom in this instance and went on in his characteristically generous fashion to offer to do anything in his power to render Reed's absence as little inconvenient to his family as possible. For one thing, he would try to get Mrs. Reed to spend the rest of the summer at his home.[21]

Reed's friends in Philadelphia had still other reasons for shaking their heads over his step. For a person who stood so high in the patriot circle of the largest city in America to accept the seemingly menial position of a secretary appeared, as John Cox expressed it in a letter to Reed, a sacrifice "the public could have

no Right to expect from a Person situated as you were." Fur-
thermore, Reed's presence in Philadelphia was deemed essential
at this critical juncture.   Cox, a member of the Philadelphia committee of inspection and correspondence which Reed had headed,
said the latter's absence was felt painfully at committee sessions:
"No man was ever more missed, nor can we possibly do without
you." [22]

But Reed himself, despite the apparent suddenness of his decision, must have weighed all these considerations carefully.   His
duty to his wife, her aged mother, and his three young children
demanded circumspection.   Aside from his professional income,
which would of course deteriorate during an absence from his
clients, he had no income sufficient for the support of his family
for any extended period.   As Washington's secretary he was to receive a very modest salary of sixty-six dollars per month, one he
later described as "too inconsiderable to be mentioned in comparison with what I then received from a very lucrative practice." [23]   Washington himself, in response to some unfair insinuations regarding Reed's financial situation as secretary, wrote the
latter, "What can your brethren of the law mean by saying your
perquisites as Secretary must be considerable?   I am sure they
have not amounted to one farthing."[24]   The simple fact that
Reed, for his family's sake, could not long remain absent from his
law practice was, without doubt, the most important consideration in the qualified assent he gave to Washington's request,
qualified because from the first he promised no more than temporary service with the commander in chief.

Reed himself entertained no doubts as to which service, that
at the general's side or that as committee leader in Philadelphia,
was of greater value to the patriot cause.   From the first Washington had made clear to Reed that he sought the latter not as a
mere clerk but, to use words he later expressed to Reed, as a confidant who "can think for me as well as execute orders." [25]   Not
a man to wheedle another, Washington must have nevertheless
pressed Reed warmly during their ride from Philadelphia to New
York and impressed upon the latter forcibly the need he had for
his services.   To Elias Boudinot Reed wrote that Washington

"expressed himself to me in such Terms that I thought myself bound by every Tye of Duty and Honour to comply with his Request to help him through the Sea of Difficulties." The general had also broken down Reed's fears that he would be inadequate to a position of importance in the strange new world of military affairs and had given Reed, as he told Boudinot, a "well grounded Expectation that I could be of real Service." [26]

Then too, the escape from the realm of planning to that of action, of remonstrance to action in the field, constituted, perhaps, an exhilarating prospect. Reed's letter to Pettit of August 20 illustrates this outlook:

I have taken too active a part in what may be called the civil part of opposition to renounce the public cause, when it seems to lead to danger, with Honour. I have a sovereign contempt for the character which can plan measures it has not spirit to assist in the execution of.[27]

It was with all these balancings of pros and cons behind him that Reed rode out of New York City with Washington on the afternoon of June 26. Up the length of Manhattan Island the party went, across King's Bridge, and then stopped for the night nearby. The next morning at New Rochelle General Schuyler made his adieus and the escort of the Philadelphia Light Horse finally turned back too. Washington, Lee, Reed, Mifflin, and Griffin pressed on. New Haven was reached on the 28th, Wethersfield on the following day. On the 30th the party crossed into Massachusetts at last and proceeded, with ever-changing escorts, via Springfield, Worcester, and Watertown, where the provincial congress was in session, finally reaching Cambridge Sunday afternoon, July 2.[28]

Two days later, July 4, 1775, in the second general orders issued by Washington as commander in chief, the appointments of Reed and Mifflin were officially announced: "Thomas Mifflin, Esqr. is appointed by the General one of his Aid-de-Camps. Joseph Reed, Esqr. is in like manner appointed Secretary to the General." [29] Reed was not given a commission in the Continental Army. Technically he was a civilian aide of the general's. He was, however, habitually addressed at Cambridge as "Colonel

Reed," the title being derived from his rank in the Philadelphia association.

Reed probably never worked harder in his life than he did during those first hectic weeks at Cambridge. The number, variety, and complexity of the organizational problems facing Washington and his staff were staggering. For the first week Reed acted, as he later wrote Elias Boudinot, as "Secretary, Adjutant General, and Quarter Master, besides doing a thousand other little Things which fell [to me] incidentally." Totally inexperienced in military affairs as he was, Reed confessed that he would have as soon thought of being an Indian interpreter as assume these tasks had not Washington's patient instructions and a hasty perusal of military tracts given him a grasp of fundamental concepts.[30]

The time and energy Washington expended in thus schooling Reed was an investment which returned high dividends. The general had chosen Reed to be his most intimate assistant not for his military knowledge but because he recognized in the young Philadelphian a rare combination of talents. These were intelligence, discretion, an ability to deal with men of high rank, both civil and military, an outlook not narrowly provincial, orderly habits, and, finally but certainly not last in importance, the ability to write clearly and, if need be, eloquently. Reed's good education, his legal training, his travel and intercolonial contacts, even his experience in the keeping of records gained as deputy secretary of New Jersey—all these eclipsed his lack of a soldier's background and equipped him admirably for the important contribution he was to make in the turbulent summer of 1775.[31]

From the first, Reed's facility with the pen was a great asset to Washington. He composed the letters signed by Washington in the famous exchange with the British command in Boston concerning the treatment of American prisoners. He drafted letters to the Congress, to the governors of Connecticut and Rhode Island, to the legislature of Massachusetts, to General Schuyler, to Benedict Arnold approving his order of march for the Quebec expedition, and to many others. He probably wrote the address to the people of Canada in which Washington invited them to unite with the thirteen colonies in an indissoluble union and to cooperate with the invading armies under Schuyler and Arnold.[32] Among the Reed manuscript collection in the New-York Historical Society are the drafts of twenty-four such letters written for Washington's signature. In addition, many of the letters now among the Washington papers in the Library of Congress which were signed by the general during the first four months at Cambridge are in Reed's handwriting. Others, written by a clerk, bear additions in Reed's hand as well as the commander in chief's signature. At times, as in the case of a letter of July 10 to General Schuyler,[33] Washington made additions to Reed's draft, but more often than not he was satisfied to accept the latter's effort without revisions. It can occasion no surprise, therefore, to find the general writing to Reed after the Philadelphian left his staff, "I feel the want of your ready pen greatly." [34]

Washington, of necessity, kept his secretary so occupied with official correspondence during the first weeks at Cambridge that Reed had neither the time nor the inclination to do much letter writing to his own circle of family and friends. Not until July 26 did he write a full letter to his wife and it was well into August before he began a regular correspondence with Charles Pettit and with friends in Philadelphia, notably John Cox. By the time he wrote the letter of the 26th to Esther, the early excitement had worn off and the day-to-day duties had become, as he expressed it, "a plain kind of jog trot life that is very tedious at times without you." [35] Mrs. Reed, for her part, accepted her husband's unexpected absence as cheerfully as possible. She was proud that Washington had reserved an important place in his military family for her husband and happy too that the duties of this position did not expose his person to danger. Fastening this early in the war upon the patriotic attitude which she sustained until her death in 1781, this daughter of England wrote her brother that "I think the Cause in which he [Reed] is engaged so just, so Glorious, and, I hope, will be so victorious" that all private interests had to take second place.[36]

Though Reed described for Esther the military situation at camp and the chances of a British attack, she was more interested in his own health and living conditions. Her concern was par-

ticularly acute since her husband had been troubled by an intermittent fever prior to his departure from Philadelphia. During
the journey to Cambridge, Reed threw off this malady and thereafter, despite the sometimes taxing nature of his duties, seemed
to thrive on the Massachusetts air. He wrote Pettit in August
that he "never enjoyed better health in my Life," and Esther,
writing to Dennis late in October, when Reed's return was expected daily, reported that every Philadelphian who had seen her
husband at headquarters returned to tell her he had grown so fat
she would hardly recognize him.[37]

These last reports may have been exaggerated, but the living
conditions for Washington and his staff at Cambridge were comfortable, luxurious indeed, if contrasted with those of later peri-
ods of the war. Though military supplies, notably powder, were
woefully low, food was plentiful and reasonable in cost and the
general health of the camp good.[38] As to lodgings, Reed was
quartered with the commander in chief throughout his stay at
Cambridge, first at the residence of the president of Harvard
College, Samuel Langdon, the so-called Wadsworth House, later
at the dignified John Vassall home.[39]

From the close contact into which Washington and Reed were
thus thrown, friendship soon emerged. Surrounded at Cambridge by men who, with few exceptions, were total strangers to
him, the general felt the need of a confidant whose friendship and
faithfulness he could trust. Reed filled that void, never abusing
the confidence Washington placed in him. The warmth of the
relationship between the two men, though not capable of docu-
mentation for the period they were together at Cambridge, is
clearly evident from the correspondence which ensued after Reed
had returned to Philadelphia in November. In writing to Reed
Washington signed himself "Yours affectionately" or "Your affec-
tionate humble servant" in place of his usual closing, "Your
obedient and humble servant." He called Reed "my good friend"
and, in asking Reed to send him word of any criticism of his
leadership, stated that the latter could in no better way "give a
more convincing proof of your friendship." [40]

In urging Reed's return to Cambridge in these letters, Wash-

ington confessed that he had not been able to find a successor
"with whom I would choose to live in unbounded confidence." [41]
No better proof of the closeness of the relationship between the
commander in chief and his secretary is to be found than the freedom with which Washington revealed his thoughts and indeed
his emotions in these letters.   Manifestly, this absence of the reserve and caution which was so characteristic of the general in
his correspondence with other men was the fruit of the candor
and trust which had been built up while Reed worked by his side
at headquarters.   The much publicized reserve of Washington
has been attributed by Douglas Southall Freeman to self-protec-
tion against the possibility of misrepresentation.   Washington,
Freeman tells us,

never permitted himself to write freely to any persons except Reed
and his brother "Jack" [John Augustine Washington] . . . In letters to
these two, he now was free of the awkward self-consciousness that
sometimes had distorted and obscured his meaning. . . . If he talked as
he wrote to those whose discretion he trusted, he conversed with confidence, with vigor, with candor, and even with some of the quality he
most had lacked, humor.[42]

Another student of the Revolution, Allen French, was equally
struck by the freedom of expression in Washington's letters to
Reed.   He commented that it was therefore the historian's gain,
though Washington's loss, that Reed returned to Philadelphia.
He wrote that the general confided to the latter not only his difficulties and perplexities but also the emotions which the Virginian so rarely allowed himself to express.   In French's opinion
Washington, at this time, was more outspoken to Reed than to
anyone except his wife.[43]

The wholeheartedness with which Washington admitted Reed
to his confidence at Cambridge and in his subsequent correspondence placed heavy responsibilities upon the latter.   While at headquarters Reed had found that "flattering and pleasing" as this
confidence was, it exposed him not only to envy, but also to the
ill will of those who saw in him a convenient target for the rancor
they dared not vent upon Washington himself.   As Reed wrote
Pettit after his return home,

The Service I really did to the Publick did not save me from the Malevolence of some who, upon the same principle that a Minister is accountable for a King's Faults, attributed to me every Measure of the General's which they did not like.   And if he censured their conduct, instead of amending it they ascribed his Censure to ill offices done them by those about him.[44]

All the while, as the summer of 1775 drew near its close, the work of fashioning a fighting force went forward.   By early September Reed could write confidently that the British army in Boston would be destroyed if an attempt were made to break through the American positions which encompassed it.[45]   But the British forts, unfortunately, were of great strength too.   Thus, though the secretary shared his commander's burning desire to deliver a resounding stroke, he wrestled with the question as to whether it would be wise to risk defeat and a disheartening of "our Troops so young" by ordering an assault against obstacles which would test the best of veteran soldiers.[46]

As Reed's grasp of military affairs became surer and as the respect between Washington and himself ripened into friendship, the general assigned to him such confidential tasks as the examination of the papers of Dr. Benjamin Church.   The latter, hitherto considered one of the most trustworthy of the patriot leaders in Massachusetts, was found to have been corresponding in cipher and through the agency of royal officials in Rhode Island with persons behind the British lines in Boston.   Church was examined before Washington and a board of generals and, unable to explain his actions satisfactorily, was put under close guard until Congress or the Massachusetts assembly, of which Church was a member, should decide his fate.[47]   From his place of imprisonment in Cambridge, Church wrote two bombastic letters to Reed.   "Am I in the Bastile, Sir," he thundered, "or in a Land struggling for the rights of Freemen?"   From rhetoric Church switched to the law, claiming the protection of no less than Magna Charta, the British Bill of Rights, and habeas corpus, and attacking as ex post facto law the Articles of War drawn up by Congress.   That Reed's reply, the text of which has been lost, infuriated Church, is disclosed by his second letter.   Reed had evidently remarked that

the arguments used by Church in his defense were "such as may
serve any *Spy* upon Earth," added that these explanations would
destroy his reputation even if they saved his life, and concluded,
and to this Church apparently took the most violent exception,
by expressing his pity.[48] "Acquit or execute me!" Church cried
in the second letter, but he was not destined for either fate.   In
November the Massachusetts assembly formally expelled him,
after which, at the order of Congress, he was imprisoned in Connecticut. Some two years later he was permitted to leave America
for the West Indies, but the ship on which he sailed was lost at
sea and he apparently perished with it.[49]

Important as it was to Washington that he should have a discreet aide who could be assigned confidential tasks, Reed's greatest
value to his commander did not lie in this field of the unusual but
in relieving the harrassed Virginian of a multitude of details that
piled up daily on the headquarters desk. Very few of the general's aides throughout the war were as able or as willing as Reed
showed himself to be in assuming responsibility for minor decisions, in displaying personal initiative, and in cultivating the
breadth of vision "to comprehend at one view," as Washington
later wrote Reed, "the diversity of matter which comes before me,
so as to afford that ready assistance which every man in my situation must stand more or less in need of." [50] After Reed left Washington's service, the latter urged his return by complaining that
"at present my time is so much taken up at my desk, that I am
obliged to neglect many other essential parts of my duty: it is
absolutely necessary, therefore, for me to have persons that can
think for me, as well as execute orders." [51]

Reed's initiative and ability to handle the details of projects
with but general directions from Washington is clearly seen in the
very important services he performed toward launching a navy
for the Continental forces. On September 2 Washington commissioned Nicholson Broughton a captain in the Continental
Army and directed him to take a detachment of soldiers with
maritime experience, proceed aboard the schooner *Hannah* at
Beverly, Massachusetts, and put to sea to prey on cargo ships
bringing supplies to the British forces in Boston.[52] Washington

then authorized Captain John Glover of Marblehead to fit out other vessels to assist the *Hannah*. After the project had gained some headway through September, the general apparently turned over to Reed the task of coordinating from headquarters the work of Glover, Colonel Stephen Moylan, mustermaster general of the Continental forces whom Washington sent to aid Glover, Ephraim Bowen of Plymouth, the above-mentioned Captain Broughton, and other captains. Reed supplied information as to the availability of crews and ordnance, sent word when British ships were expected off Boston or the St. Lawrence, and set the terms at which the Army would buy or rent vessels, the terms at which prizes would be handled, and the terms on which provisions for the ships would be purchased.[53] He settled quarrels over rank, scoured the camp at Cambridge for a surgeon to join Broughton's crew, and requested that Glover decide on a flag which the American ships would all fly, suggesting the one of "a white ground, a tree in the middle, the motto 'Appeal to Heaven' " which was already in use on American floating batteries.[54] A hundred other details the secretary handled deftly, and, in every letter, there was the vigorous call for speed. "Lose no time," he wrote Glover. "Everything depends on dispatch." [55] A few days prior to his departure for Philadelphia Reed had the satisfaction of hearing from Salem and Plymouth that three sailings which he had done so much to prepare for had finally taken place.[56]

Reed's desire to bring these naval efforts to fruition was one of the factors which extended his stay at Cambridge considerably beyond his original intention. In July he had written his wife that he would return for the fall term of the courts which began at the end of August.[57] But August came and went without offering Reed an opportunity to leave headquarters. Thoughts of departure early in September were set aside when Washington drew up plans for an attack upon Boston. Reed wrote Pettit on September 11 that this project was to be discussed at a council of war that day. If approved, he continued, he could not leave until he saw the plan through.[58] But the council of war unanimously advised Washington against an attack. Though the commander in chief accepted this decision for the moment, he by no means abandoned the idea of an offensive operation. His refusal to consider the matter closed undoubtedly frustrated Reed's plan for leaving Cambridge. Then, at the close of the month, came the Church affair and soon after that Reed became involved in the naval preparations we have already considered.

Not until October 30, therefore, was Reed finally able to set out for Philadelphia. To Washington the loss of Reed's services, even for a temporary period, was so vexing that he attempted, by writing to Richard Henry Lee in Philadelphia, to prevail upon Reed's opposing counselors in pending cases to agree to postponements of trial dates.[59] Reed did not make any promises as to how soon he would resume his duties as secretary, and for his part Washington refused to consider the post vacant, for as he later wrote to Reed, "whilst you are disposed to continue with me I shall think myself too fortunate and happy to wish for a change." [60] On this rather uncertain basis Reed took his leave of his esteemed chief and of new friends gained during the four months at Cambridge—Stephen Moylan, Nathanael Greene, Edmund Randolph, and many others—and, on October 30, took the road for Philadelphia.[61]

Reed wasted little time enroute. On November 4 he wrote to Washington from New York City. His letter of the 7th to the general was written at his home.[62] Even so, he had the opportunity, as he rode down the New England roads to New York and then across the familiar route through Jersey to Philadelphia, to ponder on the developments in which he had played an important part. An army had been created, an infant navy was in the making, an invasion of Canada was in progress. Would these positive, aggressive acts succeed where petition and remonstrance had failed and convince the king's government that America's grievances must be redressed? Or would force merely beget more force? If the latter was the case, would the struggle necessarily turn, and quickly so, to one for independence?

Reed's opinion as to the desirability of and the necessity for independence did not crystallize during his stay at Cambridge. On August 21, writing to Thomas Bradford, he had endorsed the views expressed by John Adams in his intercepted letter to James

Warren in which he proposed that the Americans draw up a constitution for a new government at once and then negotiate with Britain. These views, Reed declared, marked out "our true line of conduct . . . if we expect peace and reconciliation on proper terms." [63] Reed thus regarded the displacement of the existing colonial governments not as a desirable prelude to independence but as a step to a position from which better terms for a reconciliation with the Mother County could be secured. To Pettit he expressed the opinion that even in Massachusetts there was no general desire to do more than restore imperial relationships to the "old Ground of 1762." [64] Yet when he wrote to Pettit again on October 8, Reed's mind was evidently confused. He stated that republican governments were generally the best for mankind but "unless the tyranny and folly of ministers press us into the formation of some new system, I think we may yet return to our old ground of 1763." This would be, Reed continued, a "most desirable state if with it we could return to our former unsuspecting confidence and affection for each other. But that is to be wished rather than expected." In the same letter is a vigorous statement which, if not balanced against the foregoing views, would lead one to regard its author as a strong advocate of independence. Reed wrote, "I have no notion of being hanged for half courage; when a subject draws his sword against his prince, he must cut his way through, if he means afterwards to sit down in safety." [65]

It is unfortunate that so very few of the letters Reed wrote from Philadelphia to Washington have been preserved. Washington's letters to Reed, climaxing in that of February 10, 1776, in which the general stated his belief that America should inform Britain that it was prepared to "shake off all connexions with a state so unjust," [66] are of great value in charting the toughening of the general's own attitude. Reed's letters undoubtedly touched as freely upon that great topic, but only faint hints as to the nature of his remarks are to be gleaned from Washington's replies. On November 20, 1775, for example, Washington expressed his agreement with Reed's observation that whether the ministry would push America to extremities depended in great part on the people of England: a hostile reaction by them to a war against the colonists was indeed America's best hope.[67]

If Reed was undecided in his own mind on the question of independence when he left the camp at Cambridge, the political situation he found in Philadelphia upon reaching home was hardly designed to promote either clarity or unanimity of thought. Reed found leisure time as much of a luxury for him at home as it had been at Washington's headquarters. His compatriots in the city had constantly pressed for his return, and thus despite his absence with the army Reed was reelected to membership in the Philadelphia committee of inspection and observation on August 16 and subsequently was made one of the four co-chairmen. Then, when the Pennsylvania assembly met for its fall session, Reed was also elected a member of the thirty-two-man committee of safety headed by Benjamin Franklin.[68] Thus Reed found many public duties awaiting him upon his return to Philadelphia. Added to commissions with which Washington had entrusted him, including that of acting as host to Martha Washington as she passed through Philadelphia in November en route from Mount Vernon to Cambridge,[69] and an attempt to repair the damage done his law business by his unprovided absence, these tasks pushed thoughts of returning to headquarters further and further from Reed's mind.

Washington, however, refused to lose Reed to the Pennsylvania patriots without a struggle. In his letter of November 20 to Reed he remarked on the unsatisfactory performance of those filling in for the latter, confessed that he missed him badly, and concluded that he hoped Reed could return soon. These sentiments were reiterated in Washington's letters of November 28 and December 15.[70] Reed's replies were apparently indefinite. The reluctance with which he viewed a return to military life "unless some new events . . . make it more my duty" found expression in a letter to Charles Pettit. Citing the dangerously high enemy-making potential of the position as the commander in chief's closest confidant, Reed concluded that his lack of superior military talents made civil endeavors preferable to those of the camp and the field.[71]

On January 23, 1776, Washington asked pointedly whether he

could entertain any hopes of Reed's return to his staff, stating that he knew of no replacement "with whom I would choose to live in unbounded confidence." [72] Then, fearing that his demand for a decisive answer might force Reed to resign, Washington wrote a week later to soften his previous remarks and to let the latter know he did not wish to precipitate a resignation nor even Reed's return before his situation was "ripe for it." [73] At this time the Philadelphia patriots played a trump card in their rivalry with the general for Reed's services. On January 26, 1776, with their enthusiastic backing, he was elected to a vacancy among the city's representation in the provincial assembly. The vacancy was created when Thomas Mifflin won reelection for a fourth term in the elections of October, 1775, but resigned this place to remain with the Continental Army as quartermaster general.[74] Washington, with characteristic courtesy, congratulated Reed on his election though fully realizing that this was the "coup de grace to my expectation of our seeing you resident in this camp again." [75]

Reed took his seat in the assembly on February 16, two days after a quorum was obtained for the winter session. He was not afforded any orientation period. He was named to one committee that same day, to a second the following day, added to the very important committee on grievances on February 21, and a week later was made a member of the committee selected to revise the regulations for the military association of the province.[76] Reed's vote, his skill in drafting reports and resolutions, and his persuasiveness in discussion were much needed by the patriots trying to make the assembly a fit instrument to lead Pennsylvania in the common struggle. These men realized that the body's equivocal position in the past had created a mounting demand among the more radically minded Whigs, particularly in Philadelphia and the west, that the assembly be ignored and governmental power be vested in a provincial convention. This body would be elected by true patriots only and would give to the western counties and the working classes of Philadelphia the representation they lacked in the proprietary legislature.

No one was more conscious of this dissatisfaction than Reed. On the same day on which he took his seat in the assembly, February 16, he was also elected again to the committee of inspection and observation for the city of Philadelphia, ranking second only to Franklin in votes received.[77] From precisely this body emanated the most vocal demands for a coup against the assembly's authority. Once again Reed took the middle road, striving to have the assembly adopt a more popular program and, at the same time, striving to restrain impatient patriots from precipitate internal revolution. He wrote to Pettit that plans were laid to force measures through the legislature which would perfect the organization of the militia, increase the number of seats in the house in order to provide more equitable representation of the city of Philadelphia and of western counties, and liberalize the instructions binding Pennsylvania's delegates in the Continental Congress.[78]

The first success in effecting these plans came over the representation grievance, and it came none too soon. Late in February the Philadelphia committee, over Reed's opposition, voted to issue a call for a provincial convention. Only quick action by Reed and other patriot leaders in the assembly staved off such a step. On the basis of a promise that Philadelphia and the western counties would be given increased representation immediately, the committee was persuaded to issue a circular letter on March 4 canceling its call for the convention which was to have met on April 2. Reed and his associates were able to make good on their promise. On March 8 the house resolved to create seventeen new seats, four for Philadelphia, the remaining thirteen to be divided among eight western counties. Reed was a member of the committee chosen the following day to draw up the bill embracing these changes. This was passed March 14 and was signed by Governor John Penn on the 23rd. Thanks to unshakable Quaker opposition, however, the act did not relax the suffrage qualifications. Thus, when elections were held for the new seats in April, the conservatives maintained their voting superiority in Philadelphia, elected three of the four new assemblymen, and thereby retained a majority in the assembly despite the fact that twelve of the thirteen new representatives from the west were warm supporters of the revolution.[79]

Meanwhile, the efforts to push through the other measures

Reed had mentioned in his letter to Pettit were going forward. On February 28 a fifteen-man committee, of which Reed was a member, was appointed to revise the regulations for Pennsylvania's counterpart of the minutemen, the associators. The committee was also to consider the petitions pouring in from the province's revolutionary committees asking that non-associators be obliged to pay extra taxes. On March 5 the house was persuaded to vote to enlist 1,500 men for service until January 1, 1778, in the defense of the colony. This is as far as the assembly would go, and since the patriots had been working for an authorization of 2,000 men, the success here as in the reapportionment of seats was somewhat circumscribed.[80]

In the matter of liberalizing the assembly's instructions to the Pennsylvania delegation in Congress, the revolutionary party met with complete failure at this session. The instructions in force, drafted the previous November, had strictly enjoined that the province's representatives "dissent from, and utterly reject, any propositions, should such be made, that may cause or lead to, a Separation from our Mother Country or a Change of the Form of this Government." [81] Now, four months later, the call for independence was steadily growing in strength, in Pennsylvania as well as in Congress. Reed, for example, wrote Pettit on March 3 that he viewed separation from Britain as "a certain event." [82] The conservative majority in the assembly, however, refused to recognize this trend. On April 6 they voted down a request of the Philadelphia committee that the November instructions be withdrawn. A vote to adjourn until May 20 followed immediately.[83]

This was not only a bitter defeat for the patriots, but for Reed it was also a blow to plans he had formulated for an early return to military service. The Congress had given a concrete endorsement to Washington's persistent efforts to regain Reed's services by voting on March 1 to raise the salary for the secretary's post from sixty-six to one hundred dollars per month, citing in particular "the extraordinary services at present attending the office by reason of the General's direction of the naval department." [84] This action enabled Reed to consider abandoning his flagging law practice again for a return to the army without materially sacri-

ficing his family's interests.[85]   On March 3 he wrote Washington
that he would be with him for the summer's campaign.   In a
letter written to his brother-in-law Pettit on the same day, Reed
remarked that he intended to set out for camp as soon as the
assembly session had ended and he had settled his family in some
country retreat.   The latter project was quickly effectuated, for
within the week Reed wrote to Washington that he had taken a
house in the country.   The house, which he had succeeded in
renting for £40 per year, was one in Burlington, New Jersey,
which had been the residence of Governor William Franklin.[86]

The news of the British evacuation of Boston removed the
necessity for great haste in rejoining Washington, but Reed continued to plan on moving Esther, the children, and Mrs. DeBerdt
to Burlington at the end of March and then to meet the general
at New York City, the undoubted field for the next campaign.
But the assembly session dragged on into April and when adjournment did come on April 6 it was accompanied by the galling defeat which continued the negative instructions to Pennsylvania's
delegates in Congress in force.   The house was to reassemble on
May 20.   Preparations for that event and for a new attempt at
rescinding the vexing injunctions were deemed essential to these
plans, and Reed's departure from Philadelphia was postponed.

Thus Washington, now at New York after his successful dis-
lodgment of the British from Boston, was again disappointed.
Reed evidently wrote him that he was still determined to join the
general for the summer campaign but could not count on leaving
Philadelphia until sometime in June.   This news finally obliged
the commander in chief, beset as he was by the manifold problems of organizing the defenses of New York City, to fill the secretary's post which had been held open for Reed's return since the
previous November.   In his general orders of May 16, 1776, Washington announced the appointment of Robert H. Harrison of
Maryland as his secretary "in the room of Joseph Reed, Esqr.
whose private concerns will not permit him to continue in that
office." [87]   Even as he issued this order, however, Washington was
surveying other offices which Reed might assume at a later date,
offices of a nature which would again permit him to have Reed
at his side.

In Philadelphia, meanwhile, the demand among the patriots for the convocation of a new provincial congress to displace the uncooperative assembly was coming to a head again.   This time it could not be sidetracked, as it had been in March, by requests of moderates that nothing be done until the assembly had reconvened and had been given another chance to amend its conduct. The campaign of the radicals to seize power from the assembly was aided enormously when, on May 10, the Continental Congress passed a resolution inviting the people of the colonies to ignore their colonial governments and to establish new ones "where no government sufficient to the exigencies of their affairs hath been hitherto established." [88]   Pursuant to this invitation the Philadelphia committee issued a call on May 18 for a mass meeting to be held in the State House yard on the 20th, the same day the assembly was scheduled to reconvene.   A large number of Philadelphians responded to this call and gave evidence of their temper at the very outset by electing as chairman one of the most militant Whigs in the city, Daniel Roberdeau, commanding officer of the second battalion of the Philadelphia associators of which Reed was lieutenant colonel.   Using the resolution of Congress as a springboard, the meeting, after duly noting the assembly's refusal to rescind the November instructions, resolved that that body was not competent in the meaning of the Congressional resolution, that the assembly itself certainly did not possess the authority to form a new government, and that therefore a provincial convention be held to assume that great task.   The Philadelphia committee was authorized to issue the call for this conference and did so immediately by forwarding the above resolutions to the county committees throughout the province and setting June 18 as the date and Philadelphia as the place.[89]

The assembly, which obtained a quorum for the new session on May 22, was now clearly doomed.   Only a complete about-face by its conservative elements could have preserved its influence.   This did not come.   Reed and other moderates realized now that they could no longer hope to use the existing government to carry on the war against Britain.   But they did have one immediate aim which almost alone led them to keep their seats for the moment: they wished to free the hands of the province's delegates in Congress for a vote on independence by securing a withdrawal of the assembly's November instructions. For two weeks this battle was waged without success. But on June 5 a vote was finally carried for the appointment of a committee to draft new instructions. Reed was one of its seven members. The committee's report was debated on the 6th and referred back to committee for further consideration. The revised report was debated on the 7th and all positive references to a vote for independence were stricken from this version. On June 8, by a 31-12 vote, the old instructions were withdrawn and the new set adopted. The latter authorized Pennsylvania to concur in "further compacts between the United Colonies . . . [and in] such treaties with foreign kingdoms and states, and in adopting such other measures as shall be judged necessary." Weak as they were, the new instructions did at least remove the clear-cut prohibitions of the previous ones and permitted Pennsylvania's vote to be cast for independence when the resolution for that end was carried in Congress on July 2.[90]

With their aim accomplished by the vote of June 8, Reed and the other Whig delegates abandoned the assembly to its fate.[91] Reed had far more vital concerns on his mind now. On June 3 General Washington, in Philadelphia for conferences with the Congress, sent for Reed and pressed him to accept the post of adjutant general of the Continental Army. Although Reed had been hoping to rejoin Washington in some capacity, this proposal came as a complete surprise. The vacancy in the office was due to the promotion of the incumbent, Horatio Gates, to the rank of major general in preparation for an independent field command.[92] Reed, knowing little of the adjutant's duties, asked a day to weigh the offer. Washington agreed to this and worked with some members of Congress to allay Reed's fears of his lack of military knowledge for the post. Washington was fully cognizant of Reed's limitations in this sphere, but in his mind these were clearly outweighed by the perceptiveness, tact, and social grace which Reed had demonstrated as his secretary at Cambridge.[93] Reed was won over. On June 4 he informed the general that he would accept the post; the next day his appointment, carrying the rank of colonel and a salary of $125 per month, was voted by Congress.[94]

Washington left Philadelphia for New York City on the 4th and Reed hastened to conclude his affairs in Philadelphia and follow him. Esther and the children had already been moved to the house in Burlington. Attendance at the assembly was necessary until the new instructions were approved on June 8, but with that done the last important obstacle to departure was removed. A few hectic days at Philadelphia followed: the affairs of his law office to be put in order, a few last services for the Philadelphia committee to be performed. By the afternoon of the 11th he was in Burlington. There he drew up an inventory of his personal estate and made a will,[95] tried to convince Esther that he would have as little time with her if he remained caught up in political and militia duties in Philadelphia,[96] and, for the first time in months, was able to spend some unhurried hours with young Martha, Joseph, and Esther. But the British were expected to appear off New York at any time now and thus the respite with his family was brief. On June 15 Reed made his farewells and, acompanied by his servant "Jack," set out to join the army. That night he stopped with the Pettits at Perth Amboy and crossed to New York City the next day to assume his new responsibilities for the start of an ill-fated campaign.[97]

CHAPTER VI

1776: The Brink of Disaster

THE fortunes of the Continental Army and those of Joseph Reed during the campaign of 1776-77 display a remarkable parallelism. Each lacked the training and background to meet successfully the tasks entrusted to them. Each suffered at times from a lack of resolution, each narrowly escaped despair when winter came and the British were on the Delaware, and in each hope, strength, and a new determination were inculcated by the stirring events of Trenton and Princeton. Those brilliant thrusts, however, meant recovery only, not final victory. For the army, Brandywine and Valley Forge, Savannah and Camden, and the dreary months at Newburgh still lay ahead. For Reed, too, the recovery was incomplete. His misgivings, shaken confidence, and signs of hopelessness in the days before Trenton were to be exaggerated and pointed to again and again in subsequent years by political foes who sought to depict these weaknesses as treason. The somber details of this campaign, then, have an even darker sequel in Reed's life story, and therefore necessitate careful analysis.

Reed had no inkling of this troubled future when he reached New York City on June 16, 1776, to assume the duties of adjutant general of the Continental Army. From the very first, however, he felt unsure of himself in the new post and troubled by his ignorance of the highly technical aspects of his functions. Technical they certainly were, for it was the adjutant general who was responsible for the security of the camp, for recruiting men and maintaining a record of the numerical strength of the army, for issuing the commander in chief's orders to officers of all grades, for receiving reports and dispatches from all commanding officers, for issuing commissions, and for caring for hundreds of other details in the management of the army. Of the adjutant general it was truly said that "it is far more easy to define what is not

than what is his duty." [1] Washington's choice of Reed for this
post, though a tribute to the latter, seems to have been unwise,
for if any office in the army required a man seeped in the military
life, it was the adjutant general's.

Reed's sense of inadequacy in his new post was augmented by
the vastness and complexity of the task of defending New York
against the impending British attack, by his lack of acquaintance-
ship with the current members of Washington's military family,
and by personal perturbations. He had misgivings over leaving
his wife during her pregnancy,[2] and was worried by his brother
Bowes's presence, despite the latter's uncertain health, with the
New Jersey troops at New York.[3]

Reed's initial reactions were very unfavorable, particularly so
because he spent his first week in New York in crowded lodgings
in the lower section of the city. He wrote his wife on June 21:

My situation is far from a pleasant one and is attended with an expense I do not relish. However, I shall in a few days go up to headquarters, when I hope to find myself more at ease; if not I shall turn
my thoughts most seriously to getting out of the Army. The office I
am in has not much severe duty, but it is so entirely out of my line,
that I do not feel myself so easy with it as one of a different kind.
Perhaps a little time will reconcile me better but at present I confess
I do not much like it.[4]

Four days later, Reed did move up to join Washington at headquarters, the Mortier mansion located some two miles north of
the lower end of Manhattan. The cordial reception he received
from the commander in chief and the staff officers brightened his
outlook somewhat. He wrote Mrs. Reed that he tried to appear
cheerful but, stating that "to you alone I unbosom myself," he
confessed to an unusual depression of spirits: "the Week I have
been here seems to be a Month." [5]

The event which lifted Reed from these doldrums was the
appearance of British ships off Sandy Hook on June 29. He was
immediately dispatched by Washington to hurry the militia of
New Jersey into positions designed to guard against an enemy
movement up the west shore of New York Bay and the Hudson
River. He visited Elizabeth and Perth Amboy (where he saw

Pettit again) and reported back to Washington on July 1. This activity was a tonic. Reed wrote Esther upon his return to headquarters that he felt more composed and at ease than at any time since assuming his new post.[6]

The movements of the newly arrived enemy forces were anxiously studied during the next few days. Reed expected a landing on Long Island, yet was hopeful that if this were delayed, the swelling forces of the Continental Army would be able to cope with General William Howe's troops. When on July 3 the British landed on Staten Island instead and soon afterwards began constructing defense works, it became evident that no major attack would be forthcoming until the arrival of reinforcements en route from England convoyed by the general's brother, Admiral Richard Viscount Howe. Reed counted each day of British inactivity with satisfaction. In an overly optimistic vein he wrote on July 3, "The summer is now pretty well wasted. If this army [the British] can be kept from penetrating into the country, or getting possession of this place [New York City], America is saved." [7]

But Reed also felt that political as well as military consideration had prompted General Howe's inactivity. As early as the previous February, word had reached America that Parliament had, in December, 1775, authorized the appointment of royal peace commissioners. Few in the rebellious colonies put much hope of redress in this action. Reed wrote Dennis DeBerdt on February 24 that the commissioners would receive "a very cool reception unless they bring other offers than those of pardon." [8] On March 3 he had written Washington that "no man of understanding expects any good from the commissioners," but followed this by a letter on March 15 in which he expressed fears that artful behavior by the British might cover up the lack of substance in their peace bid and might divide the Americans.[9]

In England, meanwhile, friends of America had been striving to have the peace commissioners granted powers adequate to their mission. All such efforts failed. On May 3 King George formally named the Howe brothers as the commissioners. The instructions handed Admiral Howe conferred no power to act until a colony or part of a colony had ceased all opposition to royal authority. Not until all extralegal armies and revolutionary congresses and conventions had been totally disbanded could there be any negotiation on redress of grievances. As Lord George Germain, Dartmouth's successor as Secretary of State for the Colonies, explained in Parliament, the commissioners were forbidden to treat with "rebels in arms" and had no authority to negotiate concerning "the terms of the Submission of the Colonies, or on the Right of Taxation." [10] In essence, the Howes were merely empowered to grant the royal pardon to those who would renew their allegiance to the British government.[11]

None realized the weakness of their position as peace commissioners better than the Howe brothers themselves. Before leaving England, therefore, Lord Howe attempted to secure letters to prominent American leaders from their friends in England, letters which would introduce him as a friend of America and paint a hopeful picture of his powers to effect an honorable reconciliation. One Londoner from whom he obtained such an endorsement was Dennis DeBerdt; the letter, written May 3, was addressed to Joseph Reed.

Much transpired to render the Howe commission's chances of success even more illusory before this letter reached Reed on July 15. On July 9, at Washington's orders, the brigade majors of each of the brigades of the Continental Army at New York City trooped into Reed's office to receive copies of the Declaration of Independence that this document might be read "with an audible voice" before the assembled troops at six o'clock that evening.[12] Reed's correspondence at this juncture supplies no direct manifestation of his reaction to the parting with Britain. This issue, however, was one which had long troubled him. As early as March he had concluded that separation was inevitable, but confessed that "we are not yet so familiarized to the idea as thoroughly to approve it. . . . The Congress are paving the way to a declaration of Independence, but I believe will not make it until the minds of the people are better prepared for it than as yet they are." [13]

Four months later Reed's own mind was apparently not yet

entirely reconciled to the necessity of the momentous decision. He seems to have been appreciative of the need for foreign assistance to prosecute the war successfully, but unconvinced that independence was an indispensable prerequisite to such aid.[14] The reception of DeBerdt's letter on July 15 kept alive a gnawing doubt that it was still too early to abandon all hope of reconciliation with Britain.

The letter itself was ideally suited to foster such doubts and thereby perform exactly the function Lord Howe had in mind in obtaining and forwarding it. To what degree the false prospects it painted were due to deliberate misrepresentation by Howe to DeBerdt, or to DeBerdt's own eagerness to exaggerate the commissioner's powers, is not a vital point, for false the representations surely were. "Lord Howe goes to America as a mediator, and not as a destroyer," DeBerdt wrote. He assured Reed that Howe "has power to compromise and adjust" and asserted that the commissioners were anxious to meet the American leaders "on the wide field of argument [rather] than in the chosen ground for battle." DeBerdt begged Reed to use his weight toward arranging a conference and stated that no unreasonable concession would be demanded by the commissioners.[15]

That Reed was unduly impressed by DeBerdt's words is clear, but he was not guilty of a complete lapse of judgment. He showed the letter to Washington and then forwarded a copy to Congress through the person of Robert Morris, a member of the Pennsylvania delegation who had been a forthright opponent of declaring independence at this time. Reed's own letter enclosing DeBerdt's offers a clear picture of his thoughts. He did not think the Howes could offer anything more than unconditional submission. Yet he thought their overtures for negotiations ought not to be summarily rejected. If such negotiations revealed that the commission had no power to correct grievances, then "it must be evident to the whole world that resistance cannot be called our choice." The revelation would close off vain hopes and "have a happy effect to unite us into one chosen band, resolved to be free or perish in the attempt." If, on the other hand, contrary to all indications to date, the Howes *were* found to possess adequate powers to effect a reconciliation, Reed implied that negotiations should be pressed despite the Declaration of Independence. He stated as his private judgment that "if the two great cardinal points of exemption from British taxation and charge of internal government could have been secured, our happiness would have been best promoted by preserving the dependence." And even now, if those points could be secured, he intimated a belief that the link to the Mother Country might be reforged and the costs of the struggle to date be regarded as well spent.[16]

Morris's reply to Reed's letter indicated close agreement with the latter's outlook. He wrote, "I think that good policy requires that we should hear all they have to say . . . because if they can offer peace on admissible terms, I believe the great majority of America would still be for accepting it." Morris went on to admit, however, that a majority in Congress were not of this view. He told Reed that he had not laid DeBerdt's letter before Congress because another letter from DeBerdt "on the same subject and in a similar style," addressed to a delegate from New Jersey, James Kinsey, had been read before the house on July 18 and had been very harshly received.[17]

While Reed and Morris were corresponding over DeBerdt's letter, the Howes were striving to open direct peace negotiations with Washington. The first attempt came on July 14 when, under a flag of truce, a British naval officer came up the harbor with a letter for Washington. The general sent Reed, accompanied by Colonel Henry Knox and Lt. Colonel Samuel Webb, an aide-de-camp, to meet the officer with instructions not to accept any letter which was not properly addressed to him as commander in chief of the American forces. The letter proffered by the British officer was inscribed simply "George Washington, Esq." and Reed refused to receive it. The interview terminated, Reed related, after the officer asked "under what title General—but catching himself, Mr. Washington chose to be addressed," and Reed replied that General Washington's rank in the American Army was well known.[18] An almost comic touch enlivened the British efforts to circumvent this rebuff over titles. On the 17th a letter addressed "George Washington, Esq, Etc, Etc" was

proffered and again refused. Then, on July 19, the Howes sent
an aide under another flag of truce to request that Washington
grant an interview to General Howe's adjutant general, Lt.
Colonel James Patterson. Reed and Webb met this flag of truce
and Reed agreed to the meeting, setting the next day, at noon,
as the time. About 11 A.M. on the 20th the same two American
officers met Patterson and conducted him to the meeting place at
Knox's headquarters in the Kennedy house, Number 1 Broadway.
Reed was present during Patterson's conversation with Washington and, at the latter's direction, made notes of what had transpired once the conference was concluded. Patterson, addressing
Washington as "Your Excellency," apologized for the failures to
address properly the letters sent the latter. After some discussion
concerning treatment of prisoners, Patterson turned the conversation to the desire of Lord and General Howe to effect an accommodation in their roles as royal peace commissioners. Washington remarked bluntly that the commission seemed to possess only
the power to grant pardons and stated that those who defended
their indisputable rights had no need of pardon. Patterson gave a
vague reply, declined an invitation to partake of a light meal which
had been prepared, and the conference thereupon broke up.[19]

Patterson's evasiveness on the matter of the commissioner's
powers did not escape Reed. While conducting the British officer
from the Kennedy house he remarked that it was odd that the
peace commissioners should be the king's military and naval commanders,[20] and from this time on apparently viewed with mounting skepticism DeBerdt's glowing estimate of their ability to
proffer any serious plan toward reconciliation. Reed wrote Pettit
on August 4 that the Howes had been so cautious in avoiding par-
ticulars concerning the peace they spoke of so warmly as to convince him "much against my inclinations, I confess, that they have
no serious intention of relinquishing one jot of their despotic
claim over this country." [21]

But military duties prevented prolonged speculation on these
points. The British were steadily building up their strength on
Staten Island. On August 7 it was learned that Sir Henry Clinton's army, having failed in its attempt to capture Charleston,

South Carolina, in June, had now joined Howe. Within the
week the enemy was again strengthened by the arrival of Hessian
mercenaries, some 8,000 in number. Reed viewed the impending
test of strength with anxiety. "We have neither such an army nor
such a council as last year," he wrote to Mrs. Reed, "and yet we
want [i.e., need] it more." [22] He was worried by the failure of the
New England regiments to reach their full complements, by the
tardiness of the Jersey militia in coming forth, and by the growing number of men unfit for action due to sickness. But, un-
knowingly prophetic, he voiced confidence that "unless taken by
a greater surprise than I hope we ever shall be, we shall do very
well." [23]

Finally, on August 22, Howe's army uncoiled from its strong-
hold on Staten Island and struck toward New York City by landing on Long Island at Gravesend Bay. Washington rushed reinforcements to General John Sullivan, who had replaced the ailing
Nathanael Greene as commander on the island only two days
before, but remained on Manhattan himself. Four tense days
followed, with only minor skirmishing. Washington and his staff
were not yet sure that this operation was Howe's major thrust.
But during the evening of August 26-27 Howe led the main body
of his army, some 10,000 strong, in a wide encircling movement
around the loosely held left flank of the American army. By
daylight of the 27th this force was poised to the rear of Sullivan,
who was being engaged frontally by British and Hessian columns
under Generals Grant and DeHeister. At 9 A.M., about an hour
after Washington, accompanied by Reed had crossed from Manhattan to Long Island, Howe sprang his trap. By noon the
American forces had been completely routed, Sullivan himself
had been taken prisoner, and heavy casualties had been sustained.
Reed apparently took no part in the morning's action, but he
undoubtedly helped Washington rally the remnants of the broken
army behind the defense line on Brooklyn Heights. Feverish
activity was pressed to prepare for an assault by the British that
afternoon. But the onrushing columns of the enemy halted
before the American redoubts and then inexplicably drew back
out of cannon range.[24]

The night after the battle was a troubled one for Washington and all his officers, Reed among them. For the latter, the distressingly heavy casualties among Pennsylvania's regiments and the number of distinguished officers from the state who were missing in action—notably Colonels Samuel Miles and Samuel Atlee of Lord Stirling's brigade—deepened the perturbation produced by the expectation of a British assault at any moment.[25] But Howe did not attack that night, nor the next day, nor the next. The tension continued to mount at the temporary headquarters in Brooklyn, augmented always by Washington's fear that the British fleet would, with a favorable shift in the wind, succeed in moving into the East River and put its power between New York City and the army at Brooklyn. Such fears finally led Washington to convene a council of war on the afternoon of August 29 and there it was unanimously agreed that an evacuation to Manhattan be attempted that night.[26] The already exhausted officers and men mustered their last reserves of strength and, by dawn of the 30th, the movement had been carried out with the loss of but four stragglers who were captured. The respite which this perfectly executed withdrawal provided was badly needed. Writing from New York to General William Livingston on the 30th, Reed stated that he had not had his uniform off since the evening of the 26th and had had no sleep at all for two nights.[27]

The success of the evacuation of the American army could not, however, offset the losses it had suffered in the battle of Long Island, losses in leaders, in troops, in material, in confidence. As Freeman wrote in his biography of Washington, "Only the bravest and most philosophical could say with Joseph Reed, 'Our comfort is that the season is far advanced, and if a sacrifice of us can save the cause of America, there will be time to collect another army before spring, and the country will be preserved.'" [28]

Reed found this philosophic outlook difficult to sustain. The shock of battle had not steadied the untrained American troops but had, on the contrary, made Reed's task of maintaining discipline and order within the army even more difficult. Officers as well as men in the ranks deserted or pretended sickness. Plunder-

ing of the army's stores and of the inhabitants of New York became a serious problem. Reed regarded the militia from Connecticut and Massachusetts as particularly troublesome, and found
that his attempts to enforce discipline among them, a difficult task
where "so great an equality and so thorough a levelling spirit
predominates," stirred up a resentment against him which reached
even to the Congress.[29] These animosities were intensified by the
events surrounding the opening of hostilities on Manhattan
Island. Howe's forces made their landing on September 15 at
Kip's Bay on the East River, an area defended by some nine regiments of Connecticut militia, a small brigade of Massachusetts
militia, and a brigade of Connecticut Continentals. Without
firing a single organized volley these troops beat a disorderly
retreat inland, despite Washington's own efforts to rally them.
Reed's comparison of this disgraceful action with the courage
displayed by Maryland and Pennsylvania troops during the battle
of Long Island, a comparison made to none but the New England
officers themselves in pursuance of his duty as adjutant general,
made the breach a wide and prolonged one.[30]

The hectic flight of September 15 from lower Manhattan ended
with the American army taking a stand at a naturally strong position on Harlem Heights. The next morning, the 16th, a probing
attack by the British along Morningside Heights led to a sharp
engagement, the so-called battle of Harlem Heights, in which
Reed and, oddly enough, Connecticut rangers played stellar roles.

Reed was with Washington that morning at the Morris house,[31]
used as headquarters since the 14th, when news began coming in
of threatening movements by the British. He received permission from the general to ride down to the American advance
guard to see whether a major attack seemed to be in the making.
Washington had already ordered out some reconnaissance parties
and it was with one of these, that composed of about 120 rangers
commanded by Lt. Colonel Thomas Knowlton of Connecticut,
that Reed made contact in a "no man's land" some two and a
half miles south of headquarters and about one mile south of the
most advanced American outposts. Reed had just reached Knowlton when the British discovered the presence of the American

party and opened a heavy fire. The rangers returned it vigorously, but were soon obliged to fall back, which they did in good order, to avoid being surrounded. Reed was so impressed by the sturdy resistance Knowlton's men were offering that he galloped off to find Washington and seek support "for the brave fellows who had behaved so well." Just as Reed reached Washington, who had come down from the Morris Mansion to the main American line, the British who were pursuing Knowlton's force "appeared in open view and in the most insulting manner sounded their Bugle Horns as is usual after a Fox Chase. I never felt such a sensation before," Reed stated in an account written to his wife, "it seemed to crown our Disgrace." Perhaps Washington felt the insult too, for after some hesitation he gave Reed permission to lead a Virginia regiment to join forces with Knowlton's rangers and attempt to cut off the British force by moving around their left flank to their rear while other troops now set in motion by the commander in chief engaged the enemy frontally.

Unfortunately for these plans and for Reed, for whom this was his first experience in leading men into action, the encircling movement, thanks to an error by some subordinate officer who misdirected the party from the route Reed had intended, turned in on the enemy's position too soon and caught the British not in the rear but on their left flank. Heavy fighting at once ensued. Major Andrew Leitch, commanding officer of the Virginia troops, received three wounds and had to be carried off the field. A few minutes later Reed saw Colonel Knowlton fall, mortally wounded. He mounted the latter on his horse and brought him to safety only to hear later that the colonel died within the hour.

The action waxed even hotter, for though the British were driven back they were soon reinforced. Washington also, greatly heartened by the courage his men were displaying, committed more regiments to the battle. Reed played a conspicuous part in the action and had two narrow escapes himself. The first came when a bullet hit his horse's fore-shoulder, narrowly missing Reed's leg. The second was more harrowing, for here Reed's life was threatened by an American private, Ebenezer Liffenwell of Durkee's Connecticut regiment, whom the adjutant general attempted to halt as the former ran away from the battle, gun in hand. Liffenwell raised his musket, aimed at Reed, and pulled the trigger, but the piece misfired. Reed in turn fired at the soldier who, to quote Reed, "had the same good luck." Reed then drew his sword and, after wounding Liffenwell on the head and hand, subdued him.[32]

The battle of Harlem Heights finally ended with a further British retreat in the midafternoon. With some difficulty, so stimulating had been the novelty of driving back British troops in an open field engagement, Reed and the other officers restrained their troops from further pursuit and drew back to the American lines. The morale value of the day's action was high. Reed stated that the encounter had not inflicted a serious loss on the enemy but "it has given Spirits to our Men [so] that I hope they will now look the Enemy in the Face with Confidence." [33]

That American soldiers would stand up and fight against British regulars in an open field was settled by the action of the 16th. Five days earlier another question had been settled: whether the powers possessed by the royal commissioners, Admiral and General Howe, were substantial or whether, as was suspected, the power to grant pardons was virtually the only one they had. Adopting the viewpoint which Reed had often expressed, namely, that proving these suspicions to be true would "silence those opposers of the public [i.e., patriot measures] . . . and animate our own men, [for] seeing every hope gone, they would rely upon their own strength," [34] Congress sent Benjamin Franklin, John Adams, and Edward Rutledge to confer with Lord Howe. Their meeting, held on Staten Island on September 11, was productive only of the clear revelation that the commissioners had nothing of importance to offer. With this revelation, Reed set aside all lingering thoughts of a reconciliation between Britain and America.[35]

From September 16, the day of the battle of Harlem Heights, until Washington's evacuation of Manhattan Island which began when Howe landed in Westchester on October 12, only the slightest of skirmishes marred the watchful calm. For Reed this period was not, however, a tranquil one. Desertions and discipline remained acute problems. Concerning the latter, Reed revealed in a letter to his wife that his sense of propriety was seriously shocked when he saw a cavalry officer from Connecticut, a captain, shaving one of the enlisted men on the parade grounds near headquarters.[36] Though this was but a trivial example, the same letter reveals that Reed was deeply upset by the fact that his attempts to inculcate alertness, a sense of duty, and discipline in the army had made him, in the eyes of many, "odious and detestable." Sensitive as always, this situation and the ardent requests from Mrs. Reed that he return home, if only for a brief time to be with her at her child's birth,[37] led him to plan the resignation of the adjutant general's post at the end of the campaign. He was certain that a successor could be found "more skilled in military matters, and of more temper to bear the rubs and obstacles which ignorance and imprudence are constantly throwing in my way." [38] The inaction of the British after September 16 and the natural strength of the American position on Harlem Heights led Reed to think that perhaps Howe was content with his capture of New York City and was prepared to settle his army there for the winter. Thus, when a committee from Congress visited camp late in September, Reed informed its members of his desire to relinquish his office, but only when the campaign was ended. Two weeks after the committee left camp Reed wrote to Charles Pettit:

I am sorry to say too many officers from all parts leave the army when danger approaches. It is of the most ruinous consequences. It breaks the spirit of those who remain and are obliged to do the duty of the absent. They should be ordered back without exception and even compelled [to return].[39]

Howe's landing in Westchester burst the bubble of Reed's dream that "the enemy would go into winter quarters, satisfied with the summer's business." [40] Now all plans for a return to his family and for freeing himself of an office he found onerous and distasteful were cast aside as the commander in chief, removing from Manhattan all troops but those garrisoning Fort Washington, tensely sparred for position with the British in Westchester. On October 20, Reed and Colonel Rufus Putnam, Washington's chief engineer, carried out a reconnaissance toward White Plains. The next day Washington began shifting the main body of the army to that strategic area and began throwing up fortifications. The general, however, showing at this time some confusion of thought and lack of decisiveness,[41] failed to fortify Chatterton's Hill, an eminence which commanded the right flank of his line. On October 27 Howe's army appeared before White Plains, driving in the American advance guard. The general alarm in the American camp was given by Reed since Washington and his generals were away at the time seeking out additional defensive positions. But the British did not launch their attack until the next day, October 28. That morning Washington sent Reed to order the small militia force on Chatterton's Hill to begin entrenching and also dispatched reinforcements to that point. But these moves came too late. About 10 A.M. the British opened a heavy cannonade. The first casualty suffered among the militiamen on the hill threw them into a panic. They had barely been rallied when Hessian and British troops crossed the Bronx River and asaulted their position. If Washington had been hoping for a resistance of the mettle displayed at Harlem Heights he was sorely disappointed. Chatterton's Hill was, instead, a repetition of Kip's Bay: the militia fled early, the veterans were then unequal to the task of holding the broken line of defense.[42]

With the hill firmly in his grasp General Howe again chose to procrastinate rather than follow through with a direct, full-scaled assault on the American army. Washington held his ground grimly for three days, but on October 31 withdrew northward to a stronger position at North Castle. Then, on November 5, Howe inexplicably turned his army southward, back toward New York City. Washington, hampered now by the "weary confusion of mind to which he was coming in his consideration of strategical plans," [43] reacted haltingly. He decided he must cross the Hudson to block any British drive through New Jersey toward Philadelphia. But, and here the commander in chief's clouded judgment was evident, he left some 7,000 of his rapidly dwindling troops under General Charles Lee in Westchester and another 4,000 further up the Hudson under General William Heath.

Most dangerous of all, he failed to order that the garrison of Fort Washington on Manhattan Island be withdrawn and joined to his forces in New Jersey, accepting Nathanael Greene's estimate that the fort could be held, despite his own serious misgivings. Washington could not resolve what he frankly described three years later to Reed as "that warfare in my mind, and hesitation which ended in the loss of the garrison," [44] and a British assault on November 16 led to the capitulation of the fort's 2,818 officers and men.

Reed's confidence in his chief was badly shattered by the latter's indecisiveness at this critical time. That Reed did not reveal his sentiments freely and forcibly to Washington himself, as he had done in the past, was unfortunate. That he chose to reveal them to Charles Lee was a near catastrophe. The noisy, self-assured Lee had written to Reed before the fall of Fort Washington criticizing Greene for increasing rather than reducing the garrison there.[45] On November 20, the day Washington's army fell back behind the Hackensack River, Reed replied, stating that Washington wanted Lee to bring his strong force of over 7,000 men across the Hudson and join the commander in chief's dwindling army, now reduced to about 4,000 men. The text of that letter has been lost: it was Reed's misfortune that the indiscreet letter he sent off the next day to Lee was not. In this Reed wrote that he earnestly wished to see Lee "where the principal scene of action is laid." He continued:

I do not mean to flatter or praise you at the expense of any other, but I confess I do think it is entirely owing to you that this army, and the liberties of America, so far as they are dependent on it, are not totally cut off. You have decision, a quality often wanted [i.e., lacking] in minds otherwise valuable . . . and I have no doubt had you been here the garrison of Mount Washington would now have composed a part of this army. . . . General Washington's own judgment, seconded by representations from us, would I believe, have saved the men and their arms, but unluckily General Greene's judgment was contrary. This kept the General's [Washington's] mind in a state of suspense till the stroke was struck. Oh! General, an indecisive mind is one of the greatest misfortunes that can befall an army; how often have I lamented it this campaign.[46]

All this was pleasing indeed to the vainglorious Lee. On November 24 he wrote a reply thanking Reed for the latter's "most obliging, flattering letter" and seconding the adjutant general's sentiments concerning the danger of indecisiveness in war, a "much greater disqualification," Lee wrote, "than stupidity or even want of personal courage." Lee then went on to explain why, in defiance of Washington's orders, he had not yet set about crossing the Hudson and rejoining the commander in chief. However, he promised he would do so soon, for "I really think my Chief will do better with me than without me." [47]

Before this letter reached headquarters, now at Newark, New Jersey, Reed had been dispatched by Washington to Burlington to impress upon the governor of the state, William Livingston, the army's urgent need of reinforcement. Reed probably set out from camp on November 24, together with Thomas Mifflin who was proceeding on a similar mission to Philadelphia.[48] Several days later Lee's bombastic letter to Reed reached headquarters. Washington, anxious for word of Lee's movements and never anticipating that its contents were other than official business, opened it and read its revealing lines.

The general was undobutedly hurt by the revelation that his adjutant general and his second in command were exchanging criticisms of his conduct. Washington knew Lee well enough by this time not to feel greatly surprised at his egotism. Reed, on the other hand, had been a trusted confidant and a friend. This disclosure that he had revealed to another opinions which he had not manfully expressed to his chief pained the latter deeply. Washington now hastened to forward the Lee letter to Reed and to explain how it was that he came to open and read contents which "neither inclination or intention would have prompted me to." He thanked Reed for performing the mission to Burlington and wished him success. Humanly imitating Reed's failure to be candid, Washington did not reveal his mortification nor ask Reed to explain exactly what the latter had written in the letter Lee found so flattering.[49]

Two days before Washington sent off the Lee letter and his own note to Reed, the latter had again moved to resign the office of adjutant general. The committee of Congress to whom, two months ago, he had expressed the wish to be replaced had not effectuated this desire. Now, on November 28, Reed wrote from Burlington directly to John Hancock, president of Congress. He referred to his previous request and then continued:

As the season will not admit of further military operations (unless the Enemy should attempt an Incursion into this province to harass and distress us, in which case I shall most cheerfully devote myself to any further service) I beg leave to inclose the Commission with the highest Sense and warmest acknowledgements of the favour done me.[50]

Four days later Reed again wrote to Hancock, again from Burlington, begging leave to retract his resignation. He said that he now realized he had been mistaken in believing that the enemy would not, at this late season, attempt to carry their offensive through New Jersey. Consequently, he was anxious to return to his army post "until a Successor is appointed or Operations shall cease beyond all Doubt." [51] By December 2, Reed undoubtedly had learned that Washington was in full retreat toward the Delaware and this may be the only explanation necessary for his about-face. William B. Reed, however, states that on December 1 Reed received an urgent plea from Washington begging him to keep his post. There is no such letter in the Reed collection in the New-York Historical Society, nor any reference to it among Washington's papers. That there was such a letter must therefore be doubted, though, as Freeman states in his biography of Washington, the possibility cannot be altogether ruled out.[52]

Although impatient now to rejoin Washington, Reed was worried about his family's safety. Neither Burlington, their present location, nor Philadelphia itself seemed to offer a sure haven before the advancing armies of the enemy. Finally, a remote retreat was chosen at Evesham, a small hamlet southeast of Burlington on the edge of the pine barrens.[53] After making arrangements for evacuating his wife, children, and mother-in-law there, Reed set out for Trenton where he rejoined Washington and the remnant of the army on December 3 or 4.

The reunion with his commander in chief was undoubtedly rather embarrasing for Reed, the more so, perhaps, since his Bur-

lington mission had proved a failure. The New Jersey legislature, appalled rather than provoked by the invasion of their state,
had fled from Princeton to Burlington and then to Haddonfield
where they adjourned on December 2. During these movements
the body had failed to take any decisive effort toward securing
reinforcements for the army.[54]

Despite these gloomy tidings, and despite the Lee letter incident, Reed was well received by Washington and was again admitted into the circle of the general's closest advisers. The warm
intimacy of the past, however, was absent. While under the grim
shadow of complete defeat in these early weeks of December,
neither man had the time nor the inclination to advert to the Lee
episode. But Reed, at least, missed the friendship of the past.
After the Trenton and Princeton campaigns were over, after he
had been replaced as adjutant general, and after the armies finally
had settled themselves in winter quarters, he wrote Washington
that he "could have wished to have one hour of private conversation with you on the subject of a letter to me written by General
Lee before his captivity.[55] I deferred it in hopes of obtaining
from him the letter to which his was an answer." Reed stated
that what he had said therein contained "nothing inconsistent
with that respect and affection which I have and ever shall bear
to your person and character." [56]

On June 4, 1777, Reed wrote again in this vein, conscious, as
he said, of the difficulty of regaining lost friendship but conscious
too of "never having justly forfeited yours." Reed commented
that he was saddened by comparing Washington's most recent
messages to him with the warm, candid letters which the latter
had written from Cambridge and then New York in early 1776.
"Let me entreat you to judge of me by realities, not by appearances," Reed wrote. "Whatever may be my future destination
and course of life I could not support the reflection of being
thought ungrateful and insincere to a friendship which was
equally my pride and my pleasure." [57]

Washington's reply indicated that he too was ready and eager
to restore the old relationship. He was, he wrote, perfectly convinced of the sincerity of Reed's protestations of respect and

friendship. "Truth it is," he continued, "I felt myself hurt by a certain letter . . . not because I thought my judgment wronged by the expression contained in it, but because the same sentiments were not communicated immediately to myself." Washington went on in this letter to give tangible evidence of his high regard for Reed by urging him to accept the command of the cavalry of the Continental Army with the rank of brigadier general.[58] Reed did not accept this position, however, and in fact saw service in the campaigns of 1777, 1778, 1779, and 1780 only as a volunteer without a commission or, as in the latter two instances, as commanding officer (by virtue of his office as president of the supreme executive council of Pennsylvania) of the Pennsylvania state militia. Circumstances, therefore, prevented the reestablishment of that full intimacy which had existed between Washington and Reed at Cambridge in 1775. Reed's official position as chief executive of his state from 1778-81 rendered much of their correspondence more formal, but among the official dispatches are letters [59] which continue to indicate that Washington thought of Reed as a confidant and friend.

These repairs to a damaged friendship were all in the future in December, 1776, when Washington's every thought had to be devoted to keeping an army in the field and Philadelphia safe from capture. On December 7, abandoning hope that Lee's force would join his before the British under Cornwallis moved on Trenton from New Brunswick, he evacuated his army across the Delaware River to the Pennsylvania side opposite Trenton. Reed was with the general during that withdrawal and then, the following day, was sent to Philadelphia bearing dispatches to the Congress urging the greatest possible exertions in forwarding supplies and reinforcements.[60] Here Reed was more successful than he had been in New Jersey. Militia were rushed to join Washington and another detachment under Colonel John Cadwalader was gathered together at Bristol, some ten miles downstream from Washington's main camp.[61]

Reed did not tarry long in Philadelphia. Washington needed him in the field to check the army's arrangements for guarding against an enemy crossing of the Delaware. Reed felt that it would be impossible to guard adequately every mile of the river and thus emphasized to the general the necessity of gaining accurate intelligence of the British movements. In a letter to Washington of December 12, apparently written at or near Coryell's Ferry fifteen miles up river from Trenton, he sent information gained from one scouting party of cavalry officers and mentioned that he was awaiting the return of a spy he had sent to Trenton. Reed predicted in this letter that the British would attempt a crossing, probably somewhere near Pennytown, New Jersey (half way between Trenton and Coryell's Ferry), which Lord Cornwallis had occupied.[62]

Two weeks before Reed had erred in thinking the British had terminated their campaign for the winter. Now the enemy again upset his predictions, this time more happily, by halting at the Delaware. Washington's care in removing all available boats from the Jersey side of the river undoubtedly contributed to this decision, but probably of greater importance was General Howe's satisfaction with the almost effortless occupation of New Jersey and a reluctance to wage an uncomfortable winter campaign simply to seize Philadelphia and administer the coup de grâce to the rebellion when that could be done in the spring. On December 13 Howe gave orders for the withdrawal of most of his force from the Delaware to winter quarters in New York City, New Brunswick, and Perth Amboy. A force of about 3,000 men, however, was left behind along the Delaware under the command of Colonel Carl von Donop with orders to establish cantonments at Trenton, Bordentown, and Burlington. General Howe was somewhat uneasy about these arrangements, feeling the chain of posts was "rather too extensive." But he determined upon holding them to protect the Tories of central and western New Jersey and those Jerseymen who had taken advantage of the proclamation he and Admiral Howe had issued on November 30. This manifesto granted the royal pardon and protection to all who, within sixty days of its date, would lay down their arms and give their promise to "remain in a peaceable obedience to his Majesty." [63]

When Howe and Cornwallis returned to New York City, the latter abandoning the threatening position north of Trenton which had so worried Reed, the focal point of operations shifted to Trenton and the area south of it. About December 15, Reed was therefore sent to Bristol to assist Colonel Cadwalader, now an acting brigadier general, in organizing the Pennsylvania militia there. He was also to ferret out news concerning the enemy forces at Bordentown and other places south of Trenton and to serve as a convenient personal link between Washington's head-quarters and Philadelphia, still an important nerve center despite the flight of Congress from that city to Baltimore on December 13.

Reed's activities from the time he joined Cadwalader at Bristol until Washington's brilliant counterstroke at Trenton have been the subject of much controversy. Six years after this memorable December of 1776 Reed's political enemies in Pennsylvania un-leashed an attack upon him which centered about the charge that he had abandoned hope of American victory at that time and had spoken about applying to the British for pardon under the terms of the Howe proclamation of November 30. Only the timely success at Trenton, Reed's enemies were to claim, had kept him from doing so. The story of this controversy of 1782-83 is part of Reed's subsequent career, and since no documents contem-poraneous with the events now being discussed here were brought forward at that time, it will be reserved for future consideration.

However, the charge that Reed had not only contemplated "going over" to the British but that he had actually sought and obtained protection from the enemy in New Jersey before the battle of Trenton (after which, it was asserted, he reverted to the American cause) was made upon the basis of supposed documen-tary evidence by the nineteenth-century historian George Ban-croft in his *History of the United States.* The evidence cited by Bancroft was the mention by the Hessian commander, Colonel von Donop, in both a letter of December 21, 1776, and in a diary notation of the same date, of a "Colonel Reed" who had "Lately received a protection." Bancroft assumed this was Joseph Reed. But subsequent research by William S. Stryker, an authority on the Revolutionary history of New Jersey, established beyond doubt that the Reed of whom Donop wrote was not the adjutant general but Colonel Charles Read of the Burlington County militia, who indeed did submit to the British (he was the son of Joseph Reed's old rival for the deputy secretaryship of New Jersey) and was arrested and imprisoned by the Americans when this became known to them. Bancroft then retracted his charge in a later edition of his history.[64]

Bancroft's careless error is explainable in part by the fact that Joseph Reed and Colonel Donop had been in touch with one another, not on apostacy by Reed but on the matter of constituting the town of Burlington a neutral ground. On December 11, after occupying Bordentown, Donop had marched on Burlington with the intention of establishing a base there. But American gunboats on the Delaware River opened fire upon the town when he entered it, and as he lacked heavy artillery he complied, for the time being, with the pleadings of the townspeople, among whom were several staunch Tories, that he withdraw to save the town from the cannonading. While awaiting heavy artillery from Perth Amboy, Donop stationed his force north and east at Bordentown and Black Horse, Burlington itself remaining something of a no man's land.[65]

Reed, extremely anxious to obtain details of Donop's movements and strength, took advantage of this situation to cross several times to Jersey and reconnoiter personally. He entered Burlington more than once on these scouting trips. While there, inhabitants of the town urged him to seek an agreement with the Hessian commander neutralizing the area. On December 20, therefore, Reed addressed a note to Donop from Bristol. Refering to the "peculiar situation of the Town of Burlington, exposed to hostilities from both parties," he stated that Washington wished to make a proposition on this subject and he offered, for that purpose, to meet the following day at whatever time and place Donop selected. Donop sent back a reply with Reed's messenger stating that he could not meet Reed at present but apparently not closing the door to a later conference. For, in a second letter to Reed, written on December 24 from Mount Holly which his troops had occupied the day before, Donop offered to meet the American adjutant general at the Antrim farm, halfway between Mount Holly and Burlington, at noon the following day.[66]

Donop's note reached the American camp at Bristol Christmas morning. But Reed was not there. He was in Philadelphia consulting with General Israel Putnam on the diversionary crossing into New Jersey which Washington wanted the latter to carry out as part of the projected stroke against Trenton. Cadwalader, who received Donop's note, was anxious that the enemy commander's suspicions not be aroused by a failure to reply immediately. Therefore, in a well-written, casual-sounding note to Donop, he stated that Reed was "not at this Post at present," that he was expected back by the next afternoon, and that Reed would then "request you to name another time and place." [67] But the swift-moving events of the Trenton-Princeton campaign prevented and indeed made unnecessary any such meeting.

The inception of this campaign is eloquent testimony to the valor and dogged spirit of Washington and his men. Despite the bitter defeats and inglorious retreats of the past months, despite the dwindling size of the army and its shortness of even food and clothing, despite or perhaps because of the harrowing knowledge that many of the soldiers would quit the service when their enlistments ran out at the end of December, the commander in chief had not given up hope. He could face these grim realities and write that unless a new army were speedily recruited "the game is pretty near up" [68] and yet, at the same time, rather than simply breathe a sigh of relief that Howe had not pursued him across the Delaware, begin to plan to take the offensive himself.

Washington's resiliency of spirit was a great inspiration to his subordinates, Reed among them. Charges made six years later that Reed had sunk deep into the slough of despair are not borne out by his words or actions at this time. On December 22 Reed sent a long letter to Washington from Bristol which did indeed paint a black picture of what would ensue *unless* "an offensive attack" were made now, before the army dissolved. "Delay with us is now equal to a total defeat . . . we must not suffer ourselves to be lulled into security and inaction." Begging pardon for the freedom with which he expressed himself, Reed urged his chief to "consult your own good judgment and spirit and not let the goodness of your heart subject you to . . . opinions from

men in every respect your inferiors." All this was not mere
rhetoric. Reed went on to tell Washington that he, Cadwalader,
and the other officers at Bristol had decided to lead their force
across the Delaware the next morning, December 23, and move
against Donop's position at Black Horse.[69]

Washington was formulating his own plans for the blow against
the Hessian garrison at Trenton when he received Reed's letter
with its news of the projected attack from Bristol. He called the
adjutant general to headquarters, outlined his own scheme, and
pointed out that greater effectiveness could be obtained if the as-
saults were timed to be simultaneous. In this way Cadwalader's
attack would prevent Donop from coming to the aid of the Trenton garrison.[70] Reed returned to Bristol, informed Cadwalader
of Washington's wishes, and that same night or early the next
day, the 23rd, crossed into New Jersey with his friend Colonel
John Cox. They sought out Colonel Samuel Griffin, commander
of a body of some 600 militiamen which had been harassing
Donop from the south. But Reed and Cox found Griffin ill and
his force much too weak for offensive operations. Reed did learn,
however, that these militiamen had already contributed something to Washington's attack by drawing Donop from the river
to Mount Holly, seven miles inland and eighteen miles from
Trenton.[71]

After the meeting with Griffin, Reed and Cox crossed back to
Bristol. There, on the 23rd, the former received word from
Washington that the time for the attack on Trenton had been
fixed at one hour after daybreak on December 26. "Prepare, and
in concert with Griffin, attack as many of their posts as you possibly can with a prospect of success," Washington ordered. He
went on to enjoin strict secrecy and asked that he be informed
"by a careful express the plan you are to pursue." [72]

On the 24th, after receiving this information and exhortation,
Reed rode from Bristol to Philadelphia to urge upon the military
governor of that city, General Israel Putnam, that he join the
assault against Donop by crossing the Delaware at Philadelphia
and reinforcing Griffin's small force. The situation Reed found
in Philadelphia, however, was discouraging. Griffin, incapaci-

tated by illness, had returned there, leaving only about 400 militiamen in the field. Putnam was anxious to cooperate but doubted that he could cross into Jersey with more than 500 men. Reed stayed overnight in Philadelphia. The next morning, Christmas day, he wrote to Cadwalader and described Putnam's attempts to gather a striking force. He suggested that if the attack planned for the next morning could be postponed one day, Putnam would be able to take an effective part in the operation. He said that he had written Washington to the same effect and had asked that if any change of plans was decided upon, that information be sent to Bristol, to which he himself would return later in the day.[73]

Reed's letter reached Washington, but the general decided against postponing his Trenton attack on Putnam's account. At six that evening he accordingly wrote Cadwalader that "notwithstanding the discouraging accounts I have received from Col. Reed . . . I am determined . . . to cross the River and make the attack upon Trenton in the Morning. If you can do nothing real, at least create as great a diversion as possible." [74] When Reed got back to Bristol from Philadelphia, therefore, he found Cadwalader already moving his men, some 1,500 in all, to Dunk's Ferry, just below Bristol, for the crossing. A small force was sent across the river to prevent anyone on the Jersey side from warning Donop. Several officers, Reed among them, then crossed to select the best spot for landing the men and the artillery. They found to their dismay that the Jersey river bank was so choked with piles of ice that it was only with great difficulty that they reached the shore with their horses. It was manifest that the artillery could not be brought ashore through the ice and even doubtful that the men could be disembarked safely. Cadwalader's officers urged him not to proceed without his cannon, and after waiting at the river until shortly before dawn of the 26th, he reluctantly withdrew the few troops which had made the crossing and marched his men back to Bristol. There he sent off a message to Washington describing his rebuff by the elements.[75]

Reed, however, in order to discern the latest movements of the enemy, remained on the Jersey side when Cadwalader withdrew his men. Accompanied by Colonel Joseph Cowperthwaite of the Philadelphia associators, he made his way to Burlington and remained there briefly before rejoining Cadwalader at Bristol.[76] Not until the sound of cannon fire from the direction of Trenton reached their ears did any of the men at that camp know that Washington had not been turned back too by the ice-choked Delaware. After anxious waiting, news reached them about noon that the general had been victorious. Cadwalader now dashed off a second letter to Washington stating that he would make another effort to cross the river, this time somewhat above Bristol, at six the next morning. He would move against the enemy post at Bordentown and suggested that if Washington marched toward the same place from Trenton, "we might perfectly surround the troops at Bordentown and take every single man." [77]

Although Cadwalader received no reply from Washington, he carried out his plan, crossing at Minnick's Ferry a mile above Bristol on the morning of December 27. While the ferrying operation was still in progress, Cadwalader received the disturbing news that Washington and his army were no longer on the Jersey side but had crossed back to Pennsylvania with their prisoners after taking Trenton. These unexpected tidings left Cadwalader uncertain as to what he should do. To his officers he proposed a retreat back to Pennsylvania, but Reed opposed this strongly, suggesting the occupation of Burlington. At this time word was received that Donop, upon hearing of the disaster to his garrison at Trenton, had evacuated both Mount Holly and Black Horse. This news convinced Cadwalader that it would be safe to remain east of the river and, following Reed's proposal, he now marched to Burlington. Reed, with Colonels Cox and Cowperthwaite, rode off to try to locate the enemy. When they reached Bordentown, situated on the Delaware eight miles above Burlington and six miles below Trenton, they found that this town too, Donop's main base for the past two weeks, had been abandoned.[78]

After sending Cowperthwaite back to tell Cadwalader of what had been found at Bordentown, Reed, having as yet caught no sign of Donop's men, moved ahead cautiously. Cox was probably still with him. Before daylight on December 28 Trenton was reached and it, too, was found abandoned by both sides. Reed sent word of this, probably by Cox, across the river to Washington. This news, Cadwalader's progress, and news that Putnam had finally been able to move a sizeable force under General Thomas Mifflin from Philadelphia into Jersey prompted Washington to cross to Trenton again. On December 29 he sent over a body of cavalry to operate as a scouting force under Reed's command. The main body of the army followed the next day.[79]

But enemy troops were also on the move now. The confusion which had gripped them after the battle of Trenton gave way to purposeful activity as Cornwallis took the field again and led reinforcements from New York into Jersey. On the 30th Reed and a small party of the Philadelphia Light Horse troop reconnoitered toward Princeton. They brought back news that the British were clearly building up strength there for an advance against Trenton. They also brought back twelve British dragoons and a British commissary officer, captured in a neatly executed stroke some four miles from Princeton.[80]

This news and other intelligence received by Washington led him to concentrate his forces at Trenton. Cadwalader and Mifflin were ordered to join him there and had done so by January 2, 1777. That same day reports reached Washington that the British were on the march from Princeton. Reed, whose detailed knowledge of the local terrain was very helpful to the general, reconnoitered along the upper Assunpink Creek, which flowed through Trenton to the Delaware, while Washington set his defenses along the south side of the creek at Trenton itself. The superior British forces under Cornwallis pushed through to the opposite bank that afternoon, but deferred their assault on the American position until the next day.[81]

When the sun rose on the morning of January 3 Washington was gone. In a brilliantly executed night maneuver, again aided by Reed's knowledge of the roads and streams of the area, the American army had moved stealthily northeastward around Cornwallis's left flank, falling upon the British post at Princeton shortly after dawn. A sharp action there put the enemy to flight toward New Brunswick. Washington took a very personal role in leading his men to this victory and it is probable that Reed was also in the thick of the battle. In 1782 Washington wrote the latter that "your Conduct at Princeton evidenced a Spirit and Zeal which to me appeared laudable and becoming." [82]

The weariness of his men after their all-night march and the knowledge that Cornwallis would be hurrying back from Trenton after him led Washington to call off a close pursuit of the enemy routed at Princeton and to draw off northward to Somerset Courthouse that evening, to Pluckamin the next day, then on to Morristown where, in a position of natural strength, the army finally went into winter quarters with all but easternmost Jersey cleared of the enemy.

Now that the campaigning had ended, Reed did not resume his office as adjutant general. Washington's general orders of January 13, 1777, noted the appointment, on a temporary basis, of Colonel George Weedon, of the Third Virginia regiment, to that post.[83] After acting for Washington in the Princeton-Burlington area in disposing American forces in cantonments there, and after arranging too for for harassing raids on British foraging parties and for an intelligence network, Reed returned to Philadelphia.[84]

The campaign now concluded, redeemed at the very last by the victories of Trenton and Princeton, had convinced Reed, as the mere declaration of independence had not, that a reconciliation with Britain was totally impossible. The toughening of his attitude is candidly revealed in the letter he wrote from Philadelphia to Dennis DeBerdt. The "inhumanity" with which the British generals conducted the campaign, particularly in New Jersey, and the "most inhuman ravage, in which age and sex have indiscriminately suffered," had, Reed said, "created such an Inveteracy between the two countries as no Reconcilement can ever efface." The submission demanded by Britain was denounced as one which "scarcely leaves a Shadow of Liberty." No man, Reed continued, who thinks himself bound to "transmit to his Posterity the Blessings of Freedom unimpaired [can] make the ignominious Sacrifice." [85]

These statements by Reed and, more convincingly, his actions in the Trenton-Princeton campaign are too forthright to permit a belief that he could have been guilty of abandoning the American cause and swearing his fealty to Britain in February, 1777. Neither his contemporary foes nor later detractors such as Bancroft ever made such a claim. A suggestion that Reed did just that, however, was made with the publication of one of the British protection forms issued under the terms of the Howe proclamation of November 30, 1776, made out to a Joseph Reed. This document, bearing the date February 21, 1777, was published in 1943 by Ellsworth Eliot, Jr. in a brief monograph entitled *The Patriotism of Joseph Reed*. The author, apparently unaware that this document was a typical British protection form, simply assumed that it was made out for the Joseph Reed who is the subject of this study and yet concluded that its existence was unknown to him.

That the document is one of thousands issued under the terms of the Howe proclamation is unmistakable. Signed by Captain Henry Fox, aide-de-camp to General Howe, the paper, in ordering that "no person presume on any account to molest or injure Joseph Reed in his person or property," follows the standard text for such forms.[86] Though bearing no date on its face, the document does bear the notation "Joseph Reed, Sworn Feby 21, 1777" on the reverse side. This too is typical of the Howe forms. Originally, a person obtained one simply by declaring that he would be obedient to the royal government. But so many rebels were captured in arms in December, 1776, and early January, 1777, with these forms in their pockets that a solemn oath of obedience and submission was thereafter required to secure one. Even those who had already obtained protection were required to take this oath, a circumstance which explains why the "sworn" notations were made on the back of these forms after they had originally been issued.[87]

That this document was not issued for our Joseph Reed is equally clear. Its date alone strongly supports this conclusion. Why would Reed, on February 21, after the victories at Trenton and Princeton had been won and most of New Jersey regained, give up the fight and "go over" to the enemy? Even the initial appearance of the Joseph Reed for whom the document was issued came after those victories, for Fox did not become Howe's aide until later in January or possibly, indeed, early February.[88] Again, it seems impossible that the Reed who from Philadelphia wrote the determined letter of February 20, quoted above, could be the same Joseph Reed who appeared before a British officer the very next day and was sworn to royal allegiance. But not only these factors of time, not only the state of mind revealed by Reed in that letter, and not only his vigor in the recent campaign and the new hope which its closing fostered all militate against this assumption of identity. General Howe himself, writing to Lord Germain in March, stated that not a single major figure of the revolutionary party had taken advantage of the proclamation he and his brother had issued.[89] The man who had so recently been the adjutant general of the American Army would certainly have been considered a major figure.[90]

February, 1777, saw Joseph Reed looking forward to new service for his state and his country, not backward to a tie which he now regarded as destructive of freedom. Back in Philadelphia, he found that much had transpired since he left the city to become Washington's adjutant eight long months ago. An attempt to familiarize himself with the new political situation there and to keep abreast of the surging political developments soon engrossed his attention.

CHAPTER VII

Camp or Council?

ON July 8, 1776, while Reed was busy familiarizing himself with his duties as adjutant general of Washington's army at New York, there had occurred in Philadelphia two closely connected events which symbolized the revolution against Britain and the internal revolution in Pennsylvania. Each presaged the death of the proprietary government of Penn's colony and the birth of the new state government which was to bid so persistently against Washington for Reed's services. For on that day the Declaration of Independence was proclaimed in the State House yard, and on that same day men went to the polls throughout Pennsylvania to elect a constitutional convention to form a new government "on the authority of the people only." [1]

The convention, which convened a week later, was hardly representative of Pennsylvania as a whole. It had been called by an extralegal provincial convention composed of the more radical Whigs, its members had been elected by a very small portion of the population, again the radical element, and its own membership, drawn from this same source, was rescued from complete obscurity in reputation only by the presence of Benjamin Franklin, David Rittenhouse, George Ross, James Smith, and one or two others among its ninety-six members.[2] Conspicuously absent were members or representatives of the Quaker and eastern aristocracy which had long held the reins of government in their hands. It is not surprising, then, that the state constitution framed by this convention abruptly tore control of Pennsylvania politics from this group, working thereby an internal revolution more violent than that which accompanied the establishment of new governments in any of the other twelve states.

The Pennsylvania constitution of 1776 "established the most democratic state government in America at the time." [3] It removed property qualifications for the suffrage and for office-holding and it reversed the old system of apportioning seats in the legislature by now giving the western counties equality until a census could permit proportional representation. It vested all legislative power in a unicameral body elected annually. It established as a plural executive a board for whose president the legislature balloted, it denied this executive a veto, it provided for rotation in office, and it rejected the principle that judges should hold office during good behavior, substituting fixed terms up to seven years. Despite the abrupt departure from the former charter and despite the doctrinaire features contained in this new constitution, its framers closed the door to ready modification by permitting amendments only once every seven years.[4]

This constitution for the "Commonwealth of Pennsylvania" was promulgated September 28, 1776. The torrent of criticism which fell upon it was basically a protest against the internal revolution it embodied, a protest led by the conservatives of Philadelphia and the eastern counties whose political monopoly it shattered. Their efforts to destroy or significantly revise the constitution on the one hand, and the efforts of the democrats to implement it on the other, evoked "one of the bitterest political struggles ever witnessed by an American State."[5] In this political warfare Joseph Reed was a central figure.

As was the case in the early resistance against Britain and again in the matter of independence, Reed was reluctant to eschew compromise and throw himself wholeheartedly into either partisan camp. His actions as a member of the Pennsylvania assembly in the spring of 1776 indicated a desire for an orderly modification of the proprietary government rather than such an abrupt departure from precedent as the radicals of the convention were to achieve.[6] By June he realized that such a hope was in vain, and the prospect of turbulent change was for him an unpleasant one. Writing to his wife to inform her of his acceptance of the adjutant general's post, Reed had confessed that one of the factors which weighed in his decision was the apprehension that "this Province will be a great scene of party and contention this summer."[7] Reed's correspondence during that summer of 1776 unfortunately contains no expression of opinion as to the developments at Philadelphia. This was calculated caution, for writing his wife in October he again manifested his desire to stand apart from the partisan contest there:

> If there was no other objection to going to Philadelphia, the Part I should be obliged to take in the very unsettled State of Things would be a very strong one. In such Times a Person in any degree active must make himself a number of Enemies whom no Distance of Time or Change of Things can reconcile.[8]

Reed found the "unsettled State of Things" in Philadelphia only slightly altered for the better three months later when he resigned his commission and returned there after the Trenton-Princeton campaign. The constitutionalists had won a majority of seats in the November election for the legislature, but deliberate abstention by the conservative anti-constitutionalist members, including the Philadelphia delegation, prevented the house from securing a quorum. The anti-constitutionalists also blocked the organization of the supreme executive council. This paralysis continued until Washington's victories on the Delaware briefly assuaged party strife. In January, 1777, the assembly was able to obtain a quorum, in February the anti-constitutionalists in Philadelphia permitted the election of a councilor, and on March 4 the executive board was finally able to convene. The widely respected conservative, Thomas Wharton, was elected president, and George Bryan, leader of the democrats and a major architect of the constitution, was elected vice president. The government had finally become operative, but this very fact, by disappointing the anti-constitutionalist hope that it would die aborning, reopened the political warfare.[9]

One of the many important tasks awaiting action by the supreme executive council was the establishment of the judicial system, for the power to appoint judges was vested in the president and council. On March 20, 1777, the office of chief justice of the commonwealth was tendered to Joseph Reed. The post embraced one of the three seats on the supreme court of the state and carried an annual salary of £1,000.[10]

This appointment, formally communicated to Reed on March 29, now poised two problems for him. First, it would oblige him to come to some decision as to his future career—as soldier, lawyer, or civil servant—and secondly it would also require him to come to a decision regarding his role as either a supporter or opponent of the new state government.

The second decision was the more vital one, for it would to a great extent determine the first. That was all the more true because it had be be a firm and definitive one. This the constitutionalists themselves had required when they wrote into the constitution the following oath to be taken by all officers of the government:

I do swear (or affirm) that I will be true and faithful to the Commonwealth of Pennsylvania: and that I will not directly or indirectly do any act or thing prejudicial or injurious to the constitution or government thereof, as established by the convention.[11]

Would pointing out defects in the constitution and suggesting amendments be construed an indirect act prejudicial to the constitution "as established by the convention"? Many Pennsylvanians thought it would [12] and Reed, therefore, aware of this rigid interpretation, moved cautiously in considering the appointment.

Politics aside, there were other considerations to be mulled over. Despite the reopening of the courts, the war conditions rendered a return to his law practice unattractive to Reed.[13] But a military career at Washington's side still beckoned. On January 23, only a few days after Reed left the army and returned to Philadelphia, Washington wrote to tell him that among the recommendations he had just sent to Congress for the appointment of additional brigadier generals he had included Reed's name and had specifically nominated him for the command of the cavalry of the army.[14] Washington had been much impressed by the skill Reed had displayed in reconnaissance and in leading cavalry patrols during the Trenton-Princeton campaign.

This nomination was still in suspense when Reed received the appointment as chief justice. In February Congress had elected ten new brigadiers but Reed was not among them.[15] However, no designation as to a commander of the cavalry was made, and thus the possibility that Washington's recommendation of Reed would yet be acted upon favorably remained alive.

With this possibility before him and with it apparently appearing more attractive to him (though not to Mrs. Reed) than the judicial post, Reed attended the April 9 meeting of the supreme executive council and, pleading "some conditional engagements with General Washington which he had entered into some time ago," declared that he could not accept the chief justice's post at present. He announced his wish that he might be permitted to postpone a final answer to the council until it reconvened after the adjournment then pending. The members of the council agreed.[16]

It was about this same time that Reed composed the letter to an unspecified member of Congress of which a draft is in the Reed manuscripts. It reveals that Reed attributed Congress's delay in acting upon Washington's recommendation of him for the cavalry command to attacks made upon his past conduct in the army by members of Congress, "particularly from Connecticut." He remarked that no request or recommendation made by the commander in chief had been slighted or refused in the past. "I should be sorry that this should happen to me," he wrote, and yet, rather than have resistance to his appointment and reluctance to act contrary to Washington's wishes delay the speedy filling of the cavalry post, he authorized his unnamed correspondent to withdraw his name "should my apprehension on this subject be well founded."[17]

This letter failed to wring a prompt decision from Congress. Another month went by while Reed's sensitivity to the slight, as he viewed that body's delay to be, mounted steadily. Finally, on May 12, Congress elected two new brigadier generals, Colonel Jedidiah Huntington and Colonel Joseph Reed. But Congress did not go on to designate Reed commander of the cavalry as Washington had requested.[18] The commander in chief, knowing Reed's temperament, hastened to cover up this unflattering hesitation. He wrote Stephen Moylan on May 24 to ask that the latter convey to Reed the pleasure with which he had read Reed's name in the appointment of brigadiers and to inform him that "if Congress have it not in contemplation to appoint a General of Horse but leave it to me to assign one of the Brigadiers already appointed to that command, I shall assuredly place General Reed there." But Washington found it necessary to add that since it would be disagreeable for both Reed and himself to place the former in a situation "that might be the standing of a day only, I could wish to know what the views of Congress are on this head." Washington mentioned that he would write at once to Congress himself on the matter.[19]

The commander in chief's letter to Congress of May 24 brought action by that body, but not the direct appointment of Reed which the latter's wounded pride required as a salve. On May 27 Congress empowered Washington to assign a commander for the cavalry from among the generals already appointed. Upon receiving this authorization Washington wrote to Reed. "I mean that you should act in that line, if agreeable to yourself," he stated, "and wish you in such case to repair to Camp as soon as you can." [20]

But Reed's pique had gotten the better of him. Angered by Congress's long delay in naming him a general and by their refusal to give him the command of the cavalry, he decided against taking the latter from Washington's hands and decided too to decline the commission of brigadier general. On June 7 he wrote to Congress to return with "grateful acknowledgments" his appointment as a brigadier, citing as his reasons alterations in his private affairs and "the want of time to qualify himself for that line of service," the cavalry, for which Washington had intended him.[21] A more honest revelation of his motives was made almost a year later. Writing to Dennis DeBerdt he described the offer of the cavalry command but stated that "some promotions having been made prejudicial to my claims, and other circumstances intervening, I did not accept it." [22]

Reed wrote to Washington on the 12th to inform him of his decision. The general's reply expressed his disappointment and his wish that Reed's resolve "had been otherwise." But he told Reed that there would always be a place for him as one of his military family whenever "a desire of rendering those aids to the service which your abilities enable you to do, should lead you to the Camp." [23]

All this time Reed's appointment as chief justice of Pennsylvania had remained in suspense and now the executive council was growing impatient for a conclusive answer. Timothy Matlack, the council's secretary, wrote in mid-June requesting that Reed appear and give his answer concerning the appointment. Reed, however, received the letter just as he was leaving Philadlphia with the Philadelphia associators to join Washington's army in New Jersey, and further delay ensued.[24]

The mysterious maneuvering of Sir William Howe's army in Jersey which brought Reed and his fellow Philadelphians into the field led not to an attack upon Washington's army but to the evacuation of the British-held posts in the easternmost part of the state. Reed was often at headquarters during these wearying marches and countermarches of late June and early July, serving without rank in a volunteer capacity as a member of Washington's staff.[25]

By late July Washington was convinced that Howe intended to strike at Philadelphia. He shifted his own forces to cover that target, and in doing so gave Reed the opportunity to return to the city and put in his long-delayed appearance before the executive council of Pennsylvania on July 23. In a prepared written statement he informed the council that he must decline the chief justiceship which it had offered to him.

Reed explained that his delay in reaching a decision concerning the post had been partly due to "a flattering hope of promoting a coalition," a reconciliation between the radicals and the anti-constitutionalists. His letter of June 21 to Timothy Matlack revealed that he had been discussing the matter with members of the assembly.[26] Reed, as a member of the more conservatively minded patriot group, was hopeful that the invitation tendered him to take a high office under the constitution of 1776 might be so interpreted as a gesture toward harmony by the radicals in power that other anti-constitutionalists might be persuaded to abandon their efforts to thwart the new government at every turn.

But as peacemaker Reed was again unsuccessful. The anticonstitutional group, among whom were such close companions of his as Robert Morris, Thomas Mifflin, and John Cadwalader, refused to view the offer to Reed as a peace gesture and advised him to reject the office. Reed did so, but not until he had studied the constitution carefully and had decided to decline the judge-ship on the merits of that office itself as constituted under the constitution.

In his letter to the council Reed stated that he had compared Pennsylvania's government with those in the other states and with foreign governments about which he had read. He remarked pointedly that a frame of government formed "upon the spur of the occasion" could not hope to escape defects. Therefore, he regretted all the more that amendment was possible only once every seven years. He expressed fears that unless this system was remedied the government would "sink into a spiritless langour, or expire in a sudden convulsion." Turning then to the question of the oath required of all officeholders, he declared that feeling as he did about the necessity of change he faced "an insuperable difficulty to enter into an engagement of the most solemn nature, leading to the support and confirmation of an entire system of government which I cannot wholly approve." Referring to the fact that several assemblymen had taken conditional oaths of office which departed from that prescribed in the constitution, he remarked that he could not accept that precedent as one which would banish his scruples and enable him to take office. "I can-not reconcile to my ideas of propriety," he stated, "the members of the same state being under different obligations to support and enforce its authority."

Having explained his dissatisfaction with parts of the consti-tution, Reed then went on record against the anti-constitutionalist campaign of violent abuse. He found "many excellencies" in the frame of government, "too many to be hastily and wholly relin-quished, much less branded with those epithets, which, in some instances, have been applied to it." He declared that in reject-ing the chief justice's post he by no means intended to oppose the operation of the present government nor work for its subversion. Remarking that if the people decided against alterations in the mode of government he would esteem it his duty to support it, not merely acquiesce in it, Reed concluded by tendering his services "in any line conducive to the general interest or defense, or consistent with the sentiments I have disclosed." [27]

Reed's decision, though not the latter part of his statement, was very pleasing to the opponents of the government. But political maneuverings were quickly pushed aside, temporarily at least, when within the week of Reed's appearance before the council, the British fleet carrying General Howe's army was sighted off Delaware Bay. Washington came to Philadelphia on July 31 and began intensive preparations for the defense of the city.[28] Despite previous decisions against the military life Reed, who had moved his family from Philadelphia eighteen miles up the Schuylkill valley to a farm at Norriton,[29] once again joined the army as a volunteer, serving at times with the commander in chief as an aide, but more often with the Pennsylvania militia under General John Armstrong. On August 7, undoubtedly at Washington's request, Reed sent the former a long letter with his suggestions for Philadelphia's defense.[30] Since these largely concerned the forts on the Delaware River as obstacles against a landing on its banks by Howe, their value in shaping Washington's dispositions became slight when the British commander unexpectedly landed his troops at the head of Chesapeake Bay instead, some fifty-five miles south of Philadelphia.

During the most decisive single action of Howe's march on the Pennsylvania capital, the sharply fought battle of Brandywine Creek on September 11, Reed was with Armstrong's men guarding the lower fords of the creek. The British flanking movement which won for them the battle was directed at the upper fords, however, and the Pennsylvania militia and Reed with them saw no action that day. After the American line collapsed above them, they retreated to Chester and there rejoined the main body of Washington's army the evening of the battle.[31]

From Chester Washington moved northward on September 12 to a defensive line along the Schuylkill River. Though worried by the proximity of his family to the new scene of military operations,[32] Reed continued with the army in his volunteer capacity.

September 15 and 16 he was at Swede's Ford arranging the Pennsylvania militia in defensive positions there. On the 18th he went to the Falls of Schuylkill on a similar mission at General Armstrong's request and succeeded in obtaining some sorely needed maps for Washington.[33]

But all these preparations proved to be inadequate to save Philadelphia from Howe. Displaying abilities he rarely manifested in his Revolutionary career, the British commander outmaneuvered Washington so neatly that his crossing of the Schuylkill and his subsequent occupation of Philadelphia were achieved without another battle. It was Reed who sent Washington the first definitive news of the crossing. His note of September 23, dispatched from a spot only a mile above the house his family was occupying in Norriton, revealed that he had escaped capture there by only fifteen minutes. Reed gathered together a small group of militiamen but could do no more than take two prisoners. From one of these the intention of the British army to ignore Washington and descend upon Philadelphia was learned, but by that time Washington was in no position to block such a movement.[34]

On September 28, two days after the fall of Philadelphia, Washington held a council of war on the advisability of an attack upon Howe's forces, now centered on Germantown. Reed and John Cadwalader, who was also serving Washington as a volunteer at this time, were present at the council but because of their unofficial capacities did not sign the proceedings which advised against an immediate attack.[35] Washington, however, did not long suppress his eagerness for an offensive stroke. In the days which followed the council of the 28th, Reed and Cadwalader were kept busy scouting for the commander in chief and organizing countermeasures against British patrols and foraging parties.[36] Finally, on October 3, Washington moved toward Germantown and early on the morning of the 4th launched an attack upon the British encampment there. Reed's role in the ill-fated battle of Germantown is as enshrouded as the battlefield itself was that foggy morning. His own correspondence reveals only that he was in the action.[37] An early historian of the Revolution attributes to Reed the fervent but unheeded plea to bypass the British who found refuge in the Chew mansion, a critical decision in the course of the battle, but gives no support for this statement.[38]

Although the rebuff at Germantown was the last general encounter of the Philadelphia campaign, Washington did not go into winter quarters until late December. Except for brief visits with his family, Reed remained with the army during this period, a period marked by unsuccessful efforts to keep the Delaware River below Philadelphia closed to British passage and by cautious sparring by Washington for the opportunity which never came to catch Howe off guard and attack again. Reed and Cadwalader were indefatigable in conveying orders from Washington's headquarters northeast of Philadelphia to the commanders of the American troops on the Delaware south of the city, and in transmitting intelligence reports to the commander in chief. Reed was also assiduous in transmitting news of the movements of the armies to President Thomas Wharton of Pennsylvania at Lancaster, now the seat of the state government. Reed and Cadwalader urged Washington to shift the main army south of Philadelphia to permit greater activity in support of the forts on the Delaware, but a council of war ruled out such a move.[39] Despite this rebuff, both men remained among the circle of Washington's closest advisers and continued to participate in councils of war, a fact which caused some comment at the time since neither had commissions in the army.[40] Concerning the matter of the best location for winter quarters, Washington sent a special note asking Reed for his opinion. With Cadwalader and others, Reed urged a concentration upon Wilmington, Delaware, but a greater weight of opinion favoring the upper Schuylkill led Washington to the choice of Valley Forge.[41]

Before the move to that site was effected, Reed had one of his narrowest escapes in combat of the war. On December 6 General Howe ventured forth from his positions at Philadelphia in the hope of luring Washington into a general engagement. Sharp skirmishing ensued. Reed and Cadwalader, sent by Washington to reconnoitre on the left flank of the American line, found Pennsylvania militia troops retreating in disorder there. While they were in an exposed position endeavoring to rally these men,

Reed's horse suddenly fell with a bullet through the head. Before Reed could fully recover from his fall, several British soldiers rushed toward him with poised bayonets. But a number of militiamen now came to Reed's aid, a cavalry trooper dashed up to carry him off the field, and he escaped unscathed.[42] The minor engagement in which Reed participated and other skirmishes fought that day and for the next two days were quite inconclusive. Howe then turned back to Philadelphia and Washington moved to Valley Forge.

The campaigning was now over, but the calls for Reed's services were not. While he had been serving with Washington over the past four months, both Congress and the Pennsylvania state authorities had vied with one another in attempts to lure him into civil positions. Despite Reed's rejection of the chief justiceship of Pennsylvania in July, the assembly of the state, though dominated by the radicals or constitutionalists, elected him a member of the state's delegation to Congress on September 14, 1777.[43] Undoubtedly the fact that other critics of the constitution, notably Robert Morris and James Wilson, had served the state in this capacity led to a belief that Reed would not refuse this post as he had the judicial one.

This belief was correct. Reed did decide to accept the appointment to Congress. But the military engagements described above made it impossible for him to take his seat until Washington had gone into winter quarters late in December. The assembly had made a new choice of delegates in the interval (on December 10) but Reed was reappointed to the new slate.[44]

Meanwhile Congress itself had had its eye on Reed. A letter to Washington from one of the Virginia delegates, Richard Henry Lee, reveals that Reed was among those considered for the new board of war which Congress was creating in October of 1777.[45] He was not one of the members finally selected, however. But on November 20 Congress did name him to a three-man commission for Indian affairs which was to proceed to Fort Pitt to cooperate with General Hand in pacifying the Indians on the Virginia-Pennsylvania frontier. Reed was informed of this appointment by a letter of November 23 from President Henry Laurens of

Congress but replied on the 30th that it would not be possible for him to accept the position. Congress then elected George Clymer, also of Pennsylvania, in his place.[46] The day after his selection as one of the Indian commissioners Reed figured in the debate in Congress over the appointment of a commissioner to replace Silas Deane at the French court. He, Francis Dana, and James Wilson were nominated in addition to John Adams, upon whom the choice fell a week later.[47]

After Washington settled the army at Valley Forge a few days before Christmas, Reed was able to spend two quiet weeks with his family at nearby Norriton. Close at hand were the families of other patriot leaders who had fled Philadelphia at Howe's approach, notably that of Colonel John Bayard, one of Reed's closest friends.[48]

Having learned of his reappointment to Congress by the Pennsylvania assembly in its new selection of December 10, 1777, Reed was preparing to leave for York to take his seat when Congress saved him the journey by naming him, on January 10, 1778, to its highly important committee of conference on the affairs of the army. The committeemen, chairman Francis Dana, Nathaniel Folsom, John Harvie, and Reed, were to "repair to General Washington's headquarters" and consult with the commander in chief on the multitudinous questions involved in "introducing economy and promoting discipline and good morals in the army." They were empowered not simply to make recommendations to Congress but to remove incompetent officials in the civil department of the army and to make temporary appointments to fill vacancies caused by such removals.[49]

Before the end of January the committee took up residence at the home of William Moore, some two miles north of Washington's headquarters at Valley Forge.[50] Reed was pleased to be in close contact with Washington again and also thankful that his proximity to Norriton enabled him to see his family occasionally. His trips home, however, were described by Mrs. Reed as "seldom and uncertain," not only because of the weight of business at the camp but because British foraging parties and cavalry patrols made it too dangerous for him to make prolonged visits. Norriton was located in the "no man's land" between the lines of Howe and Washington. Mrs. Reed confided to her close friend, Mrs. John Cox, that "I am easiest when he is [away] from home, as his being here brings danger with it. There are so many disaffected to the cause of this country, that they lay in wait for those who are active in it." [51]

Reed's seventeen months of army service during the war and his close association with Washington since 1775 brought him to the fore as the workhorse of the Congressional committee and resulted in his promotion to the chairmanship of the committee in place of Dana.[52] Direct contact with the sufferings of the army at Valley Forge brought home to Reed's fellow members a sense of the terrible necessity for a reorganization of its affairs which even Washington's dispatches to Congress could not have given them previously. Together with the commander in chief they worked with great harmony and diligence on the improvement of the quartermaster and the commissary departments, on means for attracting officers through the establishment of a pension system, on the great task of providing the army with full complements by drafts upon the militia for twelve months' duty, and on means of increasing the strength of the cavalry.

Reed was particularly active in the work of overhauling the quartermaster and commissary departments. He wrote the committee reports of January 28 and 29 and February 3, 5, 12, and 25 on this subject.[53] The subsequent appoinments of his brother-in-law Charles Pettit and his close friend John Cox as the two deputy quartermaster generals indicates his influence. These men were by no means foisted upon the department by Reed. On the contrary, General Nathanael Greene, whom Congress named quartermaster general, wrote Reed that he "only agreed to accept the department upon Col. Cox being joined." Greene knew Pettit only by the latter's reputation for integrity, but that his appointment as assistant pleased the general too is evident from a later letter in which Greene remarked he "was never more happy in my life at any circumstance than that Mr. Pettit belongs to the department." [54]   Reed was also instrumental in the happy selection of Jeremiah Wadsworth of Massachusetts as the new commissary general.[55]

The greater efficiency which followed the changes in the leadership of these two departments, the enactment by Congress of a plan for drafts from the militia substantially as Washington and the committee had urged, the enactment of a measure providing pensions for the widows of officers—all these beneficial moves helped produce a significant improvement in the army which took the field for the campaign of 1778.[56]   To Reed and the other members of the committee at Valley Forge must go some of the credit for this.   Not the least of their contributions at the moment was their firm support of the commander in chief at the very time when critics in Congress, supported by Generals Horatio Gates and Thomas Conway, were noisily debating his shortcomings.[57]

After two a half months of work at Valley Forge, the committee members returned to take their seats in Congress.   Reed attended his first session as a member on April 6, 1778, and was present the next four days.   In this brief period he was appointed to four special committees.   But then, on April 11, Congress ordered "that Mr. Reed have leave of absence for a few days to remove his family to a place of security." [58]

The "few days" were to stretch into six weeks.   With the approach of spring Reed had become concerned about the exposed position of his family's residence.   Located as it was between Valley Forge and Philadelphia, the renewal of hostilities between the armies of Washington and Howe would entail great danger. As early as March, Charles Pettit was endeavoring to find a place in New Jersey where Reed's family and his own, then at Trenton, might find safety.[59]   Early in April arrangements were completed for a house in Flemington, twenty miles north of Trenton.   Since Esther Reed was expecting her fifth child in May, Reed immediately obtained the leave of absence from Congress and the move from Norriton to Flemington was made late in April.   His delay in returning to Congress was due not only to his desire to be with his wife at the baby's birth but also to the contraction of a severe case of smallpox by his youngest child, nineteen-month-old Theo-

dosia. Reed's joy over the birth of a son on May 12 was sadly
tempered when, despite the ministrations of Doctor William
Shippen, Sr., the little girl died the next day.[60] This tragedy
affected Mrs. Reed badly, and Reed's presence at home was hence
required for several additional weeks.

It was the first week of June when Reed finally left Flemington
to resume his public duties. He proceeded first to the army's
camp at Valley Forge and there received word from Congress, still
sitting at York, that he and Francis Dana has been appointed to
assist Washington implement the new arrangements for the army
which Congress had enacted.[61] Before Dana joined Reed at Valley Forge, fast-moving events thrust their mission into temporary
oblivion, to await a calmer time. First Reed became involved in
the machinations of the British peace commission led by the Earl
of Carlisle,[62] and then the British evacuation of Philadelphia set
the American army in motion again and led Reed to cast aside his
Congressional toga and assume again the now familiar role of
voluntary aide to General Washington.

Signs that Sir Henry Clinton, General Howe's successor as the
British commander, was intending to evacuate Philadelphia had
appeared during the first week of June. Washington, for his part,
was determined to hang closely upon the retreating army and
seize the first favorable opportunity to bring on an engagement.
The last British soldier left Philadelphia before nightfall on June
18, and Reed, with the vanguard of the American army, entered
the city that same evening.[63] Washington had feared that Clinton
would avoid an action by transporting his army from the Delaware to New York by sea. But the British commander decided
to march his men across New Jersey. Upon learning that, Washington moved across the Delaware too and pushed eastward on a
line parallel to the enemy's retreat route. On June 23, Reed
joined Washington at Hopewell, bringing news of the enemy
movements which he and Stephen Moylan, his associate of the
early days of the war at Cambridge, had obtained during a reconnaissance south of Trenton.[64] John Cadwalader also joined the
army at this time to serve alongside Reed again under Washington.

Five days later at the battle of Monmouth, June 28, both men saw action. From the time of General Charles Lee's retreat, Reed was "with the General [Washington] at his Desire or reconnoitering in Front, but chiefly the former." [65] Once again he narrowly escaped being a casualty. For the third time in the war his horse was killed under him, and yet, for the third time, he himself was unscathed.[66] That both Reed and Cadwalader distinguished themselves at Monmouth is indicated by Washington's subsequent revival of his request that Congress name either of them to the command of the cavalry. Oddly enough, Reed had to handle this matter himself as a member of the Congressional committee on army affairs. His report of September 7 to Congress on Washington's request recommended the election of Cadwalader to the post, "the other gentleman [i.e., himself] recommended by the General having turned his views to civil life, and wholly declining this service now." Congress did appoint Cadwalader but he declined on September 19, expressing the opinion that the war was nearly over.[67] Reed's recommendation of Cadwalader at this time is notable, for unfortunately it stands as the last sign of a close friendship soon to be transmuted by political rivalry into intense bitterness.

After the battle of Monmouth Reed did not accompany Washington's army to its new position astride the Hudson, but returned to Philadelphia where Congress was now meeting again and took his seat on July 15. One of his first acts was to sign his name to the engrossed copy of the Articles of Confederation. On June 27, while Reed was away with the army in New Jersey, the Pennsylvania delegation in Congress had presented the order of the state's assembly that they "accede to, ratify, confirm, and agree to the said Articles of Confederation." They signed the engrossed copy of July 9 and Reed added his signature after his return.[68]

In the hot summer session of 1778, his role, as always, was a very active one. He was quickly reappointed to the committee on army arrangements which was to join Washington at the camp. At first he thought he and the other members could leave before the end of July, but the press of business prevented this.[69] In the last eleven meeting days in July Reed was appointed to no fewer than nine committees, two of which concerned the reception of the French minister, M. Gerard, and the entertainment for him on August 6.[70] The heavy burden of work (and/or the rich food and drink at the diplomatic reception) brought on a week's illness during which Reed was confined to his house.[71]

Reed returned to his seat on Saturday, August 15, and then left for the army's camp with other members of the committee on arrangements early the following week. The committee, of which Reed was chairman, reached Washington's headquarters at White Plains, New York, on the 23rd. Of the quarters to which he was assigned Reed commented that they were not only hot and dirty but that "I never met with such a Combination of Smells and every one offensive." But the army itself looked good, far better as to "clothes, discipline and zeal for service" than Reed had ever known it.[72] The committee labored with Washington over such knotty problems as the relative ranking of officers, the question of the bounty to be paid new recruits, supply matters (Charles Pettit was at headquarters too at this time in his new capacity as deputy quartermaster general), and von Steuben's plan for equalizing regimental strength.[73] After two intensive weeks of work the committee concluded its sessions at the camp. Reed left White Plains about September 10, probably stopped off to see his family at Flemington, and was back in his seat at Congress on the 15th. He was in constant attendance there until October 12.[74] The year's campaigning was obviously at a close, and now his labors in Washington's behalf as the leader of the Congressional committee on the army were also completed. His martial duty, so strongly bound up with his desire to serve Washington personally, seemed fulfilled. Thus Reed now turned irrevocably to that other field of service which had beckoned him so persistently. On October 12 he resigned his seat in Congress to plunge into the maelstrom of Pennsylvania politics.[75]

CHAPTER VIII

Integrity, Soft Words, and Hard Cash

ON June 6, 1778, while Reed was returning from his leave
of absence to resume his Congressional duties at Valley
Forge, three men reached Philadelphia from London, three men
whom Reed had never met and was never to meet, but whose
mission was, incidentally, to involve him in one of the most unusual incidents of the Revolution. The men were Frederick
Howard, fifth Earl of Carlisle, William Eden, a member of the
British Board of Trade, and George Johnstone, member of Parliament and a former governor of British West Florida. Their task
was to end the revolution and nullify the recently signed Franco-
American alliance by offering America a reconciliation on terms
which barely stopped short of independence. This Carlisle commission represented Britain's last effort to save by diplomacy its
tottering empire in America. The desperate nature of the mission led its members to turn to any expedient—real concession
and misrepresentations, words of peace and threats of even more
violent war, talk of honor and attempts at bribery—in their attempt to prevent a failure which, they sensed, would be conclusive. When failure did loom up before them they turned
particularly to that last weapon, bribery, and Joseph Reed was
one of those whose services in their behalf the Carlisle commission attempted to buy.

The appointment of a peace commission as well as the substance of the concessions they were to offer the Americans were
embodied in measures introduced in the House of Commons by
Lord North on February 17, 1778. The commission's membership, Carlisle, Eden, Johnstone, and also the two Howe brothers,
was arranged between that time and early April.[1] Of all of those
only Eden had a training and background which fitted him for
the difficult assignment. Carlisle, aside from his friendship with
Charles James Fox, had little to recommend him; Johnstone,

though he had spoken occasionally for America in Parliament before hostilities, was ignorant and impetuous; and the naming of Admiral and General Howe to a peace commission was a major blunder.[2] Richard Jackson, whom Reed had met in London in 1764 and who had been a close friend of Benjamin Franklin during the latter's years of residence in England, was offered a place on the commission but declined.[3]

The powers tendered to the commission by the royal instructions of April 12 were worthy of better agents. They embodied significant concessions concerning freedom of the colonies from Parliamentary taxation and from a standing military force, the abolition of quit rents, popular elections for the colonial royal governors, appointment of judges for good behavior, and other American grievances which might well have forestalled the Revolution if offered in 1774 or 1775.[4] As to the effectiveness of these proposals in 1778, even the commissioners themselves were dubious. Carlisle believed the offers must be "supported at the same time by the most active and spirited military operation," and on April 10, twelve days before the commission left for America, Johnstone told the House of Commons that at least the concessions would promote disunity among the rebels.[5]

To another audience in London at the same time, however, Johnstone expressed himself in a far more idealistic vein. Taking a leaf from the book of Admiral Howe's efforts to prepare the way for the peace commission of 1776, Johnstone sought to establish avenues of contact with American leaders through their friends in England. In this endeavor Reed's brother-in-law, Dennis DeBerdt, anxious as ever to heal the breach with America and naive as ever too, again became a dupe. Though admitting his "credulity and misinformation" [6] in the Howe commission affair, he not only proceeded to write Reed and also James Kinsey of New Jersey to introduce Johnstone and the concessions to be offered in glowing terms, but he met with Johnstone and helped the latter draft an unctuous letter to Reed.[7]

DeBerdt's letter to Reed introduced Johnstone as "a Commissioner of *Peace,* and a steady proved friend to America and its just rights," a man who "has been steady to your cause in Parliament, and, in general, voted against the oppressive acts. . . . He despises the men, censures their measures, and abhors the cruelty and vindication with which some acts of our military have disgraced the page of history." Johnstone, DeBerdt continued, had told him that Reed was "the *very man* he had wished on arrival [in America] to commune and consult with." The commissioner had written a letter which, DeBerdt stated, he read "with astonishing pleasure. . . . May the truth of every line fill you with consolation, . . . and as you have nobly fought, act more nobly *and forgive*." [8]

Johnstone's accompanying letter to Reed, dated April 11, opened with flattering tributes to Reed's use of sword and pen "in vindicating the rights of mankind and of that community of which you was a part." It described the establishment of the Carlisle commission and proclaimed that its object was "a fair and cheerful concurrence in adjusting every point to their [i.e., the Americans] utmost wish not inconsistent with a beneficial union of interests." Then, following an assertion that Reed might surpass the glory he had won on the battlefield by showing magnanimity in meeting with the British on the peace terms now offered, Johnstone hinted that Reed might be rewarded by something more substantial than glory for such cooperation:

The man who can be instrumental in bringing us all to act once more in harmony, and to unite together the various powers which this contest has drawn forth, will deserve more from the King and the people, from patriotism, humanity, friendship, and all the tender ties that are affected by the quarrel and reconciliation than ever was yet bestowed on humankind.[9]

The commissioners reached Philadelphia on June 6. On the 9th George Johnstone sent to Valley Forge his letter to Reed, DeBerdt's covering letter, and other letters from DeBerdt and his recent bride to the Reed family. Reed found them waiting for him at headquarters on the 11th.[10]

Reed's first reaction was one of extreme displeasure that his brother-in-law had permitted himself to be used again by the British government. To protect DeBerdt's name in America he decided that he must try to prevent any more than a synoptic disclosure of his letter's contents.[11]   But as to the letter from Johnstone, Reed decided without hesitation that this communication could not be considered a private one but must be revealed in its entirety to Congress.   First he showed the letter to Washington, and then, on June 15, sent it together with some extracts from DeBerdt's letter and the draft of an intended reply to Johnstone, to Henry Laurens, president of Congress.   His own letter covering these enclosures reveals something of Reed's hostile reaction to the Carlisle commission.   He cited, as a warning, the "base duplicity" of the former Howe commission and went on to indicate a view that no negotiations for peace could proceed until the British had withdrawn their military and naval forces.   He labeled as "an insidious manoeuvre to distract and divide us" a suggestion in DeBerdt's letter that Britain would grant America her independence if a new Congress, chosen *after* the people had heard the propositions of the Carlisle commission, claimed it.[12]

The form and expressions to be used in the reply to Johnstone, a first draft of which Reed had sent to Laurens, reached the proportions of a major issue for Reed.   He felt that some reply was necessary if for no other reason than to thank Johnstone for forwarding the family letters.[13]   On June 13, two days after receiving the commissioner's message and after showing it to Washington, he composed two drafts of his answer.   Both breathe the same total rejection of any abandonment of the struggle for complete independence.   Neither, however, gives any indication that Reed had read anything improper into the words Johnstone had addressed to him.   In varying degrees, and here lies their chief difference, the drafts express admiration for Johnstone's labors as a spokesman in Parliament of the cause of America, the ex-governor being coupled with Chatham, Barré, and Camden in this regard.[14]

On June 15 Reed sent one of the drafts to Washington for the latter's perusal.   Washington read it over the same day and sent a note to Reed asking that the latter see him before he transcribed a fair copy, since "there are some parts of it which might receive a small alteration."   Washington said that "all correspondence of this nature must and will be weighed and scanned with a scrupulous exactness, and even compliment, if carried far, may not pass entirely uncensured." [15]

Reed saw Washington as the latter had requested, abridged the flattering expressions, and left the letter at headquarters to be forwarded with other communications to Philadelphia.[16]

In its final form, Reed's reply to Johnstone deprecated the latter's exaggerated estimate of his services in the Revolution, retained respectful mention of the commissioner's "seasonable though unavailing efforts to . . . place us on the great and generous scale of equal freedom with yourselves," but gave no encouragement whatever toward further personal communications on the subject of a reconciliation. Reed stated unequivocally that "you will so soon receive the sense of Congress on this important point, that any opinion from me would be equally useless and improper." [17]   He expressed the hope that if Congress's decision was "unfriendly to your present views," Johnstone would work to have Britain "give up her visionary schemes of conquest and empire for the solid benefits she may yet derive from our amity and commerce."   If Johnstone's nation proved as deaf to him in this plea as to his others in the past, Reed invited the commissioner to "come to America, the future asylum of the brave and virtuous from every quarter of the world." [18]

Johnstone never got Reed's letter. Plans set in motion for the evacuation of Philadelphia by Sir Henry Clinton, General Howe's successor as commander of the British forces, though temporarily postponed by the arrival of the Carlisle commission, were underway again by June 15, and for Johnstone and the other commissioners the 16th was their last day in that city.[19] Reed's letter, left at American headquarters on the 15th, did not reach Johnstone before the latter's departure, and seems indeed never to have left Valley Forge.

By the 16th the Carlisle commissioners had been reduced to desperation. To begin, the evacuation of Philadelphia which they had found in preparation upon their arrival was a stunning blow, for the retreat of the army which the commission had hoped, as Carlisle wrote sardonically, "might possibly be of some inconvenience to them [Congress] if they rejected our proposals" [20] vitiated the blend of coercion and compromise upon which the commission's fate depended. Under these circumstances Carlisle had at once attempted to contact Congress at York. On June 9 he and the other commissioners drew up a long letter setting forth their powers and proposing a meeting with Congress or a committee of Congress. The commission's secretary, Dr. Adam Ferguson, was given the letter to deliver personally, but Washington refused him passage through the American lines until he had received instructions from Congress. The commission's letter was consequently forwarded on June 11 with military mail. No answer had reached Philadelphia by the 16th, however, as the commissioners watched their last few hours there tick away.[21] It seemed that they must do what Reed predicted concerning them in a letter to his wife, "go off and commence operations in some other part of the country." [22]

To the spirited George Johnstone, this failure to elicit a response to the Carlisle proposals was particularly galling. On that last day in Philadelphia he made a final effort to gain a favorable hearing for the peace plan by dangling promises of material gain before two members of Congress, Robert Morris and Joseph Reed.

For Morris, to whom he had previously written from England, Johnstone now composed a new letter. Its message was but thinly veiled:

I believe the men who have conducted the affairs of America incapable of being influenced by improper motives.   But in all such transactions there is risque, and I think that whoever ventures should be secured; at the same time, that honors and emoluments should naturally follow the fortune of those who have steered the vessel in the storm and brought her safely into port.   I think Washington and the President [of Congress] have a right to every favour which grateful nations can bestowe, if they could once more unite our interests, and spare the miseries and devastations of war.[23]

Then Johnstone turned his thoughts to that contact with Reed for which, due to DeBerdt's glowing recommendation, he had entertained such high hopes. Yet he had not received a reply from Reed and now his own departure was imminent. He there-

fore made plans for a direct attempt to bribe Reed, using as his
agent a lady who was a guest at the same home, that of loyalist
Charles Stedman, where Johnstone was quartered during his stay
in Philadelphia, and who was also related by marriage to Dr.
Ferguson, the secretary of the Carlisle commission. The lady was
Mrs. Elizabeth Graeme Ferguson, American born, a leader of the
literary set in prewar Philadelphia, and sympathetic to the American cause, but now the devoted wife of Hugh Ferguson, loyalist
and lately commissioner of war prisoners for General Howe.[24]

In the Stedman parlor Johnstone laid his plans with Mrs. Ferguson. He told her that he knew Reed's brother-in-law in England and that he had hoped to enlist Reed's support in favor of
reconciliation. He said Reed could command "ten thousand
guineas and the best post in the government" for this assistance.
According to Mrs. Ferguson's account of the meeting, Johnstone
specifically told her that "if you should see him [Reed], I could
wish you would convey that idea to him." Mrs. Ferguson then
asked if Reed wouldn't regard such an offer as a bribe. But
Johnstone replied that "this method of proceeding is customary
in all negotiations; and one may very honorably make it a man's
interest to step forth in a cause." [25]

Whatever the qualms of conscience Mrs. Ferguson then had or
later developed as to serving as intermediary in the bribe attempt,
she lost little time in contacting Reed. She sent a letter to him at
Valley Forge asking that he meet her on June 22 at some house
near the camp, citing a need for advice on her husband's legal
status as a proscribed loyalist as the reason for her request.[26] But
the movement of the American army from Valley Forge following
the departure of the last British troops from Philadelphia on the
18th delayed the letter's delivery. Reed, who had entered Philadelphia on the evening of the 18th, finally received it at headquarters there on the 21st.[27] He called on Mrs. Ferguson at the
Stedman house that same evening.

The statements of Reed and Mrs. Ferguson as to what transpired during their conversation are in perfect agreement. The
latter, in seeking to protect herself against the label of "a tool to
the Commissioners," did indeed protest that Reed's published

account gave the impression that she had requested the meeting with the transmission of Johnstone's offer in mind rather than a discussion of her husband's status as the primary purpose. On the contrary, she said, an "accident" brought Johnstone's name into their conversation.[28] But there is no doubt or disagreement as to what happened once Mrs. Ferguson did transmit Johnstone's offer of the ten thousand guineas and the high governmental post. "When I came to the most interesting point of the conversation," Mrs. Ferguson related, "he [Reed] answered without hesitation, 'My influence is but small, but was it as great as Governor Johnstone would insinuate, the King of Great-Britain has nothing in his gift that would tempt me!' " Reed himself stated in his account that when Mrs. Ferguson told him what Johnstone had mentioned to her,

I found an answer was expected and gave one, "That I was not worth purchasing, but such as I was, the King of Great-Britain was not rich enough to do it." By this time the evening was pretty far advanced, and no reply being made, I rose to take my leave, which I did after expressing my concern for her private misfortunes.[29]

Before Reed had made any revelation of this incident, this "direct attempt upon his integrity" as Washington was to call it at a later time,[30] the military developments which reached their climax with the battle of Monmouth on June 28 temporarily pushed it into the background. During this brief campaign Reed, owing to, as he himself later explained, "a reluctance to expose the Lady to a criminal prosecution, or public resentment, and myself to the imputation of vanity and ostentatious integrity, kept . . . silent, except to General Washington, and two or three other Gentlemen." [31]

When he returned to his seat in Congress after the Monmouth campaign, however, Reed found that Congress had assumed a very lively interest in Commissioner Johnstone's activities as they concerned its membership. Reed, as will be recalled, had sent Johnstone's letter to him to President Laurens on June 15. When Robert Morris laid his letter from Johnstone before Congress on July 9, Congress acted on this disclosure by ordering that "all letters received by members of the Congress from any of the British

Commissioners or their agents, or from any subject of the King of Great Britain, of a public nature, be laid before Congress." [32]

On July 16, the day after Reed returned, Francis Dana, delegate from Massachusetts, told Congress that he too had received a letter from Johnstone, a copy of which, in obedience to the order, he now revealed. Written from England, this letter was similar to, but not as pointed in tone as, those Johnstone had sent to Morris and Reed.[33] Reed now felt it was incumbent upon him to reveal the bribe attempt made upon him at Johnstone's instigation. On the 18th he told the story of his meeting of June 21 with a lady (he did not reveal her name) representing the commissioner, the offer made to him, and his reply. This revelation caused quite a sensation. Congress immediately ordered that Johnstone's letters to Reed, Morris, and Dana be published.[34] The next day Reed prepared an account of the June 21 meeting for publication with the letters. All these documents appeared in the *Pennsylvania Packet* on July 21.[35]

Several weeks now intervened, during which time the Congress was occupied with other matters, particularly the reception of Gerard, the French Minister. But in August Congress turned its attention back to the Johnstone affair again. On August 11, citing the letters to Reed and Morris and Reed's narrative of the bribe offered by Johnstone through "a married lady of character having connexion with the British army," it resolved that these could not be considered other than as "direct attempts to corrupt and bribe the Congress of the United States of America" and that, consequently, "it is incompatible with the honour of Congress to hold any manner of correspondence or intercourse with the said George Johnstone, Esq." [36] Johnstone, in a lame rebuttal published in New York on August 26, could only facetiously "decline acting as a commissioner, or otherwise interfering in any message, answer, agreement, negotiation, matter or thing that may regard the said Congress." [37]

Carlisle, taking the matter more seriously, thought a formal statement necessary to counter Congress's declaration. Issued over the signatures of himself, Eden, and General Clinton (who had replaced General Howe on the commission) at the same time as Johnstone's own manifesto, it solemnly declared that the other commissioners "had not any knowledge either directly or indirectly of the correspondence and conversation alluded to till we saw it in the public papers." This statement was not meant to imply, the commissioners continued, "any assent to the construction which the Congress are pleased to put on a private letter . . . nor to insinuate a belief that any person could have been authorised to hold the conversation which the proclamation alludes to." Johnstone, as well as all the members of the commission, the statement concluded, had no other idea than that the official concessions they were authorized to offer "should rest on the broad basis of their own merits." [38]

It is possible, though unlikely, that Carlisle really had no foreknowledge of Johnstone's schemes involving Reed, Morris, and Dana. But it is perfectly obvious that Johnstone was not the only commissioner prepared to move beyond the "merits" of the royal concessions in winning adherents. The royal instructions, for one thing, authorized them to enter into correspondence not only with Washington, Congress, and state assemblies, but with "individual persons" as well.[39] That Carlisle himself had bribery, as well as a show of force, in mind as means toward accomplishing his mission is indicated in this letter he wrote to his wife from the ship evacuating him from Philadelphia to New York:

When I lay aboard the galley coming down the [Delaware] River, what do you think my bed was supported by?—a twelve pounder [cannon] on one side, and a box containing ten thousand guineas on the other. . . . I believe if the commission was suffered to the extent that these two powerful agents could carry them, there would be no doubt of succeeding.[40]

Bribery was also in the mind of John Berkenhout, a secret agent of Carlisle's who succeeded in getting into Philadelphia after the Americans had reoccupied that city. On September 14 he wrote in his diary that Timothy Matlack, secretary of Pennsylvania's executive council, "might be bribed." [41]

With this spirit prevailing, it is not surprising that the Carlisle papers contain no word of reproach concerning Johnstone's actions. Nevertheless, the latter resigned after Congress's declaration in the vain hope that his departure might remove a stumbling block to Congressional action toward a negotiation. He left New York on September 24, but his departure brought no change in the American outlook and Carlisle and Eden followed six weeks later.[42]

After Johnstone's embarkation for England, a letter addressed by him to the commission's secretary, Adam Ferguson, appeared in the *New York Gazette* of October 5. It mentioned "indisputable evidence" left in Ferguson's hands that nothing he had done "could have been conceived by the member of Congress, Joseph Reed, Esq., . . . as an attempt to corrupt his integrity." [43] The "evidence" was not described and was never to be brought forward by Ferguson or anyone else.

Upon resuming his seat in the House of Commons, Johnstone once again attempted to defend his actions in a speech delivered there on November 28. He admitted having had some "transactions where other means besides persuasion have been used," but denied that Reed ever "understood" any message from him in the nature of a bribe, not at best a very direct refutation of Congress's accusation. He maintained that the failure of Congress to have Reed reveal the lady's name proved "they know full well that no lady whatsoever could avow any authority from me." [44]

The text of this speech was printed in Philadelphia in the *Pennsylvania Packet* of March 9, 1779. Reed, now president of the executive council of Pennsylvania, decided to counter it with a full, documented account of his relations with the commissioner. From Mrs. Ferguson, whose identity as the intermediary had been deduced,[45] he obtained a statement of her conversations with Johnstone and with himself. The press of official duties delayed his publication project, however. Then, in September, 1779, Reed enlisted the aid of Thomas Paine in arranging the papers for the press.[46] With this assistance, the pamphlet, *Remarks on Governor Johnstone's Speech in Parliament with a Collection of all the Letters and Authentic Papers Relative to His Proposition . . . to Promote the Views of the British Commissioners,* appeared before the end of the year.

The entire bizarre episode had demonstrated Reed's unswerving loyalty to an independent United States. This demonstration had a significant contemporary effect on Reed's career: the widespread publicity afforded his rejection of a tempting bribe,[47] and the consequent popularity engendered among the patriots of Pennsylvania for Reed, undoubtedly played a not inconsiderable role in their decision to elevate him, late in 1778, to the highest office in the state.

CHAPTER IX

President of Pennsylvania

UNTIL the fall of 1778, Joseph Reed adhered to that aloof position regarding state politics which he assumed when offered the post of chief justice of Pennsylvania early in 1777. His decision to alter that stand, a decision based upon far more profound grounds than political ambition whetted by the personal popularity the Johnstone affair had brought him, was to lead him to high office and to significant new contributions to the Revolution. It was also to make him the focal point of bitter controversy and partisan malice.

On July 19, 1778, Reed had written Dennis DeBerdt:

I have also been strongly sollicited to accept of the Government [i.e., the chief executive's post] of this state, to which I can be unanimously appointed; but now the Liberties of my Country are secured and its Independence established, my Ambition and present Inclinations are to remain a private citizen and attend to the advancement of my Family and Fortune, both [of] which have been neglected.[1]

But three months later, George Bryan, acting president of Pennsylvania, had in his hand a letter from Reed announcing that the urgings of a "great number of my worthy, though partial Countrymen have procured my consent to serve them in the Council or Assembly as they may choose" and asking, therefore, that his resignation from Congress be accepted.[2]

Reed's decision sprang from a real fear that the patriot cause in Pennsylvania was in danger of collapse, and from a belief, well founded in the representations which reached him from many political quarters, that he could perform a signal service to his state as a rallying point for the defense of that cause. These beliefs governed his resolve to abandon the hands-off position he had previously taken in state government affairs and to employ his moderating influence to win the cooperation of its patriotic critics.

The intentions Reed expressed in his letter to DeBerdt were obviously based on wishful thinking. He had hoped that with the evacuation of Pennsylvania by the British army, the state's travail had ended, and that smooth waters stretched ahead. However, that delusion was shattered by the events of the summer of 1778. To his amazement and disgust, Reed found that men who had but recently collaborated with the British army of occupation, rather than retire now to circumspect quiescence, were boldly striving to retain the preeminence they had held under General Howe or in the pre-Revolutionary era, and, even more distressing, were being openly welcomed by the bitter anti-constitutionalists among the Whigs, such as John Cadwalader, as comrades in a program of subversion.

In a letter to General Greene, Reed stated:

New characters are emerging from Obscurity like Insects after a Storm. Treason, Disaffection to the Interests of America and even assistance to the British Interest is called openly only Error of Judgement, which Candour and Liberality of Sentiment will overlook. These are General Cadwalader's Sentiments, and that all distinction should be laid aside under a perfect oblivion for past offences, if such practices deserve the name of offences.[3]

Reed went on to tell Greene that even so valiant a soldier as General Benedict Arnold, now military commander at Philadelphia, had adopted this attitude and had invited to a public entertainment "not only Tory Ladies but the Wives and Daughters of Persons proscribed by the State and now with the Enemy at New York." Reed suggested sardonically that every Continental officer leave his uniform behind when coming to Philadelphia "and procure a scarlet coat, as the only mode of insuring respect and Notice." [4]

Reed would have been less sensitive to the machinations of those opposed to the Revolutionary cause in Pennsylvania were it not for his brief tenure in an office which served as the bridge for his subsequent rise to the highest post in the state. On August 17, 1778, the constitutionalist or "Radical" majority in the Pennsylvania assembly pushed through a resolution that "able Council" be employed to assist the attorney general, Jonathan Sergeant, in the prosecution of those who had collaborated with the British. Many Radicals, it should be noted, saw in the label of "Tory" the most effective weapon against their political opponents, no matter how innocent the latter might be of such a charge. Acting on the assembly's resolution, the council voted on the 21st to seek Reed's services in this task and offered him the attractive salary of £2,000 per year.[5] George Bryan, acting president of the state since the death of Thomas Wharton in May, wrote the same day to Reed, then with the committee of Congress at Washington's headquarters, to convey this offer. Reed sent back his acceptance on September 2.[6]

Reed entered upon his duties as the attorney general's assistant though still continuing to hold his seat in Congress for several weeks more after returning to Philadelphia from the army's camp at White Plains. Forty-five bills charging treason were drawn up for the grand jury convened for the fall term of the supreme court in Philadelphia. Twenty-three cases came to trial and the burden of prosecuting these fell heavily upon Reed, particularly when Attorney General Sergeant became confined to his home due to illness. Convictions were obtained in only two cases, those involving Abraham Carlisle and John Roberts, both Quakers.[7]

Whatever may have been his private judgment concerning the guilt or innocence of most of those whom he had been called upon to prosecute, Reed entertained no doubts as to the guilt of Carlisle and Roberts, nor any misgivings as to the justice of the death penalty which was imposed. The council, however, was bombarded by numerous petitions begging a reduction of sentence or even a full pardon for the condemned traitors. Reed felt that the men should be executed unless the assembly, with great unanimity, advised mercy.[8] Something of his reasoning is revealed in this passage from a letter he wrote to General Greene:

Out of the great Number of Pilots, Guides, Kidnappers, and other Assistants of the British Army two of the most notorious were convicted. But it would astonish you to observe the Weight of Interest exerted to pardon them and virtually every other, for none could be more guilty. But these being rich and powerful (both Quakers) we could not for shame have made an example of a poor rogue after forgiving the rich.[9]

On November 4, no strong representation from the assembly having been made and the council having remained deaf to private petitions for their pardon, Carlisle and Roberts were hanged.[10]

The extent of subversive activity which this case revealed, as well as other evidence which Reed uncovered as special prosecutor at the court session held in Bucks County late in October,[11] resulted in his decision to undertake an active political role toward bolstering the state government. The outline of that role had already been sketched in: the prospect before him was nothing less than election as president of the supreme executive council of the commonwealth.

On July 15, while Reed was in Congress, a special election in Philadelphia County to fill the vacancy on the executive council occasioned by the death of Thomas Wharton two months before, resulted in an almost unanimous vote for Joseph Reed.[12] Reed attended a meeting of the the council on the 21st, not to take his seat, but on the contrary to announce that he could not withdraw from Congress until the work of his committee on army arrangements was completed.[13] Shortly afterwards, it was discovered that his election as a councilor was invalid, for the constitution stated unequivocally that no delegate in Congress could be chosen to that office.[14] The incident, however, had revealed Reed's vote-getting ability.

Once Reed decided to seek the political offices he had so recently shunned, he took care that no technicalities would bar his path. The elections were scheduled for October 13. On October 9 Reed took the "Oath of Allegiance and Fidelity" promulgated by the Assembly in 1777, and on the 12th resigned his seat in Congress to stand for election to either the assembly or the council.[15] A seat in the second body was the greater prize, of course, for from its membership the president and vice president of the state were chosen.

The October, 1778, election gave new evidence of Reed's popular appeal. In Philadelphia County he repeated his triumph of the previous July by winning the council seat. He was also elected by the city of Philadelphia to a seat in the assembly, a position he was obliged to resign formally after that body met in order to retain the more important office of councilor.[16]

On November 24, 1778, Reed attended the meeting of the executive council, took his oath of office, and was seated.[17] With the new session of the assembly under way by this time, too, political maneuverings became feverish in their intensity. The anti-constitutionalists or "Republicans" had elected such outstanding patriots as Robert Morris, Thomas Mifflin, and George Clymer to the assembly, and though this party remained in the minority in the legislature, its position in terms of voting strength and caliber of leadership was far stronger now than in the preceding session. This opposition party felt powerful enough to begin mounting an effort toward an official call for a new state convention to modify the constitution of 1776. When the assembly session opened, twenty-four of its seventy-two members, upon being sworn in, added provisos to their oaths which permitted them to work for and even accept a seat in such a convention.[18]

This movement for a constitutional convention became linked politically with the impending election of the president and vice president of the executive council. These officers were chosen annually from the membership of the council by a joint vote of the assembly and council. The Radicals possessed the voting strength to elect whomsoever they desired, but, except for a few extremists, they realized the wisdom of eschewing blatant partisanship and of repeating, rather, the tactics employed in the election of the state's first president, Thomas Wharton, a man of rather conservative views. The anti-constitutionalist Republicans, for their part, realizing full well that they could not elect a candidate of their own persuasion (indeed there was no member of the council who could be so identified), thought it politic to offer their votes to the majority party's candidate as a gesture of harmony in exchange for an understanding that the government would permit a state-wide plebiscite on the question of calling a constitutional convention. Joseph Reed's role in these undertakings was a central one, for it was to him that the Radicals turned as their choice for the presidency.

Reed's emergence as the leading candidate for the highest office in the state was by no means sudden or unheralded. Very shortly after Wharton's death, in May, Elias Boudinot had expressed the opinion that Reed or Robert Morris would probably be the next president.[19]   In October Reed was told by General Greene that "every body wishes you to accept [the presidency] and no one more than myself." [20]   Reed set forth his own ideas as to seeking the office in his reply to this letter from Greene:

The Chair was in my offer all last Summer—neither Ambition nor Interest inclin'd me to accept it, but I now plainly see that there is a settled fixed System to subvert the Whig Interest and that in a little Time the very Name will be reproachful, if there are not very spirited exertions. . . . I am in the Council and shall now accept the Chair if offered to me with a tolerable salary because I see plainly that unless I make this sacrifice of my Interest and Ease, the Whig Interest must be materially injured.[21]

With support for him as president mushrooming among the constitutionalist faction, Reed himself began overtures to the anti-constitutionalist group "to cement the coalition of parties." [22] At the house of Gouverneur Morris, delegate from New York in Congress, Reed met with two leaders of the opposition party, Robert Morris and Edward Biddle, and obtained assurances from them that they would support his election and work for a diminution in partisan strife.[23]   In return for these pledges, Reed appears to have agreed that as president he would support or at least not stand in the way of a plebiscite on the question of a convention to amend the constitution.[24]

On December 1, 1778, Joseph Reed became the second "President of the Supreme Executive Council of the Commonwealth of Pennsylvania, Captain General and Commander-in-Chief in and over the same," under the constitution of 1776. At eleven o'clock that morning the members of the assembly had crowded into the council chamber in the State House for the joint balloting to select the president and vice president. The tally of the votes for president showed Reed with sixty-one, George Bryan with one, and councilor James Read of Berks County also with one. Bryan was next elected vice president, receiving all but one vote.[25] Reed then delivered a brief speech thanking his electors for their confidence in him and voicing his assurance that "while I make the happiness of the people the object, and the Constitution and

Laws of the state the rule of my conduct, I may not only promise myself your advice and support, but a favourable allowance for involuntary errors." [26]

Following Reed's address and a ceremony in which each member of the council and the assembly signed a declaration of his election, a procession was formed for the brief walk to the courthouse where his election was to be formally proclaimed. Led by constables with their staves and sheriffs with their wands of office, the judges of the supreme court and the members of the council and assembly, in double file, moved to the head of the stairs of the courthouse. The High Sheriff commanded silence of the large throng looking on and the secretary of the council, after reading the declaration of the election, proclaimed Reed to be president. A military band struck up a march, thirteen cannon were fired, and from the people came "repeated shouts of genuine and general joy." [27]

After this ceremony the procession of officials formed again and proceeded to the City Tavern where a lavish official banquet had been prepared at the assembly's order. Two hundred and seventy guests, including Gerard, the French Minister, and Miralles, agent of the court of Spain, sat down to the dinner and lifted their glasses to thirteen patriotic toasts.[28]

When the festivities were over and congratulatory messages from Washington, Nathanael Greene, and Anthony Wayne were read,[29] Reed was confronted with some very stern realities. He had sought the presidency in order to work for a moderate government in Pennsylvania which could defeat the "Tories and designing Whigs . . . aiming at Anarchy and Confusion" and contribute vibrant strength to the struggle against Britain, to those "virtuous Purposes we have in View." [30] Such strength required vigorous leadership. This Reed was anxious to give, and this he was personally well equipped to give. But the constitution of 1776 had not only made Pennsylvania's president "perhaps . . . the most impotent of the war executives" [31] but had given birth to a bitter opposition which divided the state and made a maximum effort in support of the war impossible.

Under this fundamental law the executive power was vested in

a president and council. The president was nothing more than
the presiding officer of the council. He, or the vice president in
his absence, and five councilors (there were twelve in all including
the president and vice president) constituted a quorum and were
empowered to make civil and military appointments, "correspond
with other states, and transact business with the officers of government, civil and military, and to prepare such business as may
appear to them necessary to lay before the General Assembly."
The president, together with the council, was given a general
power to grant pardons and reprieves except in cases of treason,
murder, and impeachment. Impeachment cases were to be tried
before both of them. During the recess of the assembly, authority
was invested in them to lay embargoes not exceeding thirty days
in duration. Even the president's high-sounding title of "Captain
General and Commander-in-Chief" was vested in that officer in
council, not in the individual. The constitution stated that the
"President shall be commander-in-chief of the forces of the State,
but shall not command in person, except advised thereto by the
Council, and then only so long as they shall approve thereof." [32]
    There were glaring omissions in these executive powers. Neither
the president alone nor the president in council possessed a veto
on measures passed by the assembly. Though the government
was born of war, the executive branch lacked the authority to
declare martial law, nor were any other "emergency" powers
granted to it. In a letter to Washington, Reed lamented that
"we have not legal power to impress a single horse or wagon, let
the emergency be what it will." [33] The appointing power, so far
as commissions in the state militia were concerned, was seriously
limited by the provision in Article 5 that all officers through the
rank of colonel were to be elected. Finally, the prohibition
against a councilor (and hence also a president) serving more than
three years in succession was to prove a source of weakness.[34]
    Joseph Reed had the distinction of being the only wartime
governor in Pennsylvania to serve the maximum three years.
That he was also the only one to give the state vigorous leadership
in the face of serious constitutional curbs upon his powers, however, is of greater importance. Alone of the Pennsylvania execu-

tives Reed ranks with governors Clinton of New York, Livingston of New Jersey, Trumbull of Connecticut, Rodney of Delaware, and Johnson of Maryland as an outstanding and energetic state executive.[35]

Indeed, it is no great exaggeration to say that not until Reed's administration did the Revolutionary state government in Pennsylvania begin to function in a coherent, sustained manner. The executive council had not become operative until March, 1777, five months after the constitution itself went into effect. The council had hardly begun functioning when Howe's invasion of Pennsylvania interrupted the full implementation of the constitution. Then, just before the British evacuated Philadelphia in June, 1778, President Wharton died. Thereupon Vice President Bryan assumed the role of acting president. When Reed took the presidential chair in December,[36] the government had not yet achieved an internal stability, and consequently had failed to win for Pennsylvania more than formal recognition and respect from Congress or from the other states.[37]

Reed's vigorous approach to the duties and opportunities of his office was immediately manifested. While the assembly was in recess between December 5, 1778, and February 1, 1779, he and the council prepared a program to bring to the legislature's attention when it reconvened. This was done despite the realization that the assembly had invariably reacted unfavorably in the past to anything smacking of leadership by the executive branch. A recent example had been its resentment and refusal to act when George Bryan, while acting as president after Wharton's death, urged the assembly to pass a law abolishing slavery.[38] But Reed, undismayed by such precedents, was determined to arouse the house to face up to the many problems crying for legislative action.

On February 5, 1779, the council adopted a message which set forth its program and sent it to the assembly. The topics suggested for that body's action included appropriations to meet the levy of $15,000,000 imposed on the state by Congress, military reforms, punishments for profiteers, the abolition of slavery, termination of the Penn family's title to the lands of Pennsyl-

vania, and the establishment of a court of appeals.[39] The recommendation concerning slavery gave rise to an immediate challenge
to the leadership of Reed and the council, for their message had
not merely made a general suggestion as to the abolition but had
announced that "we have reduced this plan to the form of a law,
which, if acceptable, we shall in a few days communicate to
you." [40] The sensitive assembly replied that it possessed the legislative function exclusively. Reed and the council countered by
quoting that part of Article 20 of the constitution which empowered them to "prepare such business as may appear to them
necessary to lay before the General Assembly." [41] In an attempt
to resolve the impasse which resulted, Reed invited the assembly
to join the members of the council in a conference. The meeting, which took place February 10, was opened by Reed who
asked the "sense of the House" on the meaning of the constitutional phrase quoted above. In the discussion which ensued,
Reed and Bryan were obliged to assure the legislators that the
council claimed no right to "prepare bills and impose them on
the House" but only that to "frame draughts or heads of bills,
which the House . . . may or may not adopt or notice at their
discretion." [42] The assemblymen present did not attack this assertion, but it is notable that the abolition measure, though recast
by a committee of the house, was not enacted that session. In
September, 1779, Reed sent another message on the subject to the
legislature but again with no success. Not until 1780 was Pennsylvania's "Act for the Gradual Abolition of Slavery" passed, a
belated victory won for the Reed administration largely because
George Bryan, the leading advocate of the measure, was a member
of the assembly that year.[43]

One of the most successful undertakings of Reed's administration was that item in the 1779 program which concerned the disposition of the proprietary lands. That this knotty and potentially explosive issue was settled with an amazing lack of friction
was due in great part to the personal leadership which Reed and
Bryan exercised. The Penn family had, of course, been stripped
of all governing authority by the constitution, but although the
opinion was general that they should also be deprived of their

title to the soil of the state, nothing had been done to implement this determination until Reed's first administration. Then the assembly reacted promptly to the suggestion by Reed and the council concerning action on this issue. John Penn, one of the proprietors and formerly the governor, was notified of the intention of the house to hold hearings on the matter. After the hearing was twice delayed at the request of Penn's attorneys, three days in March were devoted to the inquiry. A committee report drawn up after the hearing and after Chief Justice McKean had been consulted on the legal points involved laid the basis for the Divesting Act. But the assembly adjourned on April 5 before acting on this report. Thus it was the next assembly, elected in October, which on November 27, 1779, vested the proprietary titles (except the private manors of the Penn family) in the state, allowed the liberal compensation of £130,000 to the Penns, and abolished quit rents.[44]

Another important advance affecting land titles which was inaugurated at this time was the action to settle the boundary dispute with Virginia and the dispute over the Susquehanna lands with Connecticut. In the first case considerable success was achieved, in the second, none at all. On March 24 the assembly appointed Vice President Bryan, Treasurer David Rittenhouse, and the Reverend John Ewing to meet with commissioners from Virginia and arrange the boundary to the west between the two states. These men met in Baltimore with their Virginia counterparts, the Reverend James Madison and Robert Andrews, and on August 31 signed an agreement by which an extension of the Mason-Dixon line extended beyond the western limit of Maryland to a point five degrees of longitude from the Delaware River would serve as the southern boundary of Pennsylvania with Virginia. From that point a meridian drawn northward would fix Pennsylvania's western limit.[45] This settlement was ratified by the legislatures of both states in 1780. Reed and Governor Thomas Jefferson of Virginia cooperated in an attempt to implement this agreement by actually surveying the lines, but this task, in part because of the British invasions of Virginia, was not completed until after the Revolution.[46] From the governor, Jonathan

Trumbull, and the legislature of Connecticut, Reed received no such cooperation. The offer of Pennsylvania to submit the dispute to the arbitration of a Congressional commission (a technique provided for in Article IX of the Articles of Confederation) for a "full, final and friendly settlement" was rejected by Connecticut.[47]

A first-term achievement which gave Reed a great deal of satisfaction was that which improved the pay, pension rights, and the supply of clothing and food for the officers and men from Pennsylvania in the Continental Army. Before the assembly met in February, 1779, Reed had taken vigorous action to speed the delivery of uniforms and foodstuffs to the winter encampment in New Jersey.[48] When the house convened, he made good use of letters of complaint from General Arthur St. Clair, commanding officer of the Pennsylvania line, to stir that body to action.[49] Not only new appropriations for clothing and supplies were secured, but on March 13 resolutions were also adopted which guaranteed half pay for life for officers eligible for the seven-year half pay granted by Congress, provided for pensions for their widows, and extended exemption from taxation to all lands given to officers and men alike.[50] By the summer, thanks in great part to Reed's exertions, General William Irvine could write to the former: "The stores at present supplied by our State put the officers on a superior footing to any other; both they and the men, I hope and believe, have a grateful sense of it."[51] In the fall of 1779 Reed turned to reoutfitting the men of the line, a responsibility Congress had been undertaking, and received from Washington a statement of his pleasure that "the exertions of your State, since your appointment to the government, have been great and very happily directed to render the situation of your Troops, both Officers and Men, comfortable and cosy."[52]

Reed's army experience and his close contacts with Washington and former comrades-in-arms brought new energy in the marshaling of Pennsylvania's military effort. When Reed heard from Washington in March, 1779, that a major expedition was being planned to strike at the Indians and Tories who had been ravaging the frontier settlements of Pennsylvania and New York, he and the council prevailed upon the assembly to permit them to join with Washington and Congress in arranging the campaign without time-consuming referrals to the legislature.[53]   Reed left Philadelphia March 14 for a quick trip to the army's camp at Middlebrook, New Jersey, where Washington revealed his plans for the Clinton-Sullivan expedition, as it was to be called, and received Reed's pledge of firm support from Pennsylvania.[54]   Reed carried out this pledge by vigorous recruiting of troops, particularly riflemen, for General John Sullivan's command, by earmarking vital supplies for the latter, by moving more militia troops to the frontier areas, and by strengthening the post at Fort Pitt from which a diversionary attack was made in cooperation with Sullivan's advance up the Susquehanna Valley.[55]   The expedition's success, though not complete, owed much to these performances, performances which were made despite Reed's expressed opinion, official if not personal, that Pennsylvania was being asked to expend a dangerous proportion of its strength assisting its Virginia and New York neighbors on the frontier.[56]

Reed acted even more vigorously in the line of military endeavor when Washington, anticipating the aid of a French fleet under Count D'Estaing, called upon militia reinforcements from the states for a projected attack upon New York. On October 9, he obtained from the outgoing assembly an unprecedented advance authorization for the council to raise Pennsylvania's quota "on such terms as they shall find to be requisite, referring the said Council to the succeeding House . . . for approbation and legal sanction of their proceedings." [57]   Despite the fact that he had not fully recovered from an illness, Reed decided to lead the state's militia into the field in person, an intention which Washington termed "honorable to yourself and flattering to me. The example alone would have its weight, but seconded by your knowledge of discipline, ability, activity, and bravery, it could not fail of happy effects." [58]   But all these plans were cancelled when, in November, Washington learned that D'Estaing, after participating in the disastrous effort to capture Savannah from the British, had sailed back to the West Indies.[59]

In his first year as president Reed also drew upon the familiarity he had gained concerning naval matters as Washington's secretary in 1775 to breathe life into a brief effort toward expanding Pennsylvania's navy. When Congress could not grant the requests of Philadelphia shipowners for more protection against attacks by British privateers, Reed, utilizing the council's power to lay an embargo, banned all sailings for fifteen days to prevent a certain and needless loss of more ships, men, and supplies.[60] The shipowners and merchants then raised funds to lend to the state for the purchase of a state ship. On March 23 the council resolved to buy a fourteen-gun vessel nearing completion at the Kensington shipyard a few miles up the Delaware from Philadelphia. Its name, the *General Greene,* was retained after Reed declined having it named for himself.[61] After great difficulties in obtaining a crew had been solved by the drastic expedient of impressing men from the jails, the ship was ordered to sea late in May. Three cruises over the next five months netted the vessel seven prizes which brought £462,680 into the state's coffers. But mutiny aboard ship and the difficulty of holding a crew when privateer captains were enticing them to desert led Reed and the council to abandon the experiment. On October 27, 1779, the sale of the ship was ordered and this was swiftly accomplished.[62]

The shortsighted self-interest displayed by the privateer captains who doomed the *General Greene* was symptomatic of a very widespread spirit of private gain at whatever the cost to the public good and the war effort. Throughout his three years as president, Reed found success in measures of economic policy more elusive than progress in any other field. The conclusion of one student of this period that the struggle between constitutionalist and anti-constitutionalist was basically a clash of economic interests, debtor vs. creditor, the western agrarian vs. the eastern businessmen, the propertyless vs. the property holder and employer,[63] receives important substantiation from a study of Reed's administrations. It was Reed's personal misfortune to be caught between these hostile forces, for despite his service as standard-bearer of the constitutionalists, his own inherently conservative views on fiscal policy and state interference in private enterprises made of him at many times a most unwilling participant in Radical measures he could neither approve nor halt.

One of Reed's first actions on the council was to issue a strongly worded proclamation against would-be monopolists. Denounced by Washington as "those murderers of our cause," [64] these war profiteers were manipulating the prices of such basic commodities as flour. The greed Reed saw gaining ground daily angered and troubled him greatly. To Washington he wrote of this "sordid spirit of gain, a spirit of animosity and selfishness." Reed lamented that "some of our principal people seem to think all danger over, and they must recover lost time and profits: hence all the passions of avarice and ambition were let loose; and they will scarcely believe that the day of our redemption is not at hand, and all farther efforts unnecessary." [65] Reed's concern also found expression in a letter he wrote to General Alexander McDougall. "I could never have thought," he said, "that in four short years [of the Revolution] I should have heard publick Frugality, Spirit, and Patriotism laugh'd at, but so it is." He told McDougall that such men as Silas Deane, Robert Morris, and Gouverneur Morris had set mercantile and land schemes in motion whose extent savored more of "some mighty Monarch than a few private Gentlemen in a republican Government." In the name of trade, Reed concluded, "all the various Acts of Extortion and undue Gain are sanctified." [66]

Reed differed from the doctrinaire Radical of Pennsylvania in ascribing the crippling inflation not merely to the greed of a relatively few manipulators in the market but to the unchecked large-scale paper money emissions by Congress and the state alike. His letter to McDougall castigated both these emissions and the failure of federal and state governments to provide a dependable fund to pay at least the interest on the public debt.[67] On May 26, Reed took the unusual step of appearing before Congress in his official capacity as president of Pennsylvania to present a memorial, which he supported in a brief speech, urging that body to curb the depreciation of the currency by reducing emissions, by new taxes if necessary, and by loans if such could be obtained.

Congress's formal reply intensified rather than subdued the popular resentment by throwing much of the blame for the inflation on the "artifices of men who have hastened to enrich themselves by monopolizing the necessaries of life." While calling the attention of Pennsylvania to previous resolutions favoring price control by the states, Congress carefully avoided any commitment along the lines proposed in the memorial.[68]

The unsatisfactory nature of the Congressional response stimulated an already smoldering movement among the Radicals for the creation of extralegal committees to control prices and to investigate merchants suspected of hoarding and other abuses. On May 25, the day before Reed's appearance before Congress, a mass meeting called by such leading Radicals as Daniel Roberdeau and Christopher Marshall had met in the State House yard and authorized such committees.[69] A table of wholesale and retail prices was subsequently drafted by the committee providing for holding the line of May 1 until July 1 and then cutbacks to the price level of the past April. The investigators, reviving methods similar to those employed by the committee of observation and investigation of 1774-75, hauled merchants (including Robert Morris) before them and threatened those who refused to cooperate with banishment from Philadelphia.[70]

Popular feeling ran very high in Philadelphia during the summer of 1779. In June a company of militia artillerymen stationed near Philadelphia issued a manifesto proclaiming "we have arms in our hands and know how to use them" and promised that if the people's committee "find themselves inadequate to the task, our drums shall beat to arms." [71] A meeting on July 27 in the State House yard ended in turmoil when a gang armed with clubs interrupted John Cadwalader's speech against the price regulations and persisted even after a majority of all present had voted to permit him to continue.[72]

Reed did not approve of this extralegal price-fixing action, though he did think it necessary to watch "suspected Characters," men whose "spirit of Aristocracy and Pride of Wealth" led them to take advantage of economic distress. In October, in a letter to General Greene, he voiced his belief that the campaign was "impracticable from the beginning." History has proven, he said, that stringent regulation brings stagnation.[73] In a review of his political career written in 1782, Reed stated that "honest but intemperate zeal" had led to the creation of the regulatory committee and claimed that "every person concerned in them will do me the justice to say I neither originated nor conducted them."[74] That Reed did not openly oppose the movement at the time was due, it would seem, to a feeling that some show of force was necessary to frighten the manipulators of the market and to political expediency arising from his realization that the campaign was a highly popular one among many members of the council and assembly and among the electorate which supported the constitutionalist party.[75]

When the popular sentiments in Philadelphia against the merchants boiled over into serious violence, Reed reacted vigorously to protect life and property. On October 4, 1779, the "highwater mark of Radical democracy in Pennsylvania during the Revolutionary period,"[76] a mob which included many armed militiamen attacked the home of James Wilson. Wilson had incurred the hatred of the radicals by serving in a large number of cases as counsel for Tories and the Penn family against the state, and for merchants against the price control committees, and by making no secret of his bitter opposition to the constitution of 1776. Disturbances on the morning of the 4th had led a number of anti-constitutionalists to arm themselves and gather at Wilson's house at Walnut and Third Streets, later called "Fort Wilson" because of the day's incident. The Philadelphia Light Horse brigade had been alerted but relaxed its vigilance at the midday dinner hour. Reed, who was ill and confined to his bed at this time, suddenly received word in the early afternoon that the morning's mob, augmented in numbers and uglier in mood, had reformed and was marching on Wilson's house. He dressed hurriedly, sent orders that the Light Horse join him, and set out for the scene of the disorder. He found only two cavalrymen awaiting him at the appointed rendezvous but dashed on with the meager reinforcement nevertheless, for the sound of gunfire could now be clearly heard. He bore down on the mob, appearing "as if he had just risen from bed . . . his knee-buttons being unfastened, and his boots down . . . a pistol in his hand, but no sword," just as its leaders broke into Wilson's house.[77] Reed dismounted and threatened these rioters with his pistol. At that juncture the cavalry came thundering down Third Street and the mob was dispersed.[78] A number of militiamen and several of the "garrison" of Wilson's house were placed under arrest, the former being imprisoned, the latter released on high bail. Both the rioters and the defenders of the house had suffered casualties. Two had been killed in the attack and several more wounded.

The excitement engendered by the riot continued the next day. In the morning Reed received word that militia in Germantown were assembling for a march on the city to avenge the dead and wounded. He rode out, met them on the road, and succeeded in convincing them to return peaceably to their homes.[79] The president then returned to Philadelphia and employed the same diplomacy in quieting the fears of a number of the leaders of the city who had gathered in the State House. The Radicals in the assembly, realizing that their partisans had gone too far in the riot, voted that afternoon to assure Reed and the council of support in all measures to restore tranquility. This was followed five days later by a resolution commending Reed for his "spirited and prudent conduct" in the Wilson affair. When the new assembly met in November, Reed advised an act of "oblivion and indemnity" as the best method of closing the unhappy incident, and this advice was followed.[80]

Reed's arrival at "Fort Wilson" at the critical moment was later likened by an admirer to "an angel dropping from Heaven." [81] Reed seems to have expected that his action, involving as it did a risk to his own life, might soften the political animosities existing between Wilson and his friends and himself. Others wished that this would result too. General Arthur St. Clair wrote Reed that although "it was pretty generally known that you [Reed and Wilson] were not upon the most friendly terms," he hoped the incident would "remove any coolness that subsisted." These anticipations never materialized. St. Clair lamented in a subsequent letter to the president that there had not even been a return of civilities from those Reed had helped save.[82]

One among the many causes espoused by James Wilson which had brought down the wrath of Philadelphia's Radicals upon him was a defense of the College of Philadelphia against efforts toward a drastic revision of its charter which would make it a state institution. The debate on this scheme became one of the bitterest of all those which wracked Pennsylvania, for it came to be fought on tightly drawn Republican vs. Radical political lines with an added overtone of Episcopalian vs. Presbyterian interest. It had begun before Reed became president, fed by the presence of several Tories on the college's board of trustees, and by the unabashed conservatism of the other trustees and the Reverend William Smith, the provost. The Radicals came to look upon the college as "the most obnoxious citadel of conservatism." [83]

In February, 1779, the assembly ordered an investigation of the college. The report which resulted was a severe indictment of the political leanings of the trustees. The latter then made a scant concession to the growing hostility against them by ousting two of their number who had remained in Philadelphia during the British occupation and cooperated with General Howe, and replacing them with two men who were undoubtedly not Tories but who were leading Republican opponents of the state government, John Cadwalader and James Wilson.[84]

When the assembly resumed its 1779 session in September, Reed's formal message called attention to the college's "manifest attachment to the British government . . . conducted with a general inattention to the authority of the State." [85] The house needed little urging to take decisive action. A new committee returned a report on September 24 which urged rechartering of the college as a state institution. After a formal hearing before the assembly, at which Wilson appeared for the college to oppose this step, such action was authorized by a 33-8 vote. The charter was transformed by an act passed November 27, 1779, to provide for a University of Pennsylvania.[86]

Reed, who as president of the state was ex-officio a member of

the new board of trustees and who was elected its president, came
under a scorching attack from the Reverend Dr. Smith and others
for this action of his administration. Reed, however, was convinced of the need for the alteration which had been made. In
a letter written to the renowned French intellectual, the Abbé
Raynal, Reed enclosed with pride a copy of the November act
which, he stated, founded "a University on Principles of universal
catholicism, embracing all Professions of the Christian Religion
which are formed and organized among us." [87] Reed had used
his influence toward this catholicity by suggesting that the faculty
be drawn from a broad background [88] but such moderation was
little in evidence among his fellow Presbyterian trustees, many
of them officers in the government too, who fastened a strongly
sectarian grip upon the university.

While positive measures such as the creation of the University
of Pennsylvania did much to widen the breach between the Radical and Republican factions, an unreconcilable division had been
shaped at the very outset of Reed's administration by a negative
development, the abandonment of the plan to hold a state-wide
plebiscite on the question of convening a constitutional convention to amend the "Frame of Government" adopted in 1776. The
virtual unanimity in the choice of Reed as president on December 1, 1778, was undoubtedly achieved as a result of a pledge on
his part to Republican leaders [89] that he would not oppose the
execution of a resolution passed unanimously two days before by
the assembly providing that such a plebiscite be held in March,
1779.[90]

Whether Reed pledged himself to give *active* support to the
call for a convention is a moot point. The failure of the council,
after his election as president, to endorse the assembly's resolution led to accusations of duplicity on his part. Such charges
grew more bitter when the assembly, faced after reconvening in
February, 1779, by a flood of petitions from Radicals throughout
the state protesting against schemes for changing the constitution, voted forty-seven to seven to rescind its November resolution
calling for the plebiscite.[91] This action enraged the anti-constitutionalists. Reed, to allay criticism against himself, then called

a meeting at the City Tavern to which Morris, Cadwalader, and other leading critics of the government were invited, and there attempted to prove that he had fulfilled his engagements to them "to the Extent of my Weight and Influence." [92]   Reed gave as a rather weak explanation of the council's failure to act (and it was such action which, his accusers said, he had bound himself to secure) that no formal notice of the assembly's November 28 resolution was received by the council until two weeks later, and that at that advanced date he felt it improper that the council be asked to trail along in endorsing the decision of the legislature.[93]

Some anti-constitutionalists such as Robert Morris, though extremely annoyed by the revocation of the plebiscite which they had anticipated with optimism as the first step toward altering the constitution in their favor, reserved judgment as to Reed's personal blameworthiness after hearing him out. Morris wrote Reed after the City Tavern meeting to deny that he had resolved upon "a settled opposition" to the latter's administration, and then went on to say he was content to wait for the time when the people of Pennsylvania settled down to the task of establishing a good constitution.[94]

Others, however, did not adopt Morris's policy of patient waiting, nor of suspending judgment on Reed personally. Conspicuous among the fire-eaters was John Cadwalader. He asked Reed, "Why do you still hold the Chair and by your influence give support to a government that you and your friends in the opposition wanted to have altered? I really suspect you of duplicity and let me tell you the world suspects you." [95]   In addition to personal attacks on the president, Cadwalader, James Wilson, Benjamin Rush, Thomas Mifflin, Charles Thompson, and others formed a Republican Society (which Morris joined too) to continue agitation against the government. Their principles and their criticisms of the constitution were incorporated in an address signed by Richard Bache, the society's chairman, late in March.[96]

The failure of the anti-constitutionalists to obtain the constitutional convention they so ardently desired brought an added bitterness, bordering at times upon frenzied despair, to their partisan struggles with the Radicals in power. At the same time,

Reed's failure to convince his critics that the revocation of the plans for the convention was not a result of duplicity on his part destroyed whatever slight chance had existed that he personally might remain untouched by the attacks upon the government. Instead, he now became the prime target of the opposition party in Pennsylvania and of their conservative allies in Congress and in the Continental Army.[97]   The consequence, a tragic one both for Reed and for the tranquility of the state in general, was the collapse of Reed's hopes of serving as the bridge between the two rival factions.   As his own sense of moderation grew warped by the attacks upon him, he too became more and more the partisan, increasingly disinclined to attribute good motives to any who opposed him.   Within four months of his taking office, then, the angry pattern had been imposed which was to render Reed's three years as president a harrowing, enervating, and embittering experience.

Reed, of course was not left to wage the fight alone.   Support for him among the Radicals waxed in intensity as he gradually identified himself more and more firmly with their party.   The attacks upon him by Cadwalader and other Republicans evoked spirited newspaper articles and memorials from Radical societies in his defense.[98]   And the popular strength of the Radical party was demonstrated in unmistakable fashion in the fall elections of 1779.   Reed's own popularity among the electorate, their approval of the program urged by him and acted upon by the assembly, and, perhaps most important of all, the identification in the popular mind of the anti-constitutionalists with the merchant "princes" upon whom the people were prone to blame their economic distress—all these elements combined to effect a landslide victory for the Radicals on October 12.   Such opposition leaders as Robert Morris and George Clymer lost their seats in the assembly and, in fact, in the new house an organized Republican minority ceased to exist.   Every one of the newly elected councilors were Radicals.   Reed's reelection as president was thus guaranteed.   On November 11 he was chosen unanimously for his second term.   William Moore, George Bryan's successor to Philadelphia's place on the council, was elected vice president.[99]

The constitutional provision banning two consecutive terms on the council had prevented Bryan from retaining his seat, but he successfully ran for election to the assembly and swiftly emerged as the legislative leader there.[100]

This popular endorsement of Reed's first administration was regarded by him as a sweet prize, a heartening vindication of his conduct. Reed could be excused for thinking that the period which lay ahead promised greater tranquility. But mushrooming public problems and a tragic personal loss made it a tormented one instead.

CHAPTER X

The War on the Home Front

REED'S second and third years as member and president of the supreme executive council of Pennsylvania were marked by startling contrasts in both his public and private life. A grant of extraordinary powers to him by the assembly was followed within a few brief months by his party's first significant defeat at the polls; another unanimous election as president, in November, 1780, was achieved in the midst of new attacks upon him; and within the space of four months he was to gain a third son and lose his wife.

The year 1780 began auspiciously. On January 26, a court-martial sitting at Morristown, New Jersey, reached a decision which represented a moral victory for Reed and the Pennsylvania council. The court found General Benedict Arnold, erstwhile military commander at Philadelphia, guilty of misconduct on two specifications among the eight charges (four of which were argued before the court) brought against him by the state of Pennsylvania, and sentenced him to receive a reprimand from Washington.[1]

The origins of the bitter struggle which culminated in that decision can be traced almost to the very day, May 28, 1778, when the commander in chief, in anticipation of the British evacuation Philadelphia which came three weeks later, chose Arnold to be military commander of that city.[2] On June 4, Arnold, by virtue of his new authority, issued a pass to permit the *Charming Nancy,* a ship which he knew was in British-occupied Philadelphia at the time, to sail into any of the ports of the United States without "umbrage or molestation." Whether he took a financial interest in the voyage upon granting this pass has never been ascertained, but subsequently he obtained a heavy stake in the *Nancy.*[3]

Despite the pass from Arnold, the *Nancy* was captured by an American privateer and forced into Egg Harbor, New Jersey.

Arnold's financial stake in the ship and its cargo was saved, however, when the state authorities ruled that the *Nancy* was not to
be regarded as a prize. The general then decided upon the move
which embroiled him in controversy with the Pennsylvania government. To bring the *Nancy's* valuable cargo from its exposed
place at Egg Harbor to the safety (and the lucrative market) of
Philadelphia, now American held, Arnold employed the services
of a brigade of wagonmasters who, with their twelve wagons, had
been called into the state's service on October 16 and had been
ordered to Philadelphia from Chester County to serve the Continental interest. The chief wagonmaster, Jesse Jordan, reported
to the deputy quartermaster general, Colonel John Mitchell, who
sent him to Arnold for orders. From the latter, Jordan obtained
the orders to proceed, with empty wagons, to Egg Harbor. The
first inkling he had that he was not on public business came when
he was denied provisions by the commissary. But he proceeded
to Egg Harbor as instructed, loaded his wagons with sugar, tea,
coffee, nails, and other cargo from the *Nancy,* and brought them
back to the house of a Stephen Collins in Philadelphia. Collins
later testified at Arnold's court-martial that he sold the goods and
turned over about one-half of the proceeds to Arnold.[4] The transaction would have received little notice had not Arnold and
Mitchell delayed settling the pay roll and the forage accounts for
Jordan's wagon brigade.[5]

Reed and the Pennsylvania council might never have taken up
an investigation of the incident of the wagons, and certainly
would not have pressed it so emotionally when they did, if Arnold
had not already made himself obnoxious in the sight of their
party. The charge of misuse of public property, the wagons, was
prosecuted against the general with an intensity which seems
totally disproportionate if due account is not also made for suspicions of Arnold which the Radicals could not prove and seemingly deliberate affronts by him to their government which they
could not forget. He was suspected of having used the temporary
closing of the shops, ordered by him when the Americans marched
into Philadelphia, for personal gain: not until his treason two
years later were papers uncovered which proved he had entered

into an illegal agreement with Clothier General James Mease at this time.[6] He was suspected of trading in scarce commodities with Tory merchants in New York; again not until after he deserted the American cause did a partnership contract of November 2, 1778, for this purpose come to light.[7]

Then there was the ostentatious scale on which Arnold lived in Philadelphia, the menial tasks imposed by his staff upon a militia sergeant who happened to be the son of Timothy Matlack, the secretary of the Pennsylvania council,[8] the suspicious passes he issued to persons who went into British-held New York,[9] the invitations to his dinners tendered, as Reed wrote General Greene in November, 1778, to "not only common Tory ladies, but the wives and daughters of persons proscribed by the State, and now with the enemy at New York," [10] his open intervention against Pennsylvania in the celebrated admiralty case of the sloop *Active* [11] —all these incidents fanned the animosity which burst openly with the case of the wagons.

On January 18, 1779, a formal complaint from the Chester County wagonmaster concerning the incident of the past October was laid before the council. That board thereupon requested that Colonel Mitchell explain the transaction in writing. The latter's reply mentioned Arnold's role in ordering the wagons to Egg Harbor and the council consequently wrote on the 22nd to the general to inquire under what authority he had employed the public transport for private goods.[12] Arnold replied crisply that Mitchell's statement gave all the facts the council needed and that "I shall only say that I am at all times ready to answer for my Public Conduct to Congress, or General Washington, to whom alone I am accountable." [13] Reed wrote to Congress that same day, January 25, demanding the "Reparation of our Authority thus wounded" and a full investigation of Arnold's conduct.[14]

Congress acted promptly on Reed's request by naming a five-man committee, headed by William Paca of Maryland, to study the wagon episode.[15] When Reed's suggestion that Arnold be forbidden to leave the city until the charges were studied was ignored, and Arnold did leave on a trip to New York, the council broadened their attack upon him by publishing seven new accusations. These concerned his actions in the cases of the *Charming Nancy* and the *Active,* the incident involving Matlack's son, a charge of private purchases when Philadelphia's shops were closed at his own order, etc.[16]

Congress proved somewhat reluctant to take up all these new charges, with the result that relations between it and the Pennsylvania authorities became quite strained. Arnold personally had few supporters in Congress, but a number of members sided with him possibly because he was aligned against the Radicals of Pennsylvania.[17] Arnold himself was now demanding a court-martial to clear his name of the charges. After tempers in Independence Hall (both Congress and the Pennsylvania council met there) came close to the breaking point several times,[18] Congress resolved on April 3 to direct Washington to convene a court-martial on four of the eight charges brought against Arnold by Pennsylvania.[19] Washington assigned May 1 as the date for the court to convene, then changed the date to June 1 on Reed's request for more time to arrange for the presence of witnesses.[20] By the time the court met on the latter date, Arnold had not only resigned his command in Philadelphia but had opened his treasonable negotiations with the British in New York City. The court succeeded in holding but one session, however, before movements by the enemy required its members' services in the field.[21]

Not until December 23, 1779, did the court reconvene. Intermittent sessions were held through January 22, 1780. On the 21st, Arnold, his schemes for treason now far advanced, defended himself nevertheless "with the vigour of affronted innocence." [22] Nor did he in his summation overlook the opportunities for a counterblast at Reed. Referring to the events of December, 1776, he exclaimed that he "did not propose to my associates basely to quit the General [Washington] and sacrifice the cause of my country to my personal safety, by going over to the enemy. . . . That is more than a ruling member of the Council of the State of Pennsylvania can say, as is alleged and believed." [23]

On January 26 the court handed down its verdict. The charge of impropriety in bestowing the pass upon the *Charming Nancy* was sustained. The charge of making private purchases was declared "unsupported" and the general was acquitted of that as well as of the accusation of mistreating militiamen. Concerning the wagon episode, the court saw no attempt at fraud or injury to the public cause in Arnold's action, but did find his request for transportation of the goods at Egg Harbor "imprudent and improper." The sentence, in view of their findings as to the first and last charges, was that he be reprimanded by Washington. This sentence was confirmed by a twenty-three to three vote in Congress on February 12.[24] The commander in chief's reprimand appeared in his general order of April 6:

The Commander-in-chief would have been much happier in an occasion of bestowing commendations on an officer who has rendered such distinguished service to his country as Major General Arnold; but in the present case a sense of duty and a regard to candour oblige him to declare that he considers his conduct in the instance of the permit as peculiarly reprehensible, both in a civil and military view, and in the affair of the wagons as imprudent and improper.[25]

When Arnold's treason was revealed by the capture of André on September 23, seizures of the traitor's papers revealed that the council had been more correct than even they realized in their suspicions and charges. Some Pennsylvanians wrote to Reed to confess that he was right and they had been wrong in their attacks on the prosecution of the general.[26]

By the time the court-martial had reached its verdict against Arnold, Reed had settled down to his second year as president. Several actions by the assembly were making that office less of a burden than it had been when he was first elected in December, 1778. On October 9, 1779, the outgoing assembly voted to increase his yearly salary from £1,5000 to £2,000. Reed had pressed for a raise because he found, during his first administration, that he had spent some £750 of his own money for public purposes over and above his salary.[27] The assembly also acted to provide an official residence for the president. Title to the confiscated home of Joseph Galloway on Market Street was retained by the state for that purpose. Reed moved into the house in the summer of 1779.[28] In 1780 the president was also permitted to occupy "Laurel Hill," the country home of Samuel Shoemaker, a

Tory who had fled to New York City, as a summer residence.[29] The executive mansion on Market Street witnessed a particularly festive scene on June 29, 1780, when Reed's third son, born May 26, was baptized George Washington Reed in the presence of the French Ambassador, LaLuzerne, Martha Washington, and the president of Congress, Samuel Huntington, and Mrs. Huntington.[30]

Thanks to these measures Reed's personal finances may have been improved, but the same could hardly be said of the fiscal standing of the state or the United States in late 1779 and in 1780. The most pressing problem of Reed's second administration was the financial one. The extralegal citizens' committee of the summer of 1779 had utterly failed to halt the inflationary trend. Merchants continued to hoard rather than sell scarce commodities for the paper money, Continental and state, which doctrinaire Radical legislation had made legal tender but which, in the case of the Continental issue, had depreciated by the end of 1779 to a ratio of forty to one with specie.

Reed employed his embargo power to check commodity exports and thereby increase the short supply of foodstuffs in Philadelphia, and he argued before Congress, as was mentioned above, for a limitation on the emissions of paper money.[31] But neither of these efforts had any appreciable effect. Similarly unproductive of results was his plea to the newly elected assembly in November, 1779, to provide a "solid basis of truth and justice" for the state's credit.[32] An undated memorandum among Reed's papers contains his flat statement that "the supporting of any Paper Money by compulsive Methods is contrary to my opinion." [33] But the debtor outlook of most of the Radicals, particularly those from the western counties of the state, made them look with favor upon legal tender paper money and with disfavor upon any plan, such as Reed intimated, for the heavy taxation which alone would engender faith in the issues in commercial circles.

The almost total collapse of the Continental currency at the end of 1779, and the failure of an undertaking in which the Radicals had placed considerable faith, the interstate price-fixing convention held in Philadelphia in February, 1780,[34] finally produced a slight shift in the assembly toward the policies advocated by Reed, Bryan, and others. A new issue of state money was authorized in March, 1780, funded on land and including provisions for interest payments, which promised greater soundness than any previous state issue. Reed was hopeful that the legislature might forbear making the emission legal tender, but in vain. The assembly, however, did vote on May 31 to terminate the legal tender status of the Continental money.[35]

Though the new state money did not conform to all of Reed's desires, he was extremely anxious that it be supported by the Philadelphia business community without undue pressure from the state authorities. A statement by Robert Morris in May in favor of the issue augured well for its success, yet, by the midsummer, resistance to its acceptance had produced a serious depreciation.[36] Reed felt that politics lay behind the refusal of the money. Many conservative businessmen, he believed, did not want his fiscal program to garner any success, for, with the October elections for the assembly looming ahead, they wished to campaign on the Radical failure to stabilize the economy.[37]

Before the fate of the 1780 issue of state money became apparent, Reed and the council had taken steps to seek a loan in Europe. They received an authorization from the assembly on May 29 to borrow up to £200,000 in specie and a pledge that the legislature would provide by law specific funds for interest and principal payments. On July 8, the council commissioned James Searle, then a delegate for the state in Congress, to be its agent in negotiating the loan. He was directed to seek the full £200,-000, at a term of not over ten years and at not over 5 percent interest. In expectation of success, Searle was given a long list of articles he was to purchase in Europe, and was directed to forward them via the Dutch island of St. Eustatia.[38] But Searle, despite assiduous efforts in France and the Netherlands over a seventeen-month period, failed to raise any money for Pennsylvania. In France he was informed by the Company of Lyons, the firm which supplied the French army, that "we know only the Congress." Pennsylvania's inability to get Congress to guarantee its loan, and a lack of cooperation or even outright obstruction by the American ministers in Europe toward Searle's mission, made it impossible for him to succeed.[39]

When the anti-constitutionalists or Republicans won control of the new assembly chosen in October, 1780, Reed's disappointment over this partial repudiation of his second administration must have been somewhat tempered by the expectation that his own sound money views would now be reflected in legislation. The presence of Robert Morris in the new house, his position of leadership among the Republicans, and his critical attitude toward paper money seemed to guarantee this. Morris did work diligently to inculcate a new sense of financial responsibility in the assembly. But in spite of the new composition of that body's membership, much the same reluctance to face the harsh economic realities was displayed as that which had confronted Reed in the Radical assemblies of 1778-79 and 1779-80. The legal tender nature of the March, 1780, issue was reinforced by the new assembly in December, penalties for violation actually being increased. On April 7, 1781, the house, over the protests of both Reed and Morris, voted a huge new paper emission of £500,000 and then adjourned.[40] Reed struck back by calling the body into special session for May 24. At that time Morris took up his fight from the floor again, and on June 21 succeeded in pushing through a law repealing all laws making Continental and state paper legal tender except those applying to the last two state emissions, those of March, 1780, and April, 1781. At the same time, firmer support for these issues was provided through sales of some public lands, a step Reed had urged unsuccessfully ten months before.[41] With these measures, Pennsylvania's fiscal condition was at last, in the middle of Reed's third and last year as president, freed from its former capriciousness, though by no means at once restored to full health.

Before this promising event of June, 1781, however, the paper money evil had wreaked great damage to the war effort in general as well as to Pennsylvania's economy in particular. The collapse of the Continental currency had forced Congress to adopt the desperate expedient of levying "specific supplies" quotas on the states in order to support the Continental Army in the field. On February 25, 1780, Pennsylvania was assessed 40,000 barrels of flour, 200,000 bushels of corn, 14,189 bushels of salt, and 24,423 gallons of rum. This was a heavy requisition indeed, particularly when added to one for 50,000 barrels of flour made December 11, 1779.[42]

Upon Reed, as the state's "Chief Executive," fell the burden of meeting these demands. Since he had pleaded unavailingly with Congress to limit the unsound emissions which had necessitated this new expedient, Reed was quite naturally angered by the new responsibility thrust upon him. He called the system of specific supplies "absurd," and denounced it as "a scheme to carry on the war without money." [43] But to say, as one authority on this era of Pennsylvania history has, that Reed "ignored" the requisitions,[44] is not accurate. He did complain that Pennsylvania was resorted to "to make up the Deficiency" when other states failed to meet their quotas.[45] Reed's suspicions of a conservative faction in Congress, suspicions fed by the support Arnold had found among them, perhaps also led him to believe that the demands upon Pennsylvania were made unduly heavy to embarrass the Radical administration. General Greene wrote Reed from camp that the opposition would be given "a great handle to improve to your prejudice" if his exertions were not equal to the occasion.[46] It is perfectly true that Reed did not receive with good grace the calls upon his state. But the fact that Pennsylvania's effort fell considerably short of its quotas must be attributed to the prevalent economic dislocation rather than to his own apathy.

On May 30, 1780, Reed received a plea that he could not and did not ignore. Washington wrote from Morristown, New Jersey, on May 28 that only spirited exertions by the states would save the army, which had recently been reduced to one-eighth rations, and could enable it to seize the opportunity for a decisive stroke which would be afforded by the arrival in America of the French army, now crossing the Atlantic. For supplies and transport, the commander in chief said, "Pennsylvania is our chief dependence." He continued:

I speak to you in the language of frankness and as a friend. I do not mean to make any insinuations unfavorable to the State. I am aware of the embarrassments the Government labours under from the open opposition of one party, and the underhanded intrigues of another. I know that with the best dispositions to promote the public service, you have been obliged to move with circumspection; but this is a time to hazard, and to take a tone of energy and decision. . . . I wish the Legislature could be engaged to vest the Executive with plenipotentiary powers. I should then expect everything from your abilities and zeal. This is not a time for formality or ceremony. The crisis in every point of view is extraordinary, and extraordinary expedients are necessary. I am decided in this opinion.[47]

Reed laid Washington's letter before the assembly immediately. On June 1 the house voted more provisions for the army and then went on by unanimous vote to authorize the president or vice president "in Council" to declare martial law during the recess of the legislature. Later the same day the assembly adjourned. Eight days later Reed proclaimed martial law, stating that to fill the army's needs quickly, "the usual and ordinary forms must be dispensed with, or the requisitions remain unexecuted." [48]

After the assembly's action of June 1, but before Reed's proclamation, the mercantile community in Philadelphia suddenly came alive with programs to assist Washington in the crisis. At a meeting on June 8 a plan was adopted to raise funds by subscription to be used in recruiting men for the army. By the 17th this idea has been expanded under the leadership of Robert Morris to that of capitalizing a bank, again by private subscription, which would purchase supplies for the army. Congress threw its support behind this bank by pledging to reimburse those who contributed capital. Within a few days, £300,000 had been pledged by some ninety subscribers, most of whom were merchants, and many of whom were outspoken anti-constitutionalists. The quick response enabled Morris to send five hundred barrels of flour off to Washington.[49]

Reed did not oppose this measure, for assistance from whatever quarter was essential to the war effort. He, in fact, subscribed £2,000 himself. But he could not help speculating as to the motives of men who preferred to display their patriotism through this private scheme rather than through cooperation with the government. He wrote in this vein to Washington:

The new plan of a Bank seemed to go on with great spirit; and I hope will continue to do so, as it appears to be the only system which can give timely aid; but the finger of party is so manifest that I sometimes have my doubts. I have given it every forwardness in my power, and shall continue to do so, whatever my private opinion of the designs and plans, and secondary views may be. I wish the gentlemen here had done the same with the money issued by the State [the March emission], which is acknowledged by themselves to be well secured, and yet is most disingenuously evaded and depreciated. Had this seasonable and proper measure met with deserved and proper support, we should now have had 10,000 barrels of flour on hand.[50]

Nathanael Greene shared Reed's views that the bank was designed in part to embarrass the state government. He wrote to Reed that the latter's enemies were making noble and generous exertions for the army, but added that "doubtless they have something further in view than just accommodating the Troops. The Army is the great object on which all political institutions must depend ultimately." [51]

Reed drove himself unmercifully during June and July to rouse his state to greater exertions. He wrote Washington in July that he had never "gone through half the fatigue of business that I have done for these two months past." [52] In letters to the treasurers, commissioners, and militia officers of the counties, he invoked his extraordinary powers under martial law and employed threats, supplications, and insults in spurring them to decisive action.[53] Indifference or outright hostility among the people, however, continued to block fulfillment of the heavy demands upon the state. In replying to a letter from Washington urging that Reed employ vigorously the "full discretionary power" which the general viewed the declaration of martial law to embody,[54] the president described the sensitivity of all the people toward any conscription of manpower or confiscation of property—"we have had officers killed in execution of the clearest duty," he wrote—and spoke of a growing practice among the farmers to raise nothing beyond that which was needed for their subsistence and their taxes.[55]

Yet some progress was made. General William Irvine of the Pennsylvania line could write to Reed as early as June 5 that the good effects of the state's exertions were being felt at the Morristown camp.[56] The commander in chief was growing more hopeful too. Though the supplies which reached him from all sources came nowhere near his requisitions, the news that the Comte de Rochambeau had arrived safely at Newport, Rhode Island, on July 11 with over 5,000 French troops led him to call upon militia from the states, some 16,500 in all, for a new effort at his favorite target, the British base at New York City.

Reed's reaction to this undertaking was identical to that which similar plans in 1779 had produced: he would lead the Pennsylvania militia into the field himself. On August 15, Reed turned over the chair of the council to vice president Moore and set about transporting the Philadelphia levies across the Delaware and marching them to the rendezvous at Trenton, New Jersey. John Lacey, a member of the council and a brigadier general of the state militia, had already been dispatched into Berks and Bucks counties to order forward their contingents.[57] On August 16 Reed arrived at Trenton to assume command of the 1,200 troops gathered there. More men came in daily, and Reed was hopeful that he could soon muster over 3,000 for the march eastward on the route through Princeton and New Brunswick which Washington had specified.[58] Meanwhile, he and his officers busied themselves with training the militiamen and inculcating a sense of discipline among them. Reed's own presence in the field contributed to an unusual success in the second objective. Pennsylvania's chief justice, Thomas McKean, who had once commanded a militia battalion and found among his men "some of the most rude, turbulent, impudent, lazy, dirty fellows . . . I had ever beheld," congratulated the president on the order at the camp.[59]

But Reed's growing levy never proceeded beyond Trenton. The French naval forces had not achieved the superiority which was a necessary prelude to the projected attack upon New York. On the contrary, Rochambeau's army and the French squadron which had convoyed it to Newport now found themselves blockaded there by a superior British fleet. Though these developments did not cause Washington to abandon the project at once, the lack of supplies at his main depots obliged him to write to Reed on August 20 that the latter should not march to join him but might better draw back into Pennsylvania and hold his men in readiness there. The general also advised that no new contingents from the state should be called forward until the situation had been clarified.[60]

Reed consulted with his officers and decided to remain at Trenton a while longer. He gave the orders for stopping the "back country" militia in Pennsylvania as Washington had suggested.[61] Then, within the week of Washington's first letter, came another written August 26 with the crushing news that the eagerly awaited French naval reinforcements were still in Europe, blockaded at Brest. Once again the attack upon New York had to be written off for another year. Reed was advised in this letter to dismiss the militia completely. After a formal review on September 1, he did so. He then returned to Philadelphia, the reconvening of the assembly being at hand.[62] His good example in taking the field himself and the sizeable force he had gathered at Trenton quieted a number of critics, particularly at headquarters, and demonstrated, as General Wayne wrote Reed, that "the virtuous citizens of Pennsylvania are not tied down to any local spot, but when occasion requires, will cheerfully move to any point . . . under the conduct of a Governor in whose fortitude and abilities they can place the highest confidence."[63]

The disappointment of the abortive campaign of 1780 was driven from Reed's mind soon after his arrival in Philadelphia by a much sharper sense of loss. On September 18, Esther Reed, not yet thirty-five years of age, died.[64] In January, Mrs. Reed had had smallpox, but had recovered. After the birth of George Washington Reed in May, and after having Martha Washington as a house guest for a week late in June,[65] she and the children moved out from the city to "Laurel Hill," the mansion by the Schuylkill which the state had set aside as a summer residence for the president. She had busied herself during the summer with a subscription undertaken among the women of Philadelphia to raise funds for clothing the army, an undertaking of which she was named the chairwoman.[66] When her husband left Philadelphia to command the militia at Trenton, her letters to him contained no mention of illness. In fact she expressed a wish, if the camp remained at Trenton, to pay her husband a visit there, "as you know I have ever had a strong curiosity to see an army in the field." [67] She and the children moved back to Philadelphia just before Reed also returned there. Her sudden death followed soon afterwards, on September 18, and she was buried at the Second Presbyterian Church on the 19th.[68]

Esther Reed's death was a heavy blow to the troubled president. He spoke of their marriage as "the happiest" in a country of many happy marriages where "Pride and Interest do not govern in that Article." He was to wear the "garb of sorrow" for a full year and, after his last term as president came to an end, stated that were it not for the children, he would "retire into some obscure Corner, nor mix more with the vain and triffling Crowd." [69] Reed's sister Mary came to live with him after Esther's death and, assisted by Mrs. DeBerdt, cared for the three boys and two girls.[70]

Political duties crowding about him after his wife's funeral made it impossible for him to seek that "obscure Corner." The fall elections for the assembly and one-third of the council seats were only a month away. In a move designed to ferret out the reasons for the laxness of the counties in meeting their tax, supply, and manpower quotas, and also undoubtedly to permit some campaigning for the Radicals before election day, the assembly, on September 22, named Reed, Treasurer David Rittenhouse, and Speaker John Bayard to constitute an investigatory commission, and ordered that they report on their findings to the next assembly.[71]

Reed and his two companions left on their tour at the end of September and were away most of October. They visited all but the westernmost counties and found much that needed correction. The basic difficulty as Reed saw it was not a defect in the laws, but "real neglect in the execution of [them by] Commissioners, Collectors, etc." and, particularly in the case of purchasing agents for the United States Quartermaster, duplication in jobs: "There have been at one time twelve Deputy Quartermasters in this County [Northampton] only, on pay, rations, and with clerks, etc. etc. etc. Had a suitable inspection taken place twelve months ago, I am sure we should have saved many thousands, if not mil-

lions." [72] In Berks County, Reed was confronted by rioters protesting against the taxes. He acted vigorously in having a large
number committed to jail. After returning to Philadelphia he
heard with considerable anger that Chief Justice McKean had permitted the "sudden discharge" of these men. His displeasure
brought a sterner attitude by the court with the result that one
hundred and fifty-three tax delinquents were fined a total of
£1,000 in specie on November 7. The excuse offered by the accused was interesting: their default, they said, was "a residue of
revolutionary business not to be got over entirely till time and
habit should enure us to regular proceedings." [73]

On November 9 Reed informed the new assembly that he and
his fellow commissioners were preparing the full account of their
recently completed trip. The report was laid before the house
on April 3, 1781. It contained detailed suggestions for improving
tax collections and for strengthening the militia system.[74]

Reed's tour, whatever its effect in laying a basis for new legislation, did not accomplish its secondary aim, the reinforcement of
Radical voting strength for the October, 1780, election. For the
first time since the implementation of the constitution in 1776,
the Radicals lost control of the assembly. Speaker Bayard himself failed to win reelection from Philadelphia County. The Republican numerical superiority was a very thin one, but they had
leaders of the stature of Robert Morris, Samuel Morris, and
Frederick Muhlenburg. The last-named was elected speaker.
The Radicals missed Bayard and also George Bryan, who, in what
now appears to have been a tactical political error, had resigned
from his seat in the assembly to take the appointment, bestowed
by Reed and the council on April 3, 1780, to a newly created
fourth seat on the state's supreme court.[75]

Despite the hostile complexion of the new assembly, Reed and
Moore were reelected president and vice president of the council,
the former unanimously, on November 14.[76] Thus Reed began
his third and last term as president, a term which was hardly
under way when the mutiny of the Pennsylvania line of the Continental Army confronted him with the gravest crisis of his three
years in office.

The mutiny was the product of inadequate clothing, insufficient food, long overdue pay, failure to obtain bounties promised for enlistment and reenlistment, harsh discipline, and, in some cases, coercion to force reenlistment.[77]   On the evening of January 1, 1781, about one thousand of the approximately twenty-five hundred men of the line at the Morristown, New Jersey, winter camp, poured from their huts fully armed, wounded several officers who attempted to disperse them, seized several cannon from the magazine, defied General Anthony Wayne, and marched off southwestward toward Princeton.   The other men of the line refused to act against the mutineers, and, for the most part, drifted after their comrades.

Reed received news of the mutiny from General Wayne, the line's commander in the temporary absence of General Arthur St. Clair, the evening of January 3.   That evening he and the council conferred with a special committee appointed by Congress, and ordered St. Clair and Colonel Proctor of the Pennsylvania artillery to leave the next morning for Princeton.   The next day Wayne, who had followed the mutineers to Princeton and was negotiating with the board of sergeants which had assumed leadership within the movement, dispatched a list of the latter's demands to Reed with a plea that the council appoint one or more of its members with full powers to treat with the dissidents.[78]

The next morning, January 5, the council authorized Reed and James Potter, councilor from Northumberland County and a general in the state militia, to negotiate with the troops.   After ordering that the Philadelphia militia be altered, Reed left for New Jersey that afternoon with Potter and a guard of twenty cavalrymen of the Philadelphia Light Horse.[79]   At Bristol, where they spent the night, a messenger from Wayne reached them with news that the mutineers had settled themselves at Princeton and were orderly, but that they had refused to submit to their officers. Reed sent word back to Philadelphia to hurry forward clothing, provisions, and money.[80]

Reed crossed over to Trenton the next morning.   From John Cox's house he sent a message addressed to Wayne but written more for the eyes of the mutineers in the event thy seized it. As Reed later wrote, "There was a Guard at Gen. Wayne's Quarters but [it was] not fully ascertained whether it was a Guard for him or upon him." [81] The soldiers at Princeton permitted the letter to be delivered to Wayne, but later the board of sergeants called upon him and asked and received the general's permission to see the letter. Agreement was reached that it would be read by Wayne to all the men the next morning.[82]

Reed had stated in the letter that the refusal of the men to negotiate with General St. Clair the day before had convinced him that he could not go to their camp for fear of violence upon his person. He decided to proceed from Trenton to Maidenhead, four miles from Princeton, and in his letter he invited Wayne to meet him there. The mutineers sent word to Reed that he need not fear any irregularities or ill treatment at Princeton. They also permitted Wayne to send a brief note to the president. Reed, however, decided to go back to Trenton for the night.[83]

In Trenton, Reed was joined by the members of the committee of Congress. He had written to them earlier in the day asking that he be permitted to negotiate for the state first, and then, "if new or further concession than I make are necessary, the Committee may have the opportunity to offer them." [84] This was the strategy now agreed upon by Reed and the committeemen.

The next day, Sunday, January 7, Reed rode up to Maidenhead again and there, much to his satisfaction, found Wayne and three other officers whom the mutineers had permitted to meet him. Even more encouraging was another action the soldiers had taken that morning: they had seized John Mason, a Loyalist bearing proposals for the mutineers from the British command at New York City, and his guide James Ogden, and had sent them under guard to Reed. Wayne had suggested to the mutineers that they be delivered to the president and had promised that the enemy emissaries would be returned to their custody upon request.[85]

Reed decided that he would now go to Princeton and negotiate directly with the sergeants. A note to that effect was sent off to the latter, and although signs of a dangerous change of heart on their part came with the receipt of a request that the spies be surrendered to them again, Reed, together with Potter, Wayne, and the other officers who had accompanied the latter, rode up to the college town he knew so well. Upon his arrival in the late afternoon the whole line turned out under arms to meet him, and Reed decided it was prudent to return their salute.[86]

That evening, fortified by an expression of full discretionary powers from the Congressional committee,[87] guided by a letter Wayne received from Washington advising against violent coercion, and troubled by news of British military activity,[88] Reed and Wayne sat down to bargain with the sergeants. The president found that some of them were "very sensible Fellows and reason very speciously, but Williams, their nominal Leader is certainly a very poor Creature and very fond of Liquor." [89]

The sergeants opened the proceedings with their basic demand: every man who enlisted in 1776 and 1777 was to receive a discharge at once. Reed immediately replied that such a general mustering out, without reference to the term enlisted for, was impossible. He then went on to draw up a set of counterproposals which, after being approved by Wayne, were submitted to the sergeants. The latter agreed to submit these to the men the next morning. The meeting then adjourned and Reed went back to Maidenhead for the night.[90]

The next afternoon Reed received from Wayne the line's answer to his proposals. Accepted without reservation were the pledges that no man would be detained beyond his enlistment time, that arrears of pay were to be paid up as rapidly as possible, that a pair of shoes, overalls, and a shirt would be supplied each man in a few days, and that men who had enlisted "for three years or during the war" would be discharged at once if they had served three years. The sergeants stated, however, that the board which Reed had proposed the Pennsylvania council should create to rule on disputed enlistments and pay depreciation must be altered to include an equal number of their own representatives.[91] The mutineers, though Reed was not to learn of this until later in the evening, had also agreed to march to Trenton the next day, a move Reed and Wayne had been urging upon them for several days in a desire to remove them further from the British lines.

Despite Reed's flat rejection of their leaders' demands for seats on the board of inquiry, the men proceeded to Trenton on the 9th and camped at the site Reed's militia troops had used four months previously.[92]

That evening Reed and Potter met with the committee of Congress to put into effect the pledges that Reed had made to the line. Potter, Colonel Samuel Atlee of the committee, and two officers of the Philadelphia Light Horse were chosen to constitute the board of inquiry. It was also decided to demand custody of the British spies, the possession of whom the mutineers had used with great skill as a shield against threats of coercion. Mason and Ogden were handed over the next day after Reed had curtly rejected a counterdemand that the line be permitted to remain together in arms until all promises were carried out. The spies were tried and sentenced to death that same evening by a court-martial hastily assembled by Lord Stirling across the river from Trenton in Pennsylvania. They were hanged the next morning January 11.[93]

Two days later Reed left Trenton for Philadelphia. A shipment of clothing arrived from Philadelphia on the 11th and lessened the men's fears of being tricked or coerced. But their restlessness was alarming, with the result that the board of inquiry began examining disputed enlistment cases immediately, accepting the soldier's word under oath in lieu of the official records which had not reached Trenton as yet from Philadelphia.[94]

Back in Philadelphia, Reed found that the subscription he had asked Vice President Moore to launch for immediate cash to meet the promises to the line was not going well. His feeling that he had risked his own life to go among the mutineers and had, perhaps, prevented a march on Philadelphia led him to view this recalcitrance very unfavorably. In an angry gesture which was definitely malapropos, he issued a threat on January 15 to close the port of Philadelphia if more funds were not made available at once. An embargo was executed for two days before Reed realized that he had gone too far. He issued a statement in which he described again the pressing need for specie in the emergency, went on to express regret that an "erroneous interpretation" had been placed upon his proclamation, and concluded by withdrawing the plan for the subscription altogether.[95]

The next week was a hectic one as Reed strove to gather money together to send to the state auditors, Jonathan Smith, Joseph Dean, and Jacob Morris. They had gone to Trenton to handle the financial terms of the agreement by which Reed had ended the mutiny: the payment of arrears in wages, the payment of bounties which had been promised but never received, and payments to make up for depreciation in past pay.[96] Since the sergeants were still in control at Trenton, the men having persisted in their refusal to accept their officers again, it was decided to furlough until March all those who were not being discharged. The lack of money, which made it impossible to reenlist more than a handful of the men who claimed their time was up, and the perjury of others who took advantage of Reed's concession that they be permitted to swear to their status before the records arrived, reduced the strength of the line from some 2,450 to 1,150 men. By the end of January, the mutineers' camp had broken up.[97]

When the crisis had passed, criticisms of Reed's handling of the emergency were heard. Aside from his ill-advised proclamation, most of them centered about his decision to begin the board of inquiry hearings before proper records were available at Trenton. In February or March the criticism had great worth, but at the crucial time when Reed had agreed upon that procedure, there had been no protests from Wayne or the other officers upon the scene, nor from the Congressional committee which he had taken great pains to keep informed. Much of the criticism was to come from the regimental officers who had played no role whatsoever in quelling the mutiny, officers who were understandably bitter over the long-sustained refusal of the men to submit to them, or even negotiate with them. Some of these officers had urged a complete dissolution of the line rather than the expedients used, but Reed, Potter, and the Congressional committee members were undoubtedly right in their opinion that this would be a far more dangerous precedent than the measures to which they had turned.[98] It is noteworthy that greatly disturbed though he was by the mutiny and by the failure to quell it at its inception by disciplinary means, Washington felt the Pennsylvania authorities had made the best of an explosive situation.[99]

For the officers of the line, Reed attempted a settlement of pay and other disputes in order to reduce their sense of grievance against the state government. Realizing that many of them were anti-constitutionalists, he made personal efforts to win their political neutrality if he could not win their support. He met with a number of them at the City Tavern in Philadelphia on January 29 and followed that up with a dinner for them at his home on the 31st. He succeeded in obtaining a depreciation allowance for them at this time and an ample if not munificent allowance for their travel expenses to the sites selected for the regimental rendezvous in March.[100] Yet hostility continued to run high against the Radicals and, to a lesser extent, Reed personally. In a statesmanlike letter to Wayne, written in June, Reed advised him and, in effect, the officers as a group, against a reactionary political outlook:

Property is too casually distributed in this state ever to permit that Aristocratick influence which some wish and which I admit to be the most natural to the Sentiments of Gentlemen used to the discipline and subordination of an army. A popular [i.e., democratic] Government must in the nature of things be most generally agreeable to the People of this State, and though it is probable some changes may be adopted, I am persuaded this will be the only ruling principle at all times.[101]

By the time of the Yorktown campaign, the relations between the president and the officers had improved. Colonel Thomas Moore of the line could write in July that most of his fellows felt that Reed had handled the mutiny well, though he went on to say that by some among the officers the difficulties of the state in supplying and paying them was being "craftily imputed to policy inspired by your influence." [102]

While Reed's political opponents, now in control of the assembly, failed directly to challenge his settlement with the mutineers, they did adopt a committee report on the affair which contained some implications of unwise conduct.[103] Reed and Potter wrote to the house protesting against this report but the legislature took

no action. When the assembly met again in the late spring, Reed
sent a message on June 2 asking that the original committee,
which included such Republican leaders as Morris and Mifflin,
be reappointed and directed to make a new report. This was
done. The new report, offered June 8 and adopted by the house
on the 11th, reaffirmed the original report's conclusion that Reed
and Potter had "conducted the Business so far as they were concerned with Zeal and attention to their Country." Now an additional statement was added which recognized that reports unfavorable to the president had circulated, reports which were to be
reprobated since he and Potter "did render on that occasion every
service to their country that circumstances and the nature of the
transaction would admit of." There the matter rested.[104]

The altered political fortunes of his administration and the
mutiny episode were not the only strains Reed had to bear early
in 1781. His tour of the state in October, 1780, had convinced
him that many officials appointed by Congress, particularly deputy
quartermasters, were engaging in a partisan manner in state politics on the side of the anti-constitutionalists, despite a circular
letter of 1779 issued by Nathanael Greene, then quartermaster
general, warning against such activities.[105] Reed had brought this
matter to the attention of Charles Pettit and John Cox, Greene's
(and subsequently Timothy Pickering's) assistant quartermaster
generals. When redress of his grievance was not made in what
Reed considered a sufficient period of time, there occurred an
unhappy rupture in his close relations with the former, his
brother-in-law. Undoubtedly the pressure of official business, the
constant sniping by political enemies, and then the death of Mrs.
Reed had combined to make the always sensitive Reed unusually
short-tempered and exasperated in those closing months of 1780.

Fortunately for Reed, the open-hearted Pettit took this background into consideration, and made the first overture to heal the
breach with a long and often movingly phrased letter written
December 4. Reed, in his reply of the 8th, said he read Pettit's
message with care "and with Affection too . . . [but] without drawing from it that Satisfaction which you seemed to expect." [106] The
mutiny intervened to interrupt the correspondence, but on Janu-

ary 20, 1781, Pettit sent Reed an eighteen-page letter, "as I flatter myself the Door of Reconciliation is not yet shut and the Object is too desirable to be easily relinquished," and in it set forth not only his affection for Reed but also, in great detail, the circumstances surrounding the apparent inaction on his part which had so displeased the latter. This message melted Reed's resentment, though it did not entirely convince him of the reasonableness of Pettit's actions. He brought the unhappy controversy to an end with his reply of January 26:

> Was I capable of entertaining more durable Resentments than I am, the Desire you manifest to remove them would have its Effect. Our Conceptions on this Subject are very different and will probably remain so if further Discussion was attempted. Mine may perhaps lead me to expect too much, yours to grant too little. Both may be right and wrong to a certain degree. . . . I believe we have neither of us much Time to spare for such Discussions, so that I shall only add, that if my Sister and you will come and dine with us on Sunday, it will give me much pleasure, and renew the Intercourse of Families the Interruption of which has given sincere Pain.[107]

Problems of state, unfortunately, could not be disposed of so readily. The new assembly in its spring session of 1781 did, as was mentioned above, take some measures of which Reed heartily approved toward greater financial stability. But to rouse the legislature toward more vigorous measures to recruit men and supply them for the approaching campaign was as difficult a task as it had been in 1779 and 1780. Now Washington was writing to Reed and the other governors once more, again with the plea that the promising opportunity for combined operations with the French navy and expeditionary force must not be forfeited for lack of spirited exertions in filling up the ranks, stockpiling supplies, and providing transport facilities.[108]

Reed, who had already won the thanks of Governor Thomas Jefferson of Virginia for the aid he had sent southward to Generals Greene and Lafayette,[109] made vigorous efforts to summon a maximum response from Pennsylvania to Washington's requests. In May he called the legislature into extraordinary session and in his message of May 31 stressed the necessity for fiscal relief to permit decisive action to meet the "exigencies of the State (particularly frontier defense), the requisitions of Congress, and the representations of the Commander-in-Chief." [110] On June 19, little having been accomplished, Reed felt compelled to address the house "in a language more serious and decisive than any we have ever yet adopted. . . . We have laid the state of the public wants fully before you; it was the hope of immediate relief that induced us to call you together, and though near three weeks have now elapsed, we are in the same state of imbecility and distress as when the session began." [111]

The next day the house repealed the legal tender laws. Within the following week it so accelerated its efforts that Colonel William Grayson could write of Pennsylvania to General George Weedon that "this state is doing well at present in some things; effectual measures are taking [sic] to fill up their line; their money affairs will be put on a good footing." Only eight days before, Grayson had told the same correspondent that "the Languid Assembly of this State are doing nothing." [112]

These exertions and Reed's permitted Pennsylvania to make an important contribution to the Washington-Rochambeau campaign against Cornwallis in Virginia, and, in fact, to the preliminary maneuvering there during which the reinforcement of the Pennsylvania line had greatly aided Lafayette in his cat-and-mouse game with the British commander. On August 30 Washington and Rochambeau arrived in Philadelphia on their way south. The American army marched through the city on September 2, the bulk of the French forces two days later.[113]

Then followed the weeks of anxious waiting. But they were not idle weeks, nor without new alarms, for Congress became fearful that Sir Henry Clinton would launch an attack upon Philadelphia from New York while Washington and the main American army were besieging Cornwallis. On September 10, Reed was asked to call out 3,000 militiamen to cooperate with an equal number from New Jersey against a British offensive.[114] Reed issued the necessary orders the next day, but no such move was launched by the enemy. By early October the militiamen who had answered the summons were being permitted to return to their homes though not formally discharged.[115]

One of the reasons for releasing the militiamen was the approach of the annual election for the legislature, scheduled for October 9. For Reed it marked an important milestone, for he had now served out his three-year term on the council and, because of the constitutional prohibition, could not run for a second consecutive term. This meant as well the end of his presidency, for only a member of the council was eligible for that office. Quite naturally, however, though he was not directly involved, Reed was most interested in the results of the elections to assembly and council. He took great pleasure in the choice of John Bayard to fill the council seat for Philadelphia (an election which was soon to be challenged, but unsuccessfully), but the over-all picture was not favorable. Although the Radicals and Republicans were almost evenly matched in the assembly, the latter succeeded in electing their candidate, Frederick Muhlenberg, as speaker.[116] On the brighter side was the election, on November 14, of William Moore, Reed's vice president, as president, and the choice of James Potter, the retiring president's associate during the tense days of the mutiny, as vice president.[117] Both were constitutionalists.

But a greater victory than these had occurred to bring Reed cheer as he relinquished the presidency. On October 24, the news of the surrender of Cornwallis had reached an expectant Philadelphia. As Reed stepped down from public life,[118] it was now with the heartening assurance that his country's independence, the goal toward which he had labored so diligently, was finally assured.

CHAPTER XI

Great and Bitter Fruits

FOR the first time since that June day six years before when he had set out from Philadelphia for Cambridge with George Washington, Joseph Reed was now a private citizen. With the exception of a brief month's work as a special commissioner for his state, Reed's remaining years, and these were to be lamentably few in number for so young a man, were to be spent in this private capacity. But that new and strange status was not to bring isolation from the clash of partisan political strife. Reed was not to be permitted the luxury of looking back with satisfaction from his retirement upon his contributions to the Revolution. An attack more bitter than any which had been launched against him while he held office was to break about him in 1782, an attack which saddened his last years and which called for all the resignation he could summon to avoid, as he did avoid, an abandoned bitterness.

Despite the attacks made upon Reed while he was president, he left that office with a sagacious attitude toward vilification as a natural hazard of political life. In 1780 he had written to Anthony Wayne of envy, malevolence, and slander "as the Tax which Merit and Distinction must pay." He went on to say that at first he felt hurt by attacks directed at him "and spent Time and Labour to counteract them, but I have long since learned that the best Shield is Integrity, and [the] truest Remedy, Patience." [1] That Reed took his own advice is indicated by the thoughts he revealed in a letter written in June, 1781, to his good friend, General Nathanael Greene:

I have been alternately the subject of gross abuse and extravagent panegyric: I deserve neither; I am an honest servant of my country, but I know I have made many mistakes in which my head, not my heart, was to blame. . . . The vain task of pleasing all because I wished to serve all I have now given over and have learned to be content with the approbation of my own mind. . . . But after all, and after repeated gross and illiberal attacks of every kind, from meanness to treason, for great pains have been taken to prove me in the interests of the enemy, I am still in good health and spirits, not disgusted with the service of my country, though ready to give place to any man who can serve it better.[2]

Reed wrote to Greene again several weeks after his term as president had ended. He said:

My term of office is expired, and I am now quite a private man. My knowledge of the affairs of this State might have been useful, and I should have thought it my duty to have given my service if it had been required in the line of the State, but it has not, so that I find myself in a situation more truly enviable, if peace and ease are to be envied, than I have been in for some time. I am pressed to go into Congress, but this I shall positively decline. I have not the least ambition or inclination, and can ill afford to give the public the few remaining years wherein I can be actively useful to my family. You will therefore probably, find me, when you return, a private gentleman, pursuing my profession with activity and industry.[3]

Reed's reference that his services were not "required in the line of the State" is undoubtedly to the fact that he had permitted his name to be put forward for assemblyman from Philadelphia in the October election. He did not actively campaign, however, and was not chosen.[4]

In the new assembly which met after the election, several efforts were undertaken toward naming Reed to the state's delegation in Congress. But Reed, as he forecast in his letter to Greene, refused to permit his name to be proposed formally. Toward another post in the United States government he was more receptive. This was the office of secretary at war, established in February, 1781. Reed and Generals Henry Knox, Benjamin Lincoln, Nathanael Greene, and Philip Schuyler were all considered for the appointment by Congress. Greene favored Reed for the job,[5] but the latter withdrew his name from consideration (it had been introduced without his knowledge) when it was observed by some members that only officers with continuous active field service should be nominated. Reed thought that Robert Morris's influence would win the appointment for General Schuyler.[6] But the post was voted to Benjamin Lincoln of Massachusetts on October 30, 1781.[7]

Reed had never entertained high hopes of securing the war appointment at this time, nor any other federal posts. His fellow Pennsylvanian but political foe, Robert Morris, was far too powerful now for such delusions. Reed recognized that the work Morris had performed since assuming the office of superintendent of finance in May, 1781, had brought "a real benefit" to the public.[8] While president, he had cooperated with the superintendent and had received the thanks of Morris.[9] But Reed also felt that the latter mixed a good deal of private interest in his conduct of his public post. He regarded the financier's control over Congress "humiliating" in the fiscal field, and told Greene that it was "also great, not to say irresistible, in the appointment of other officers not connected with his own [department]." [10]

A year later, when Reed's name was again raised in Congress in connection with an important office, he continued to regard an appointment impossible while Morris, "the hostile Colossus, who not only bestrides the other officers of Congress, but even Congress itself," reigned supreme.[11] Robert Livingston, secretary of foreign affairs for the Congress since the creation of the office in the summer of 1781, tendered his resignation on December 3, 1782. The names of Reed, Philip Schuyler, and George Clymer, a leading Republican of Pennsylvania, were put forward as possible successors. But to all these men some opposition developed, and the result was that Livingston was persuaded to continue to serve until May, 1783.[12] Reed, who was in New Jersey at the time his name was proposed, was not pleased by this action and wrote George Bryan that he would "put an end to the nomination" upon his return.[13] His name, consequently, was not brought forward the next year when Livingston did step down.

The failure of his halfhearted attempt to win a seat in the assembly in the 1781 election, the election of Lincoln as secretary at war, and Reed's own refusal to consider serving Pennsylvania in Congress combined to make him truly, and for the first time in eight years (if his membership on pre-Revolutionary patriot committees be considered public posts), "quite a private man."

He naturally turned to his law practice, a practice which had languished seriously since the Revolution began, and most seriously of all during his three years as president of Pennsylvania. He had not closed his office completely during the latter period, but had turned over the task of running it to a young protégé, Jared Ingersoll, Jr. Ingersoll had studied law at London's Middle Temple at Reed's advice and was invited to work for the latter when he returned from Europe (he had gone to France from England) in 1778.[14] The young man accepted, and proved able and conscientious in caring for Reed's clients during the latter's presidencies. By the time Reed stepped down from office and took up his practice again, Ingersoll was a close friend as well as a business associate. Two months after Reed resumed his profession, another link was forged between them, for in December, 1781, Ingersoll married Reed's niece, Elizabeth Pettit.[15]

Reed did not make the transition from the roles of soldier and politician back to that of attorney without some difficulty. Ingersoll was to relate later that Reed's mind did not return too willingly to the law, and the enmity which had been built up against him among many of Philadelphia's most important businessmen did not make this return or the securing of clients any easier.[16] But his ability before the bar soon manifested itself again, and by early 1782 his business was flourishing. At the supreme court's April term he argued ten cases, some in conjunction with William Bradford who had been the state's attorney general during Reed's third term as president, a number surpassed only by William Lewis and James Wilson, with thirteen and eleven cases, respectively.[17] Though Reed preferred to remain in Philadelphia now rather than follow the circuit, at times he did engage to appear at Lancaster, Doylestown, and other county seats.[18] His professional reputation had been sufficiently restored by the fall of 1782 to permit him to charge a fee of £100 to take Owen Biddle's son John into his office as a law apprentice.[19]

Though his professional duties required constant attention, Reed now had greater leisure time for his family and for avocations. His children, cared for by his sister Mary and his mother-in-law, Mrs. DeBerdt, were a source of great pleasure. They

partook of Esther Reed's sweet disposition, he wrote Dennis De-
Berdt, "and are very promising, at least in a Parent's Eye." [20]
Reed was very solicitous as to their schooling, particularly that
for his three sons. The will he wrote in 1783 reveals something
of his views on education:

As my sentiments of education differ widely from the common mode,
I desire that my boys be taught writing, arithmetic, mathematics, and
the German and French languages, in preference to all other learning, and on no account to meddle with the dead languages till they
arrive at the age of fifteen, nor then unless they discover remarkable
genius. My present intentions are that Joseph be bred to trade, but
not sent abroad till he has served his apprenticeship to the age of
twenty; Dennis to be bred to the law, under the care of my good
friends Mr. Ingersoll or Mr. Bradford; Washington is of too tender
an age yet [he was only three] to say anything of him, but that I would
have the same mode of education as to him, and that they go to
Bethlehem [Pennsylvania, i.e., to the Moravians there] at proper ages
to learn the German—to Canada, to learn French, if practicable, but
none to go out of America till twenty.[21]

The family had to move from the official presidential mansion
on Market Street, of course, when Reed's term expired. He
leased a house on Third Street from a Mr. Wallace for an annual
rental of approximately £250.[22] In addition, since the children
had so enjoyed the summer of 1780 away from the city at "Laurel
Hill," also an official residence, Reed, in July, 1781, bought a
two-story brick and stucco house nearby, overlooking the Schuylkill River and surrounded by an extensive orchard. This was
used by the family as a summer home until his death in 1785.[23]

Only once did Reed seem seriously to consider marrying again.
Late in 1782, he courted a widow, Mrs. Sarah Shaw, a sister of
Clement Biddle and sister-in-law of James Wilkinson. Reed's
overtures for marriage were "not unfavourably received, and . . .
promised an early completion." But the wedding never took
place. For reasons which are not known, Reed broke off the
connection. He wrote to Wilkinson on January 18, 1783, "Circumstances have since happened which occasioned an Interrup-
tion. Your own Delicacy will suggest the propriety of reserving
to myself my future Intentions." [24]

Wilkinson, however, was considerably incensed by what he called Reed's "very equivocal Conduct." He was also disturbed by rumors circulating in Philadelphia that his family had ardently sought the marriage for social gain.[25] In reply to Wilkinson's demand for an explanation, Reed stated rather mysteriously that he could not fully disclose the reasons for his change of heart without making "two Families forever miserable." But he gladly gave Wilkinson a statement to the effect that he had never perceived that the Wilkinson family had desired the marriage but rather had displayed "the utmost propriety and even Delicacy." [26] With this statement the whole matter was apparently closed.

The release from official duties permitted Reed to take a more active role in the affairs of his church, the Second Presbyterian Church on Arch Street, where his friend the Reverend James Sproat was pastor. While president of Pennsylvania, Reed had been elected a trustee and president of the corporation of the church, and, when his three-year term as trustee expired in 1783, Reed was reelected to that position.[27] Reed was also elected to office in another institution of which he was a member, the American Philosophical Society. A member since 1768, Reed had been asked to preside at several meetings which he attended while president of Pennsylvania. On January 4, 1782, three months after stepping down from that office, he was chosen to be one of the four councilors. In January, 1785, two months before his death, his term was renewed.[28]

The present-day student of the American Revolution has cause to regret that Reed did not execute an idea to which his membership in the Philosophical Society gave rise: a plan to write a military history of the War for Independence. Reed mentioned "some little essay towards a history of the present Revolution" in a letter to Nathanael Greene in 1781. He said he thought he himself could give a good account of the campaigns of 1775 through 1778 because of his participation in them. For the campaigns in the South, he stated he must depend upon Greene, and asked the latter "to preserve as much as possible of regular and authentic accounts of what has passed and may pass in your department with a general sketch of characters who make any considerable figure with you." In describing the project to Greene, Reed indicated that he would attempt a truly critical account in which even Washington's military role would be dispassionately weighed:

The little observations I have made of our own affairs has destroyed all the credibility of history, and I am satisfied that one half of what is read, and perhaps more, is nothing but an agreeable romance, framed according to the fancy of the historian, and the materials good or bad which he has accidentally collected. Many a victory has been gained, I firmly believe, contrary to the will and judgment of the General, who has swallowed the undeserved praise with as little compunction as if it had been gained by the skill of his manoeuvres and the full exertion of his own talents and judgments. If I should live to finish what I have begun, I shall certainly strip every Jack Daw of his borrowed plumage, which I can the better do, as I have no pretensions to plumes of any kind myself beyond what a volunteer of subordinate fame can lay claim to.[29]

Greene replied with a promise to save material for Reed,[30] and his letters of 1781-83 with their details and observations on the campaign he led in the Carolinas are an important fruit of the latter's scheme. But Reed never carried out his plan. The polemic writing to which he soon felt obliged to turn, his failing health, his nine-month absence from the country in 1784, and his early death all prevented this accomplishment. The draft of a twelve-page "Memoir of General Greene in the American Service and late Commander-in-Chief in South Carolina" written by Reed and preserved among his papers [31] is the only tangible product of his project.

Much more of a disappointment to Reed himself than his inability to write the history of the Revolution was that involving his unfulfilled hope of being named to the supreme court of Pennsylvania in 1782. The Radical forces had decided to support the chief justice, Thomas McKean, for the council seat from Chester County in that year's election, and they looked forward to electing him president too. If the plan had succeeded, Reed was to be rewarded for his three years of service as president by an appointment to fill McKean's place on the court. But the latter failed to win the Chester seat. He had not resigned his judicial post prior to the election, however, and with his retention of that office the vacancy Reed was to have filled never materialized.[32]

Though Reed did not gain the judgeship he coveted, his legal talents and his prominence in the state won for him, in the same year, 1782, the only official position he filled between the termination of his presidency and his death. This was the appointment as one of the four agents for Pennsylvania who argued that state's claims upon the Wyoming Valley against those of Connecticut before a court empowered by Congress to settle the dispute. It will be recalled that Reed, while president in 1779, had sought to inaugurate negotiations with Connecticut, but that these overtures were rejected by Governor Trumbull of the latter state.[33] In 1781, however, in the waning days of his administration, Reed had brought the matter to the fore again, this time seeking action through Congress by invoking Article IX of the recently implemented Articles of Confederation. That article set up the machinery to deal with a formal request by a state for a hearing of a dispute with another state. Under this provision agents of the two states would, by joint consent, name a court which would hear the case and render judgment. This was the procedure invoked by Pennsylvania in October, 1781.[34]

Owing to numerous delays, it was August, 1782, before the membership of the court and a date and place for the hearing (November 12, at Trenton, New Jersey) were agreed upon. The judges named by the mutual consent of the two states were William Whipple of New Hampshire, Welcome Arnold of Rhode Island, David Brearley and William C. Houston of New Jersey, and Cyrus Griffin, Joseph Jones, and Thomas Neilson of Virginia. Five of the seven so named would constitute the court.[35]

Not until November 18 were the requisite number of these gentlemen present at Trenton. On that day Whipple, Arnold, Brearley, Houston, and Griffin formed the court, Jones and Neilson failing to appear then or at any later time. To argue Pennsylvania's claims before them came a bipartisan group of five of the state's leading attorneys: Solicitor Henry Osborne, Attorney

General William Bradford, Jr., former Attorney General Jonathan Sergeant, James Wilson, and Joseph Reed. William Samuel Johnson, Jesse Root, and Eliphalet Dyer represented Connecticut.[36]

On November 22, the Pennsylvania agents presented a formal statement of their state's claims to the disputed tract, citing the charter granted to William Penn by King Charles II in 1681. The Connecticut statement, filed the same day, rested principally upon the provisions of their charter of 1662 from the same monarch which specified extension westward (except where New York was concerned) to the Pacific.[37]

Beginning November 25 and continuing through December 9, the agents of Pennsylvania and Connecticut alternated in presenting proofs for their respective claims. The Connecticut argument revolved about the prior grants made to it by Charles II. The Pennsylvania cause was based upon the inequity of splitting its territory because of the carelessness of a century-old royal grant, and it made capital of Connecticut's failure to show interest in the Wyoming lands until the formation of the Susquehanna Company in 1753.[38]

Reed, writing to George Bryan on December 3, expressed confidence that the Pennsylvania argument was the stronger and that it was making the best impression, thanks in part to some transparent subterfuges attempted by Connecticut's agents. Of the latter, Reed regarded Johnson as the ablest, "a good speaker, and . . . a man of candour." Reed thought Dyer a poor advocate since he would "submit to no order . . . [but] speaks twenty times a day, and scarcely ever finishes one sentence completely." [39]

On December 10, the final arguments, in the nature of a summing up, began. Root began that day and concluded his remarks in some two hours. Sergeant spoke at length for Pennsylvania on the 11th and 12th, and Dyer for Connecticut on the 13th and 14th. James Wilson began his summation on the afternoon of the latter day, a Saturday. That night he crossed the Delaware River to Pennsylvania, intending to return Monday morning. A severe storm, however, filled the river with ice which rendered it impassable for three days. Not until Wilson was able to return on the 19th did the hearing resume. He spoke that day, and again

on the 20th. Reed commented that his argument was "both
laborious and judicious, he has taken much pains." [40]

Johnson gave the concluding argument for Connecticut on
December 21 and 23. Reed found his performance disappointing
in the light of his earlier estimate of the man, "full of palpable
misquotations and assertions, open to the most easy detection."
All this made Reed's own task easier, for he had been given the
honor of the final summing up for Pennsylvania. He held forth
on the 24th, and, as he wrote Bryan, "finished in one day, taking
three hours before dinner and as many after. We have little
doubt of a favorable decree," he concluded. [41]

Reed's optimism was borne out by the court's ruling. After
deliberating for four days, this judgment was pronounced before
the agents of the two states on December 30:

We are unanimously of the opinion that the State of Connecticut has
no right to the lands in controversy. We are also unanimously of
opinion that the jurisdiction and pre-emption of all the territory
lying within the charter boundary of Pennsylvania, and now claimed
by the State of Connecticut, do of right belong to the State of
Pennsylvania. [42]

On January 6, 1783, the report of Reed, Wilson, Bradford, Sergeant, and Osborne was made to the Pennsylvania executive council. A proclamation was then issued giving official notice of the
court's decision. [43]

The satisfaction Reed obtained from having helped secure the
ruling in favor of his state was diluted at this time, however, by
far less pleasant emotions. These latter had been aroused by a
new attack upon him unmatched in scope and virulence by any
previous effort. It was launched by an article attacking Reed in
the *Independent Gazetteer,* the journal of the anti-constitutionalist party, on September 7, 1782. In this issue five queries were
made by "Brutus" as to the conduct of "General R—d" in December, 1776, when he was "A—t G—L of the Continental army."
The writer charged that to the American commander at Bristol,
Pennsylvania, that month, Reed had expressed thoughts of abandoning the American cause and accepting a British protection.
General John Cadwalader was that commander. [44]

What occasioned this assault upon Reed at a time when he was
no longer in public office? The answer is not to be found in any
mere personal clash between Cadwalader and himself. Since the
former was referred to in "Brutus's" queries, Reed asked him for
an explanation, and Cadwalader subsequently became the open
protagonist in supporting and amplifying the charges against
the former president. But Cadwalader denied that he himself
was "Brutus," and probably was not. That attack and the support for Cadwalader's later polemics with Reed had their origin
in the conscious plan of the anti-constitutionalist forces to push
forward their counterrevolution by discrediting and destroying
the influence of the man who had been the constitutionalist standard bearer for three years. The conscious nature of the attack on
Reed is indicated by the following letter Benjamin Rush, a leading Republican, wrote to Cadwalader while the dispute still raged
the following Spring:

The whole republican party feel themselves under obligations to you
for the finishing blow you have given to the pale faced [Radical]
faction in Pennsylvania. Our accounts from the Counties are very
flattering. Not only the faction but the constitution itself must
perish forever with Mr. Reed. Remember your promise to join us
[i.e., run for office on the Republican ticket] in the fall.[45]

The political motivation of the attack on Reed was quite apparent to observers who watched its progress from a position in-
sulated from the partisan currents of Pennsylvania. Washington
termed the news that Reed sent him of the charges "unexpected
and surprising" and acceded to the latter's request that his private
letters to Reed might, if necessary, be used "to your justification" [46] Nathanael Greene was shocked by the news when it
reached him in South Carolina. He wrote to Charles Pettit:

The attempt to traduce him [Reed], as having a design to go over to
the enemy is truly wicked. General Cadwalader never had such a
thought. I am persuaded nothing but party rage could induce him
to countenance such an insinuation. . . . The abuse and scurrility
thrown out against him [Reed] betrays so much rancour and Malice
that it destroys itself. He will live beloved and respected by every
good Man and friend to his County.[47]

To Reed himself, Greene wrote that Cadwalader's insinuations were "Infamous." He again asserted that "party rage" was directing the latter. Philadelphia, he said, "has something infatuating in its air. No character escapes abuse, and the innocent as well as the guilty are all arraigned as party or spleen directs." [48]

The Republican program which was in the Philadelphia air when "Brutus" posed his questions in September, 1782, centered about obtaining control of the supreme executive council. The Republicans, it will be recalled, had been able to organize the assembly elected in October, 1781. The council, however, had remained in the grip of the Radicals, and Moore and Potter, both constitutionalists, had been elected president and vice president that November. As the election of 1782 approached, the Republicans, confident of increasing their hold upon the legislature, raised great hopes of utilizing that strength to elect a Republican to the presidency (it will be recalled that the president was elected by the assembly and council jointly). The candidate they had in mind, a candidate who could only become so by first winning a seat on the council, was John Dickinson.[49]

Dickinson's return to the political wars in Pennsylvania (he had been in almost unbroken retirement on his farm in Delaware since 1777) indicated that the pendulum had indeed turned back toward conservatism. Had he not voted against independence in Congress on July 1, 1776, and absented himself the following day when the conclusive vote was taken? One Radical writer after another threw this record up against Dickinson in newspaper articles. Another target for attack was the latter's resignation from the army in 1776 as a result of pique when overlooked in promotions. "Virginius," writing in the Freeman's Journal, the Radical organ, of August 7, 1782, asked if one could really believe that a man who "withheld both his person and his purse from the public service" in 1776-77 was a friend to the Revolution. Dickinson was not named, but "Virginius" went on to say that such men, hostile to independence, "are coming among us." The same writer, in the August 21 issue of the Journal rebuked the Republicans for taking up "new associates" who had pursued a

traitorous conduct in 1776-77, and for daring to "advocate their
Characters, and extol their importance or public utility." [50]

The answer of the Republicans to these attacks on their candidate (Dickinson himself did not reply in the newspapers until
after his election as president, and even then his defense lacked
assurance) [51] was the attack on Reed. If Dickinson was being accused of deserting the Revolutionary cause in 1776, then Reed
must also be shown to have entertained thoughts of abandoning
"the wretched remains of a broken army" [52] during that same
campaign. The queries by "Brutus" in the *Gazetteer* on September 7 were the opening guns of this counterattack.

Reed could not and did not ignore these charges. Aspersions
upon the wisdom of his decisions as leader of the state were to be
expected from political opponents, but intimations of desertion
and treason upon his part while adjutant general of the Continental Army were in a different and far more provocative cate-
gory. Reed wrote to Washington four days after the appearance
of the "Brutus" article that he never thought the winter of 1776
"would be selected as the Season of my greatest Reproach and
that I should stand publickly charged with not only meditating
but actually expressing Intentions of deserting to the Enemy." [53]

Toward disproving these charges, Reed began by writing to
John Cadwalader on September 9, for the latter had been referred
to in the newspaper article as the one to whom Reed had expressed his treasonable intentions. Reed, realizing full well that
Cadwalader was one of his most rabid political foes, was curt:
"Prejudiced as I know you are, I shall be sorry to suppose you
capable of propagating such a Sentiment or decline the opportunity of doing Justice to my Character. . . . I need make no Apology in this Case for requesting an immediate answer." [54]

Cadwalader's reply, received by Reed the following morning,
was an eager acceptance of conflict:

I can assure you . . . that I am not the author of that publication. . . .
But, sir, I have repeatedly mentioned the substance of those queries
to individuals after the conversation alluded to happened. . . . I therefore now assert, that in a conversation with you at the time and place
[December, 1776, at Bristol] mentioned in the above publication

(signed Brutus) that you expressed the substance, and I think the very words, contained in the queries.

Cadwalader had the presumption to cite the similar accusations made against Reed by Benedict Arnold at the latter's court-martial in 1780 and to state that since Reed had not replied to these, "the world very justly concluded they were true." Cadwalader also, in effect, admitted the political background of the charges he was now endorsing by stating that Reed's past mistakes might have been buried in oblivion "if your conduct in civil life had been such as could have been approved of." [55]

Reed sent back a blistering reply immediately upon receiving this letter. He was, he said, "at a loss which to admire most, the Depravity of your Heart, or the Weakness of your Understanding. Your quoting Genl. Arnold's Testimony to vindicate your own Falsehood is perfectly consistent." [56]

After these fiery exchanges, the controversy simmered on for several days while Reed was out of town attending the Bucks County Court session, and Cadwalader departed for his estate in Kent County, Maryland.[57] Reed, before leaving, composed a forthright denial, which was published in several Philadelphia newspapers on the 11th, that he had expressed the sentiments to Cadwalader referred to in the *Gazetteer* on September 7: "I do not hesitate to pronounce it an infamous Falsehood and with the Serenity of a Christian and upon the Honour of a Gentleman solemnly declare no such Conversation as alluded to in those Queries ever passed." Reed concluded by saying he was gathering "unquestionable and satisfying Proofs" of his innocence.[58]

Reed had begun this latter task the day of his first letter to Cadwalader. He had written John Cox to ask that he recall to mind those days in December, 1776, when they performed reconnaissance work for Cadwalader in New Jersey, and particularly to recollect what Reed's sentiments then were on "the State of our Affairs and my own Intentions." [59] On September 11 Reed wrote to Washington to request "a few lines expressive of your Sense of my Conduct in the Fall and Winter of the Year 1776 and particularly whether you ever heard or at any time entertained Doubts of my Fidelity." [60] Reed also sought statements from two

Philadelphians, Thomas Smith and William Shippen, Jr., whom Cadwalader had named as men who had heard him make accusations as to Reed's intended defection.

A gratifying response from the latter two was awaiting Reed when he returned to Philadelphia on September 14. Both Smith and Shippen had written to him that they did not recollect that Cadwalader ever expressed such sentiments to them.[61] Several days later Washington's reply arrived. The commander in chief wrote:

Not knowing the particular charges that are alleged against you, it is impossible for me to make a specific reply. I can therefore only say in general terms that the employments you sustained in the year 1776, and in that period of the year when we experienced our greatest distresses are a proof that you was not suspected by me of infidelity, or want of integrity; for had the least suspicion of the kind reached my mind, either from observation or report, I should most assuredly have marked you out as a fit object of resentment.

While on our retreat through Jersey, I remember your being sent from Newark, to the Assembly of New Jersey, then sitting, to rouse and animate them to spirited measures for our support; at the same time General Mifflin was sent to Pennsylvania for the same purpose. This employment was certainly a mark of my confidence in you at that time.

Your conduct, so far as it came to my immediate notice, during the short period we lay on the west [bank] of the Delaware, appeared solicitous for the public good. And your conduct at Princeton evidenced a spirit and zeal, which to me appeared laudable and becoming a man well affected to the cause we were engaged in.

Washington concluded by granting Reed's request that his letters to the latter might be made public "if absolutely necessary to your justification." [62]

Upon his return to Philadelphia, Reed touched off a final burst in the correspondence with Cadwalader. The latter, in his note of September 12, written as he was leaving for Maryland, had mentioned that "if necessary, I shall attend [you] in person for further investigation." [63] Reed regarded this as an implied invitation to a duel. In answer he wrote back that Cadwalader's observation of him during the war, "especially in the Actions at White Marsh and Monmouth (if your short stay in the field at the

former did not prevent your making any) must have satisfied you
that Considerations of personal Safety do not prevail with me over
those of Duty." If Cadwalader wished a meeting, Reed continued, he would accept the invitation "with no other Reserve
than may be necessary to make some Family arrangements." [64]
On September 23 Reed wrote again that "if by investigation you
mean a personal interview, I will endeavour to make it as convenient as possible, and will shorten the distance between us." [65]

Cadwalader did not request an immediate interview. Replying to Reed on September 30, he stated that he would await the
publication of the documents Reed had said he was collecting,
would reserve the right to give to the public his proofs of the accusations he had seconded, and then, "this business being ended,
an interview may reasonably be expected." [66] Cadwalader sent
this message to George Clymer, also a leading Republican, to be
delivered to Reed in Philadelphia. His covering letter to Clymer
is noteworthy in its revelation of the calculated effort to compromise Reed:

This will probably close our correspondence. You may perhaps think
than I have said too much, but since things have gone so far, I had
rather be thought rash than deficient. . . . The affair *must* come to a
Crisis, and though I would wish to be *understood*, I would wish to
avoid the Law.[67]

By the time Clymer delivered Cadwalader's letter to Reed, the
latter was busily assembling the materials for his publication. He
took from his files letters from Washington of 1776-80 which
demonstrated the general's confidence in him. He also brought
out two letters from Cadwalader written to him late in 1777.
These testified to the friendship and respect the writer held
toward Reed, and also as to Cadwalader's bitterness toward the
Pennsylvania constitution and his intolerance of anyone who
would perpetuate it by taking office under it.

To these letters was added an affidavit which John Cox swore
out in answer to the request Reed had made on September 9 for
his recollections concerning December, 1776. Cox certified that
Cadwalader had displayed no suspicions of Reed while they were
at Bristol, that he had never heard Cadwalader express any doubts

of Reed's perseverance in the cause, and that, on the contrary, Reed's opinions were "much depended on" and he was "treated with the most unreserved confidence." Cox related that Reed, during frequent private conversations with him at this time, "never intimated, nor had the subscriber the least reason to suspect he had any intention of, abandoning the cause or arms of his country to join those of the enemy." [68]

Reed also obtained depositions from his brother Bowes and from Daniel Ellis, both residents of Burlington, New Jersey, in December, 1776. "Brutus" had charged that Reed had suggested that Bowes remain in Burlington, though its occupation by the Hessians seemed imminent, and swear allegiance to Britain if the enemy did take possession. In his affidavit, Bowes denied that his brother had so advised him. He swore that "during the said time or at any other his brother never intimated to this deponent in the most distant manner any advice or encouragement to seek protection of the enemy . . . and never expressed to him any apprehensions of the success of the cause." [69] Ellis, in his affidavit, swore that Reed had opened contact with Count von Donop, the commander of the Hessian forces near Burlington, at the request of the townspeople of Burlington who sought its neutralization, and that he himself had carried this innocuous request from Reed to Donop, not any request for British protection for the former.[70]

Early in November, 1782, before leaving Philadelphia to represent Pennsylvania at the Trenton hearing against Connecticut, Reed left these letters and sworn statements, together with his own commentary and defense, with Francis Bailey, publisher of the *Freeman's Journal,* for publication in pamphlet form. In a memorandum to Bailey, Reed stated that the papers were to be shown to any gentleman who wished to assure himself of their authenticity.[71] There was a delay when the manuscript of Reed's own composition was accidentally destroyed in Bailey's shop. Thus it was not until January, 1783, that Reed's defense appeared. It was entitled *Remarks on a Late Publication in the Independent Gazetteer, with a Short Address to the People of Pennsylvania on the Many Libels and Slanders Which Have Lately Appeared Against the Author.*

The documents presented therein by Reed, his honest account of his actions in the Trenton-Princeton campaign, and his success in indicating the partisan political background of the charges against him were impressive, but, for that very reason, all the less likely to end the controversy. Reed had also, in his defense, attacked Cadwalader and his political associates as friends of the Tories, and of course this charge spawned rebuttal. As Major John Armstrong wrote to his father, General John Armstrong:

Mr. Reed's pamphlet . . . will do him much honor. There is a great deal of the dignity of a retiring Governor in it. But do you imagine that a man of Cadwalader's abounding pride and deficient wisdom, will kiss the rod or sit quietly under it? Is anything so sensibly humble to be expected from him? Provocation has already produced reply—Reply will beget rejoinders—and thus the wound will go on festering.[72]

General Nathanael Greene agreed that the *Remarks* did Reed credit. He wrote the latter that "it is much admired. Everybody reads it with pleasure and conviction. I wish I had been at Philadelphia [Greene was still in South Carolina]; I would have given you all the support my little influence might have had." [73]

Armstrong was correct in predicting that Cadwalader would make a rejoinder to Reed's pamphlet. But the political situation which had given rise to the attack on the former president in the first place rendered this rejoinder as much a Republican party measure as Cadwalader's personal one. It might be thought that the Republicans had no need to continue the attack on Reed after having succeeded in their fall program for 1782 by electing John Dickinson to the council and then raising him to the presidency of the state.[74] But the attacks on Dickinson's past record did not cease with these successes. They became more biting, particularly those from the pen of "Valerius" writing in the *Freeman's Journal* in November and December. The feeling that the attack on Reed had to be continued in order to counteract the fire directed at Dickinson was undoubtedly strengthened among Republicans by a suspicion that Reed himself was "Valerius." [75] This suspicion seems unfounded. Most of the articles by this anonymous writer appeared in the Philadelphia papers while

Reed was absent from the city at the Trenton hearing. One of Reed's letters written from Trenton to George Bryan, a close friend and a leading Radical who would have shared his political secrets, mentions "Valerius," but clearly as a third person. Reed commented that this author's attacks were a "wild fire." He hoped their intensity might be reduced, and if they could be, he thought they should be continued.[76]

Another motivation which influenced the Republicans in supporting a prolongation of the Cadwalader-Reed feud is to be found in the approach of the time when the constitution and the actions of the administrations which had held office since its promulgation in 1776, Reed's among them, would be officially reviewed and judged by the council of censors. This unique body, provided for in article 47 of the constitution, was to meet for the first time in November, 1783, and inquire whether, over the past seven years, "the legislative and executive branches of government have performed their duty as guardians of the people." They were empowered to recommend to the assembly the repeal of laws which they regarded as contrary to the principles of the constitution. The censors also possessed the authority, and it was for this reason that the anti-constitutionalists were most interested in controlling this council, to "call a Convention, to meet within two years after their sitting, if there appear to them an absolute necessity of amending any article of the Constitution . . . and adding such as are necessary." [77] Control of this council, whose members would be elected in October, 1783, promised an opportunity to alter drastically the constitution, a goal sought by the Republicans since its promulgation. Popular indignation directed against Reed seemed to the Republicans to be a way to insure victory in the choice of censors. The attacks upon him (and the Radical attacks upon Dickinson as well) were thus part of the struggle for control of the council of censors which in turn would decide the struggle over the constitution.[78]

Cadwalader might not have returned to the lists himself if Dickinson had been a more aggressive controversialist. But the latter's replies to the critical attacks by "Valerius" and others, replies published in the *Pennsylvania Gazette* of December 24,

1782, and January 1, 8, and 22, 1783, were not at all to the taste of the firebrands of the party. The latter particularly reprobated Dickinson's action in printing, in his January 8 article, an apology for having mistakenly charged in a previous article that Reed had presided at and spoken at public meetings held to demand revision of the constitution.[79]

Thus Cadwalader continued as the agent for the accusations against Reed. After Reed's pamphlet appeared, he began preparing his reply. Following the technique of the former, he secured a number of letters and affidavits to bear out his charge of Reed's traitorous intentions. The sources of this testimony are revealing. Philemon Dickinson was the president's brother; George Clymer, John Nixon, Benjamin Rush, and Jacob Rush, his brother, were leading anti-constitutionalists. A statement was obtained from a Joseph Ellis of Gloucester County, New Jersey, whom Reed had prosecuted in the Greenwich tea burning incident in 1775. Another was obtained from the son of Reed's old rival in New Jersey, a man who had openly made his peace with the British in 1776, Charles Read. Not one document contemporary to December, 1776, in fact no document prior to 1782, was produced by Cadwalader. Benjamin Rush was the only one who made a direct statement that he himself had heard Reed utter defeatist sentiments in December, 1776. None of the deponents were able to state that Cadwalader had told them at that time that Reed had indicated an intention of taking a British protection. Dickinson and Nixon could only say that Reed had been gloomy. Clymer "charged" his memory on March 2, 1783, and asserted that in 1778 he had heard Cadwalader speak of Reed's weakness of 1776; so too did Thomas Pryor, also an anti-constitutionalist, on March 8. A statement from Alexander Hamilton, solicited by Cadwalader in a letter of March 2, put the date of Cadwalader's revelation in the fall of 1777.[80] Hamilton's sympathies in the political struggle in Pennsylvania, it need hardly be said, were with the conservative Republicans. Some of the replies Cadwalader received to his requests for recollections of 1776 were entirely unfavorable to his cause. These papers, though preserved among the Cadwalader manuscripts, were not included in his pamphlet. Such was the letter from Colonel Robert Harrison, Reed's successor as Washington's secretary, in which Harrison pointed out quite clearly the innocent nature of Reed's correspondence with the Hessian commander, von Donop.[81] Cadwalader was dishonest enough to ignore this information and charge that Reed "absolutely applied to Count Donop for protection." [82]

This unconvincing testimony and a long invective by Cadwalader which significantly broadened the original attack on Reed (and did much to reveal its motivation) by castigating him in bitter terms for taking office under and giving support to the Pennsylvania constitution of 1776 were published in April, 1783, under the title *A Reply to General Joseph Reed's Remarks on a Late Publication in the Independent Gazetteer.* Cadwalader hoped that the pamphlet would goad Reed into the duel which had been bruited in their correspondence of the past September: his friends advised him that it would be improper for him to challenge Reed. He had George Morgan visit Reed on April 17 to tell the latter that he had waited for him to call after the *Reply* had been delivered to him, and that he was not now planning to leave Philadelphia. Reed asked Morgan twice whether this message was "mere matter of Information" or whether it implied more than that. When Morgan replied that it was merely information, Reed made no answer.[83] In August, Reed issued another public denial of Cadwalader's charges and, in passing, attributed the actual authorship of his opponent's pamphlet to the Reverend Dr. William Smith, the former rector of the College of Philadelphia, and Dr. Benjamin Rush, for, Reed charged, Cadwalader's literary talents were "unequal to the Composition of a Single Page." [84]

Polemical writing rarely settles anything, and these exchanges of Cadwalader and Reed were no exception. Within less than three years of Reed's last declaration, both men were dead. The political struggle which had given birth to this controversy went on with new agents to personalize it. What is remarkable, however, is the persistence of the Cadwalader-Reed controversy in American historiography. Some mention of this has been made in passing in previous chapters: the charge made in 1866 by

George Bancroft, for example, that Reed had not only intended seeking a British protection as Cadwalader had charged, but had actually obtained one, a charge disproven by the research of William S. Stryker in 1876; the bald assumption made in 1943 by Ellsworth Eliot, Jr. that a British protection form made out to a Joseph Reed in 1777 belonged to the Joseph Reed who is our subject here, a charge considered in Chapter VI. Somewhat more understandable, but equally to be reprobated, were the revivals of the controversy in the 1840's and 1850's by descendants of the Reverend Dr. Smith and Benjamin Rush on the one hand (none of the Cadwalader family joined in this, interestingly enough) and Joseph Reed's grandson, William B. Reed, on the other. Their exchanges generated far more heat than light, they unearthed no new materials relevant to the subject, and in some cases complete untruths were put forward.[85] A description of their contents would be fruitless for the purposes of this study.[86]

As to Reed himself, the controversy aroused in him a determination never again to accept public office. He wrote General Greene in March, 1783, that if the latter came to see him, "I shall be found very poor, with a great many enemies, chiefly political, but much happier that I have been for many years, and if I am a competent judge, a much cleverer fellow than when President of Pennsylvania with numerous worshippers." [87] Reed abided by his determination when pressed to stand as a candidate for the council of censors that fall. His reply stated that he knew he was not one of the "happy few" who possessed the "depth of Judgment, Extent of Information, Moderation of Temper and Exercise of Candour" which that office required.[88]

Reed might have added that he did not intend to be in Philadelphia through the winter of 1783-84. Now that the war was over (the provisional treaty was ratified by Congress on April 15, 1783, and the final one signed at Paris on September 3) several circumstances turned his thoughts to a voyage to England. His health had been failing and a sea voyage had been advised.[89] His aged mother-in-law, who had been living with him thirteen years, was impatient now to return to England before she died to see her son again and the grandchildren there she had never

seen.[90] Dennis DeBerdt was equally anxious to have his mother
returned to England to join his household. His letter to Reed of
June 30, 1783, for example, stated he expected her back with him
"in the course of this year." [91]

In addition to these entirely personal factors, Reed had other
motives for the trip. The College of New Jersey, of which he had
been elected a trustee in 1781, was facing a financial crisis. No
funds existed to repair the wartime damage to Nassau Hall, used
several times as a barracks by both armies, or replace the scattered
library and scientific equipment, and hire new teachers. At a
meeting of the trustees held at the college on October 22, 1783,
it was resolved to send a mission to seek funds in Europe for the
institution. Reed and the Reverend John Witherspoon, president of the college and a New Jersey patriot leader, were asked to
undertake this venture. Both men consented, and Reed offered
to serve the trustees in England without asking any expense allowance, an offer gratefully accepted. The commission for
Witherspoon and Reed was signed that same day by the president
of the board of trustees, Governor William Livingston of New
Jersey.[92]

The affairs of the West Jersey Society, the venture in lands in
New Jersey and Pennsylvania in which Reed was a stockholder,
also prompted him to contact personally the major stockholders
in London. The society's American agent, Thomas Hunt of New
York, had died in 1778. The war, of course, had prevented the
society from taking proper action toward a successor. Reed, on
his own initiative, had stepped into the breach and had attempted
to protect the society's claims in the two states by paying the taxes
on its holdings and instituting actions to prevent the exploitation
of the timber on the lands.[93] In 1781 he had obtained a special
act from the New Jersey legislature vesting in him powers "nearly
conformable to those of the deceased Agent." Reed's effort to
obtain a similar grant in Pennsylvania was tabled by the Republican-dominated legislature in October, 1781.[94] By March, 1782,
he had laid out over £237 from his own pocket and had collected
but £57 on the society's account. His desire to be reimbursed for
these outlays, and a conviction that the society must protect its

lands against confiscation (as an alien holder) by prompt sale or by a trust arrangement conveying title to Americans,[95] made Reed anxious to meet with the stockholders in London.

On December 20, 1783, after making a will and after designating Jared Ingersoll to carry on his law business, Reed left for England aboard the *Washington*.[96] Accompanying him were Mrs. DeBerdt and Martha ("Patty"), his eldest daughter, who served as a companion for her grandmother. Dr. Witherspoon sailed in the *Washington* too. Reed bore letters of introduction from General Greene to Count Rochambeau and to Count D'Estaing in the event he had time to travel from England to France, but he was not able to do so.[97]

The *Washington* made a speedy crossing of the Atlantic, for Reed was in London by late January, 1784. Mrs. DeBerdt was happily reunited with her son, and Reed and his daughter were also warmly welcomed at Dennis DeBerdt's home. Reed and Witherspoon lost no time in contacting American diplomats in Europe to inform them of their arrival and mission. Reed wrote to John Adams, then at The Hague, and to John Jay in Paris. Cordial replies were received from each; [98] but the fund-raising campaign turned out to be a complete failure. American causes, Reed and Witherspoon found, no matter how worthy, were not popular in England or Scotland (which Witherspoon visited), and the lack of response there discouraged an appeal on the Continent. After Witherspoon returned to America and his expenses were deducted (Reed had paid his own), the miserable balance of only £5 remained from the meager donations which had been secured.[99]

This disappointment, unfortunately, was typical of the unproductive nature of Reed's trip. Aside from reuniting Mrs. DeBerdt and Dennis, and aside from making provisions for his daughter to stay in England with the DeBerdts while she attended school in London, it produced no benefit. His health did not improve, but rather, if there was any change, deteriorated.[100] The West Jersey Society affair did not go well. Though Reed attended two meetings of the board of the society, on March 8 and 25, he failed to obtain a settlement of the sums he had paid out in its name, a failure he regarded with some bitterness, for he felt he had preserved the society's interests from complete ruin.[101]

A greater disappointment concerning the society was its refusal to agree with Reed that its interests should be put up for sale. Here Reed seems to have played something of a double part. To the society he painted a dark picture of possible confiscation, disputed boundaries, and depredations by squatters.[102] To several Americans in England, he wrote enthusiastically of the "handsome American fortune" which could be secured if they would join him in offering to purchase the society's lands in America. He predicted that an offer of £10,000, which could probably be paid in installments, would be accepted by the stockholders.[103] But this bid was apparently rejected at the March 25 meeting which Reed attended, for nothing more appears concerning this scheme. After returning to America, Reed did state in a letter to DeBerdt that he now regretted that he had not agreed to the price asked by the society, for he was confident land values were on the rise.[104] Despite the collapse of his purchase plan, Reed retained his shares in the society, sixty-five of the fifteen hundred outstanding.

Augmenting these personal and financial disappointments was Reed's blighted hope, a rather naive one it would seem, that the war had cleared the air between Britain and America, and that the English would admit their error in attempting coercion of their former colonists and, without resentment, forge cordial bonds of friendship with the United States. A few weeks in England disabused Reed of this opinion. In February he wrote from London to General Greene:

The affairs of this country are so connected with ours that whatever we may wish or feel towards them, they must affect us. I find we have flattered ourselves too much in the belief of returning cordiality, and also indulged too much vanity in supposing that our conduct in the war, and final success, have created sentiments of respect and esteem. It is not so. The war [against America] was a popular one, and only ceased to be so when all hope of final success ceased. . . . The Court and its party, the army, the navy, clergy, and, in short, the general class of gentry, find the Pride of Old England so mortified by the issue of the war, that they cannot speak of the country [the United

States] and its inhabitants in any other dialect than that of rebellion.[105]

Reed expressed similar opinions to other correspondents. To John Adams he wrote that the English "seem to labour under the insuperable curse of never profiting by experience in anything that respects" America. He admitted to being disappointed by their general lack of a conciliatory spirit.[106] Reed wrote in the same vein to William Bradford back in Philadelphia, and commented that no American he met in England thought it wise for the United States to send a Minister to Britain at present for fear "he would be neglected, if not insulted." [107]

Letters from Bradford, Charles Pettit, and Jared Ingersoll brightened the gloom of Reed's seven-month sojourn in England. Bradford sent him news of Pennsylvania politics, Pettit and Ingersoll more eagerly awaited news of his children. Pettit was caring for Esther and four-year-old George Washington Reed, and Ingersoll had taken Joseph and Dennis into his household during the father's absence.[108] Reed wrote a letter to Joseph the tone of which disproves the charge of his critics that he had become worm-eaten by bitterness:

Remember my dear Boy that to be a great Man, or what is better a good Man, you must mind your Book when you are young, be obliging and kind to all your Companions, avoid all bad Language and above all never tell a Lye on any account nor take any Thing which is not your own. Think what pleasure it will be to me to find when I come Home that every Body loves and praises you, what an example it will be to your Brothers who will mind what you do. It will not be long now before I see you if I am well, and I shall not leave you again very soon.[109]

The last sentence of this paragraph has a tragic ring to it. Reed realized by the time he wrote it, May 2, that he was a very sick man, and that his voyage and stay in England had not brought a restoration of his health. On this same day he wrote to William Bradford that he wished to return to America as speedily as possible. He also said, in answer to a reference in a letter from Bradford as to marrying again, "My hour is past. I am not unreasonable in my claims upon human life." [110]

It was mid-August, however, before Reed bid adieu to the
DeBerdts and his daughter Martha, and left England for the voyage to Philadelphia. It was late September when he reached
home. Home was now at a different address, for his lease on the
Third Street house had expired while he was away and Pettit,
after refusing to renew for him at the price demanded, found
Reed a new house on Chestnut Street.[111] Reed found his children well but his sister Mary very sick and living with Bowes
Reed in Burlington. Reed had depended on her to keep house
for him and care for the children as she had done since his wife's
death in 1780, but that was now impossible. Dennis moved into
the new house with him, but Esther and George Washington continued to live with the Pettits. Joseph, Jr. was living with the
Moravians in Bethlehem, studying German in accordance with
his father's ideas on this subject.[112]

Reed's arrival in Philadelphia came just as the council of censors was dissolving itself and the 1784 political campaigning for
the October elections was coming to a climax. The fact that the
censors ruled that the constitution of 1776 be given a new seven-
year lease on life augured well for the Radicals. Reed, however,
steered clear of the "furious" electioneering. The savage Republican attacks of a personal nature, this year aimed at George Bryan
rather than himself, shocked him anew. This spectacle, and the
low ebb of Congressional power at the time, led him to express
the fear that America would "shew less Wisdom in Peace than
we did Skill in War." [113]

In the October elections, the political pendulum swung back
sharply in favor of the Radicals. The Republican majority in
the previous assembly was destroyed. In the new house the anti-
constitutionalists had barely one-fourth of the seats. The counter-
revolution was decisively checked.[114]

One result of this abrupt reversal of the counterrevolution was
a new public honor for Reed, the last before his death. In a gesture of vindication to a wronged man, his name was brought
forward for election to Congress when the new assembly met.
Reed argued against the action on the grounds of ill health and
his inability to leave Philadelphia (Congress was now sitting in

Trenton) while his family affairs were unsettled,[115] but the legislature paid no heed and formally elected him one of the state's five delegates on November 16.[116]   The ravages of Reed's illness, however, had now become crippling, and his death came before he had taken his seat in Congress.   Fittingly enough, Charles Pettit was elected in April, 1785, to fill the vacancy.[117]

The last months of Reed's life were painful ones.   By January, 1785, it was clear that he had but a short time to live.   A paralysis set in which first deprived him of the use of his limbs, and then of speech.[118]   He died on March 5, not yet forty-four years of age. He was buried on the 9th in the yard of the Second Presbyterian Church beside his wife.[119]   On the day of his funeral, the *Freeman's Journal* carried this tribute from the pen of Philip Freneau:

> No single act engag'd his manly mind
>   In every scene his active genius shin'd
> Nature in him in honour to our age
>   At once composed the soldier and the sage.
> Firm to his purpose, vigilant and bold
>   Detesting traitors and despising gold
> He scorned all bribes from Britain's hostile throne
>   For all his country's wrongs were thrice his own.
> Reed, rest in peace, for time's impartial page
>   Shall blast the wrongs of this ungrateful age.
> Long in these climes thy name shall flourish fair
>   The statesman's Pattern and the Poet's care
> Long on these plains thy memory shall remain
>   And still new tributes from new ages gain.

Conclusion

THOUGH obscured by the great controversy which closed his career, and beclouded by the very diversity of his roles in the American Revolution, the contributions of Joseph Reed to that cause entitle him to high rank among the patriots who stood beside the major figures of the era. His role was unique. While Reed was among the most reluctant of all the American leaders to accept as inevitable the break with Britain, he later became the standard-bearer of the democratic forces in Pennsylvania which effected the most sweeping internal revolution the War for Independence produced. These two positions seem irreconcilable, and Reed's critics were to charge him with opportunistic equivocation. It is certainly true that all Reed's actions from 1770 through 1783 are not entirely consistent; it is true, too, that he was envious of high public position and public esteem. But this is merely to admit that Reed was not a patriot without flaw. He was not guilty of bad faith. The moderate approach, the conciliatory effort, the sophistication which eschews extremes— this was the essence of Reed's public life, and this was, inevitably, a posture which invited periodic charges of weakness, of evasion, of betrayal.

Reed began to play his distinctive role in the troubled years which preceded the War for Independence as he labored to mark out a middle ground where American liberties and British imperial control could meet harmoniously. For while he opposed the conservatism of Galloway or even Dickinson—conservatism which balked at democracy—he simultaneously strove to moderate the fiery demands for war of Roberdeau and Thomson. Reed's letters to Lord Dartmouth and others in England testify eloquently to his appreciation of the threat poised by British policies; his actions as a leader in the provincial conventions and in the last proprietary legislature of Pennsylvania reveal with equal clarity his desire to hold open the door of reconciliation to the last.

When war came, Reed's positive services to his country were many. His contributions as Washington's secretary and confidant during those first months at Cambridge were invaluable. As adjutant general of the Continental Army in 1776 he again lifted many administrative burdens from the harassed commander in chief. In the field, Reed displayed skill and dash which, had he accepted the proffered post as commander of the American cavalry, might well have brought him the sturdy fame of a soldier-hero.

Despite the brevity of his ten-month term in Congress, Reed left his mark in that sphere of service as well. In his capacity as chairman of the committee on the reorganization of the army, he combined his legal training and his legislative and military experience to achieve reforms which won Washington's gratitude. Reed's orderly mind and his capacity for hard work made him a valued member of numerous Congressional committees.

As president of Pennsylvania, Reed again essayed the role of the mediator rather than that of the aggressive political partisan. Too perceptive and too cosmopolitan to adopt the doctrinaire outlook of the extremist, Reed used his influence toward a moderate program upon which he hoped factions might combine harmoniously. But he faced great difficulties, for his administration coincided with that period of financial chaos, profiteering, and growing war-weariness during which the cause of the Revolution sank to its lowest level. Then, too, Reed made errors of political judgment and these undermined his chances of softening the factional strife. When he found to his chagrin that the Republicans would not cooperate with him and relax their opposition to government under the constitution of 1776, he was driven to become more and more the partisan himself. But he was never the complete Radical, and the modifying influence he exerted, in fiscal policy, for example, prevented an even more divisive convulsion in Pennsylvania. Yet, Reed's very reputation as a moderate revolutionary produced the Cadwalader attack upon him. The Republicans had to discredit Reed's party, and since most

Pennsylvanians could hardly be led to regard Reed as a dangerous, wild-eyed radical, he was splashed with the opposite stain, treason to the patriot cause.

The charges and controversies which Reed's political career engendered cannot obscure his devotion to a cause which he embraced slowly and upon the basis of deep conviction. The urbanity and breadth of outlook which he possessed, and which Washington recognized and leaned upon so heavily, sustained itself above the partisanship and the provincialism of his day. An expert prognosticator of political developments, a leader in the legal profession, an eighteenth-century man with his interest in both great principles and diverse activities, Joseph Reed most significantly of all deserves the title of patriot.

Notes

CHAPTER I: THE STUDENT

1. *Pennsylvania Gazette*, Oct. 20, 1763.

2. J. W. Reed, *History of the Reed Family in Europe and America*, p. 458; Perley, *The History of Salem, Massachusetts*, III, 420.

3. Hunterdon County Wills, Folder 118J, Office of the Secretary of State, Trenton, New Jersey.

4. First Presbyterian Church, Trenton, New Jersey, Verbatim Copy of All Charters, Deeds, Records, and Manuscripts in the Archives of the Presbyterian Church of Trenton, p. 55.

5. F. Lee, *History of Trenton, New Jersey*, p. 140; Raum, *History of the City of Trenton, New Jersey*, p. 111.

6. J. Hall, *History of the Presbyterian Church in Trenton, New Jersey*, p. 40.

7. M. B. Reed, *A Family Record*, p. 8.

8. J. Reed, *Reed Family*, p. 458.

9. Walker and others, *A History of Trenton, 1679-1929*, I, 85, 102-8.

10. Rachel Bowes Sayre to Joseph Reed, May 11, 1764, Reed Manuscripts, Vol. I, New-York Historical Society. This collection will be cited hereafter as Reed MSS.

11. Charles Pettit to Joseph Reed, Dec. 20, 1765, *ibid.*

12. Boyer, *Early Forges and Furnaces in New Jersey*, pp. 39, 107, 131.

13. Hall, *Presbyterian Church*, p. 44.

14. Nelson, *New Jersey Biographical and Genealogical Notes*, p. 182.

15. Quoted in Montgomery, *A History of the University of Pennsylvania from its Foundation to A.D. 1770*, p. 139.

16. Cheyney, *History of the University of Pennsylvania, 1740-1940*, pp. 31-37.

17. Montgomery, *University of Pennsylvania*, p. 368.

18. Lippencott, *The University of Pennsylvania, Franklin's College*, p. 20; Jackson, "A Philadelphia Schoolmaster of the Eighteenth Century," *Pennsylvania Magazine of History and Biography*, XXXV (1911), 316-19; Cheyney, *University of Pennsylvania*, p. 38.

19. Walker, *History of Trenton*, II, 708; M. Reed, *Family Record*, p. 8.

20. Andrew Reed collected money in Trenton for the college in 1749. Lee, *History of Trenton*, p. 31.

21. Todd, *A General History of the Burr Family*, p. 47.

22. Wertenbaker, *Princeton, 1746-1896*, p. 25.

23. President Aaron Burr's Account Book, 1752-1758, p. 68. Princeton University Library.

24. *Ibid.*, pp. 68-69, 124-25; McAnear, "The Selection of an Alma Mater by Pre-Revolutionary Students," *Pennsylvania Magazine of History and Biography*, LXXIII (1949), 433.

25. Wertenbaker, *Princeton*, pp. 28-29.

26. Burr's Account Book, p. 68; DeWitt, "Historical Sketch of Princeton University," in *Memorial Book of the Sesquicentennial Celebration of the Founding of the College of New Jersey*, pp. 355-56. DeWitt draws heavily upon the letters of Joseph Shippen from the college to his father, 1750.

27. Burr's Account Book, p. 68.

28. DeWitt, "History of Princeton University," in *Memorial Book*, p. 358.

29. Burr's Account Book, p. 124. In 1783, in his will, Reed directed that his sons be taught German and French but "on no account to meddle with the dead languages . . . unless they discover remarkable genius." Reed MSS, Vol. X.

30. Collins, *Princeton*, pp. 34-37.

31. The college authorities desired to name the building Belcher Hall, but New Jersey's governor declined the honor and suggested the name Nassau Hall. Wertenbaker, *Princeton*, p. 37.

32. Collins, *Princeton*, pp. 38-41.

33. *Ibid.*, pp. 41-44.

34. DeWitt, "History of Princeton University," in *Memorial Book*, p. 358.

35. Burr's Account Book, pp. 124-25, 186.

36. Wertenbaker, *Princeton*, pp. 39-40.

37. McAnear, "Selection of Alma Mater," *Pennsylvania Magazine of History and Biography*, LXXIII (1949), 432.

38. Maclean, *History of the College of New Jersey from its Origins in 1746 to the Commencement of 1854*, I, 169-70. Among Reed's fellow graduates were Timothy Edwards, brother of Mrs. Burr, Nicholas Bayard of New York, Peter Faneuil of Boston, and a cousin of Reed's, Stephen Sayre.

39. *General Catalogue of Princeton University, 1746-1906*, p. 85. A notebook of Reed's, dated 1758, is in the Reed MSS.

40. Nelson, *Biographical and Genealogical Notes*, p. 197.

41. Hamlin, *Legal Education in Colonial New York*, pp. 40-46.

42. *Ibid.*, pp. 64-65.

43. Reed MSS, Vol. I.

44. Kemmerer, *Path to Freedom; The Struggle for Self-Government in Colonial New Jersey, 1703-1776*, p. 275n.

45. William Franklin to William Strahan, Oct. 14, 1763, in Hart, ed., "Letters from William Franklin to William Strahan," *Pennsylvania Magazine of History and Biography*, XXXV (1911), 431.

Chapter II: England: Law and Love

1. Edward Jones, *American Members of the Inns of Court*, pp. ix-xxx.

2. T. Cunningham, ed., *The History and Antiquities of the Four Inns of Court*, p. vi.

3. Leigh, *The Law Student's Guide*, p. 23.

4. Hamlin, *Legal Education in Colonial New York*, pp. 17, 21.

5. *The Annual Register . . . for 1763*, p. 114; John Ewing, a Philadelphia friend, in writing to Reed commented upon the latter's "remarkable Deliverance . . . when so many hundreds perished around you in the Channel." Reed MSS, Vol. I.

6. See Mrs. Rachel Sayre to Joseph Reed, May 11, 1764, Reed MSS, Vol. I. Since very few of Reed's letters from England have been preserved, details of his life there must be gleaned from allusions to his letters in the replies from his correspondents, most of which Reed kept.

7. Memorandum of disbursements, Reed MSS, Vol. I.

8. Joseph Reed to Charles Pettit, June 11, 1764, *ibid.*

9. Charles Pettit to Joseph Reed, June 22, 1764, and Richard Stockton to Joseph Reed, Oct. 8, 1764, *ibid.*

10. Sturgess, comp., *Register of Admissions to the Honourable Society of the Middle Temple*, I, 361-62.

11. Banta, *The Sayre Family*, p. 91.

12. Malone and Johnson, eds., *Dictionary of American Biography*, XVI, 406. Cited hereafter as *DAB*.

13. Boyd, ed., *The Susquehannah Company Papers*, II, 150-52. In 1768 Sayre became a partner of the Lees, Washingtons, and Calverts in the formation of the Mississippi Company. *Ibid.*, p. 153n.

14. *DAB*, XVI, 406; see also Dennis DeBerdt to Joseph Reed, Jan. 26, 1771, Reed MSS, Vol. II.

15. Andrew Reed to Joseph Reed, June 20, 1764, Reed MSS, Vol. I.

16. Joseph Reed to Charles Pettit, June 11, 1764, *ibid.*

17. Charles Pettit to Joseph Reed, May 2, 1764, *ibid.*

18. Richard Stockton to Joseph Reed, April 8, 1764; John Coxe to Joseph Reed, June 25, 1764; William Franklin to Joseph Reed, Sept. 23, 1764, *ibid.* See also Joseph Reed to Richard Stockton in the

Bancroft transcripts of Joseph Reed papers at the New York Public Library.

19. See, e.g., Abraham Hunt to Joseph Reed, April 10, 1764; Moore Furman to Reed, June 23, 1764; Daniel Coxe to Reed, Feb. 2, 1764; and Richard Stockton to Reed, Nov. 26, 1764, Reed MSS, Vol. I.

20. William Franklin to Joseph Reed, Sept. 23, 1764; John Coxe, Jr. to Reed, June 25, 1764; and Charles Pettit to Reed, March 14, 1764, *ibid.*

21. Joseph Reed to Charles Pettit, June 11, 1764, *ibid.*

22. Charles Pettit to Joseph Reed, June 22, 1764, *ibid.*

23. Moore Furman to Joseph Reed, June 23, 1764, *ibid.*

24. Richard Stockton to Joseph Reed, April 8, 1764, *ibid.*

25. John Coxe, Jr. to Joseph Reed, June 25, 1764, *ibid.*

26. Joseph Reed to Richard Stockton, June 11, 1764. Bancroft transcripts, New York Public Library.

27. Thomas Ruston to Joseph Reed, April 30, 1764, Reed MSS, Vol. I. Ruston later practiced in London. See Butterfield, *John Witherspoon Comes to America*, p. 94.

28. Reed apparently visited Bath at least twice, early in the spring of 1764 and again during a tour he made in September. See Daniel Coxe to Joseph Reed, July 11, 1764, and Peter Wikoff to Reed, Jan. 19, 1765, Reed MSS, Vol. I.

29. *DAB*, V, 180; Burns, *The Colonial Agents of New England*, p. 8.

30. William Shippen, Jr., for example, was a frequent guest of the DeBerdts in the summer and fall of 1759.

31. Esther DeBerdt to Joseph Reed, Nov. 9, 1765, Reed MSS, Box 1.

32. W. B. Reed, *The Life of Esther DeBerdt, Afterwards Esther Reed of Pennsylvania*, p. 34. Cited hereafter as W. B. Reed, *Esther.*

33. Ellet, *The Women of the American Revolution*, I, 47.

34. W. B. Reed, *Esther*, p. 23.

35. Stephen Sayre wrote to Reed on Feb. 20, 1765, "I would lay my Life that he [DeBerdt] could not have found an objection of ever so trifling a nature had that grand one been removed, The Want of Money." Reed MSS, Vol. I. See also Pettit to Reed, Dec. 20, 1764, *ibid.*

36. Esther DeBerdt to Joseph Reed, "Saturday Morning," 1764, Reed MSS, Box 1.

37. This change of heart occurred by early November, [1764], for on Nov. 9 Joseph and Esther saw the Lord Mayor's Show in London together. See Esther DeBerdt to Joseph Reed, Nov. 9, 1765, Reed MSS, Box 1. That Mr. DeBerdt did not consent to an engagement is indicated in Esther DeBerdt to Joseph Reed, Feb. 22, 1765, *ibid.*

38. Feb. 22, 1765, *ibid.*

39. Bowes Reed to Joseph Reed, June 22, 1764, Reed MSS, Vol. I.

40. Charles Pettit to Joseph Reed, Dec. 20, 1764, *ibid.*

41. Abraham Hunt to Joseph Reed, April 10, 1764, *ibid.*

42. In writing to Reed on April 11, 1764, Moore Furman mentioned "the Sparing manner in which you are Supply'd." *Ibid.*

43. Reed MSS, Vol. I.

44. Daniel Coxe to Joseph Reed, July 11 and Nov. 10, 1764, *ibid.*

45. See Esther DeBerdt to Joseph Reed, Nov. 1, 1764, Reed MSS, Box 1.

46. W. B. Reed, *Esther*, p. 27.

47. See Joseph Reed to Esther DeBerdt, Feb. 26, and March 4 and 7, 1765, Reed MSS, Vol. I. John Macpherson, the trusted confidant of Joseph and Esther, was captain of the *Britannia*. Joseph's father and perhaps he himself had owned shares in privateering voyages made by Macpherson in this ship during the war with France. See Charles Pettit to Joseph Reed, March 14 and Dec. 20, 1764, *ibid.*

CHAPTER III: THE COLONIAL COUNSELOR

1. See Charles Pettit to Joseph Reed, Dec. 20, 1764, Reed MSS, Vol. I; Esther DeBerdt to Reed, June 28, 1765, Reed MSS, Box 1; and Kemmerer, *Path to Freedom*, pp. 280-81.

2. W. B. Reed, *Esther*, p. 72; New Jersey Deeds, Liber A-B, p. 51, Office of the Secretary of State, Trenton. Amwell is now Hopewell, N. J.

3. Reed to Esther DeBerdt, Jan. 13, 1766, W. B. Reed, *Esther*, p. 70.

4. The property was described in an unproductive advertisement for sale in the *Pennsylvania Journal*, March 8, 1764. See *Documents Relating to the Colonial, Revolutionary and Post-Revolutionary History of the State of New Jersey*, XXIV, 330. Cited hereafter as *N. J. Archives.*

5. Hunterdon County, Minutes of the Court of Common Pleas, Vol. X, Hall of Records, Flemington.

6. New Jersey Supreme Court Minutes, Vol. "1765-67," pp. 136, 172-76, Standard Master's Office, State Annex Building, Trenton. On the Stamp Act's impact see Reed to Esther DeBerdt, Jan. 13, 1766, W. B. Reed, *Esther*, p. 72.

7. Hunterdon County Minutes, Vol. X.

8. See Reed's advice to Charles Pettit, who was to follow him in the legal profession, in his letters of Jan. 14 and Feb. 25, 1775, Reed MSS, Vol. III. Reed's brother Bowes also became an attorney.

9. Quoted in Watson, *Annals of Philadelphia and Pennsylvania*, I, 320.

10. See *N. J. Archives*, XVII, 500-512, and Burlington County, Minutes of Court for Common Pleas, Vol. "1767-83," p. 89, County Clerk's Office, Mount Holly.

11. R. Field, *The Provincial Courts of New Jersey*, pp. 164-70; Fisher, *New Jersey as a Royal Province*, pp. 256-60.

12. W. B. Reed, *Esther*, p. 115.

13. See Esther's letters of Nov. 15 and Dec. 8, 1765, and that of Feb. 7, 1766, to Reed, Reed MSS, Box 1.

14. See Esther DeBerdt to Reed, Aug. 8, Sept. 19, and Nov. 9, 1765, *ibid.* Reed did become DeBerdt's attorney in the colonies, empowered to collect balances, etc. See DeBerdt to Reed, Feb. 15, 1766, *ibid.*, and DeBerdt to Sayre, July 29, 1766, in DeBerdt, *Letters, 1757-1770*, ed. by Matthews, p. 318.

15. See Sayre to Reed, June 19 and Sept. 3, 1766, in W. B. Reed, *Esther*, pp. 85-87, and Esther DeBerdt to Reed, July 4, 1767, Reed MSS, Box. 1.

16. DeBerdt, *Letters*, p. 440.

17. See Esther DeBerdt to Reed, Nov. 7, 1766, and Feb. 3, 1767, Reed MSS, Box 1, and Stephen Sayre to Reed, Oct. 13, 1768, Reed MSS, Vol. I. DeBerdt was instrumental in winning over Dartmouth to advise the Stamp Act's repeal. See Clark, *British Opinion and the American Revolution*, pp. 193-94, and Thomson, *The Secretaries of State, 1681-1782*, pp. 46-54.

18. Morgann (1726-1802), a protégé of Lord Shelburne, became Under Secretary of State to the latter in 1782, secretary to the British peace commission in 1783, and later the first Marquis of Lansdowne. He was also noted as a writer. Stephen and Lee, eds., *Dictionary of National Biography*, XIII, 939.

19. Reed MSS, Box 1.

20. See *N. J. Archives*, X, 5, and Esther DeBerdt to Reed, July 7, 1767, Reed MSS, Box 1.

21. On Charles Read see Woodward, *Ploughs and Politicks*, pp. 153-56. A contemporary said of Read that "no man knew so well as he how to wiggle himself into office, nor keep it so long, nor make so much of it." Diary of Aaron Leaming, 1775 notation, Historical Society of Pennsylvania.

22. Dec. 23, 1767, Reed MSS, Vol. I. See also Reed to Pettit, Dec. 2, 1767, *ibid.* The Perth Amboy office was entrusted to Revaude Kearny, a great-uncle of General Phil Kearny. Whitehead, *Contribution to the Early History of Perth Amboy*, pp. 90-91.

23. That estimate was given Esther DeBerdt by Stephen Sayre. See her letter to Reed of Dec. 10, 1767, Reed MSS, Box 1.

24. Reed to Morgann, July 20, 1769, Etting MSS, "Generals of the Revolution," III, 61, Historical Society of Pennsylvania; Reed to

Morgann, Oct. 1, 1769, Reed MSS, Vol. I; *N. J. Archives*, X, 114. Pettit held the office into 1776 and then became first secretary of the independent state of New Jersey. *Ibid.*, 133n.

25. See Esther DeBerdt to Reed, Feb. 19, 1767, and July 4, 1768, Reed MSS, Box 1.

26. Appleton, "The Agents of the New England Colonies in the Revolutionary Period," *The New England Quarterly*, VI, 2 (June, 1933), 373, 377; Burns, *Colonial Agents of New England*, p. 13; DeBerdt, *Letters*, pp. 301-2.

27. See Esther DeBerdt to Reed, Feb. 8, 1769, Reed MSS, Box 1.

28. DeBerdt, *Letters*, p. 387; W. B. Reed, *Life and Correspondence of Joseph Reed*, I, 41n. Cited hereafter as W. B. Reed, *Reed*.

29. Quoted in W. B. Reed, *Esther*, pp. 140-41.

30. Pratt, "Autobiographical Notes of Matthew Pratt, Painter," ed. by Hart, *Pennsylvania Magazine of History and Biography*, XIX (1895), 462-63. Pratt was a passenger on the *James* with Reed.

31. Reed to Pettit, April 25, 1770, Reed MSS, Vol. II. See also DeBerdt, *Letters*, p. 299.

32. See Reed to Pettit, May 7, June 8, and June 25, 1770, Reed MSS, Vol. II.

33. W. B. Reed gives May 22 as the wedding date, *Esther*, p. 150. For the correct date and the names of the witnesses (Dornier DeBerdt and Mary Palmer) I am indebted to Professor Mark H. Jackson, LeMoyne College, Syracuse, N. Y., who secured in London a letter from the Reverend Allan V. Wintersgill, Aug. 1, 1952, citing this date from the parish records. St. Luke's is still standing.

34. Reed to Pettit, June 8 and July 13, 1770, Reed MSS, Vol. II.

35. *Pennsylvania Gazette*, Nov. 1, 1770.

36. See W. B. Reed, *Esther*, p. 159; Reed to Pettit, Dec. 20, 1770, Reed MSS, Vol. II.

37. Esther DeBerdt to Dennis DeBerdt, Nov. 14, 1770, W. B. Reed, *Esther*, pp. 158-59.

38. See Esther Reed to Dennis DeBerdt, Jan. 17 and June 15, 1771, and Feb. 29, 1772, W. B. Reed, *Esther*, pp. 165, 168, 171; Reed to DeBerdt, Jan. 4, 1772[3], Reed Letterbook, p. 36, New-York Historical Society; Second Presbyterian Church of Philadelphia, Register of Baptisms, p. 16, Presbyterian Historical Society, Philadelphia.

39. Oct. 28, 1773, W. B. Reed, *Esther*, p. 185.

40. E.g. Joseph Galloway, John Dickinson, and Nicholas Waln. See Esther Reed to Dennis DeBerdt, Feb. 29, 1772, W. B. Reed, *Esther*, pp. 170-71.

41. Philadelphia Court of Common Pleas, Docket (1761-71), pp. 124-32, Historical Society of Pennsylvania; and see Reed to Pettit, March 9, 1771, Reed MSS, Vol. II.

42. *DAB*, II, 123. A second Constitutional Convention delegate who served his legal apprenticeship under Reed was Jared Ingersoll, Jr. Ingersoll married Reed's niece, Elizabeth Pettit.

43. See Reed's "Estimate of My Estate, July 4, 1774," Reed MSS, Vol. III, and Dallas, comp., *Reports of Cases Ruled and Adjudged in the Courts of Pennsylvania before and since the Revolution*, p. 34.

44. J. Adams, *Works*, ed. by C. F. Adams, II, 378.

45. See "Estimate" and Reed to Pettit, Feb. 11, 1774, Reed MSS, Vol. III.

46. "Estimate," *ibid.*; New Jersey Deeds, Liber A-H, p. 401, Office of Secretary of State, Trenton; Memorandum, Dec. 20, 1774, Jacobs Papers, II, 603, Historical Society of Pennsylvania; Reed Letterbook, pp. 90-94, 104, Reed MSS.

47. DeBerdt to Reed, Nov. 14, 1772, Nov. 3, 1773, Reed MSS, Vol. II; "Estimate," Reed MSS, Vol. III; Reed to DeBerdt, Aug. 31, 1773, Letterbook, p. 60.

48. See DeBerdt to Reed, March 4 and Nov. 14, 1772, Reed MSS, Vol. II; also "Mr. DeBerdt's Terms of Doing Business" (n.d.), Reed Letterbook, p. 328.

49. DeBerdt to Esther Reed, Nov. 17, 1772, Reed MSS, Vol. II.

50. Dec. 5, 1775, Reed Letterbook, p. 135; see also Reed to DeBerdt, May 4 and Sept. 26, 1774, *ibid.*, pp. 99, 105.

51. Second Presbyterian Church, Transcript, Minutes of the Congregation, II, 251, 256-57; transcript, Minutes of the Corporation, I, 24, 44, Presbyterian Historical Society, Philadelphia.

52. Lesley, comp., *Early Proceedings of the American Philosophical Society*, p. 6.

53. See President Witherspoon of the college to Reed, March 18, 1772, and Reed to Pettit, April 14, 1772, Reed MSS, Vol. II.

54. Jan. 14, 1775, Reed MSS, Vol. III.

CHAPTER IV: THE PATRIOT WHO WOULD BE PEACEMAKER

1. Schlesinger, *The Colonial Merchants and the American Revolution*, p. 231.

2. *Ibid.*, p. 247.

3. Marks, *England and America, 1763-1783*, I, 281.

4. Clark, *British Opinion and the American Revolution*, pp. 193-94.

5. Thomson, *The Secretaries of State*, pp. 58-59. Arthur Lee wrote Sam Adams in 1772, "Lord Dartmouth is too insignificant for you to regard what he says." Richard Henry Lee, *Life of Arthur Lee*, I, 222-23.

6. Esther Reed to Dennis DeBerdt, Oct. 20, 1772, W. B. Reed, *Esther*, p. 178.

7. Reed to Dennis DeBerdt, Jan. 4, 1773, Letterbook, p. 63.

8. *Manuscripts of the Earl of Dartmouth,* Historical Manuscripts Commission, Eleventh Report, Appendix, Part V, II, 166. Cited hereafter as *Dartmouth MSS.*

9. Copy sent by DeBerdt to Reed, Reed MSS, Vol. II.

10. Reed to DeBerdt, July 24, 1773, Letterbook, p. 53. For note to Dartmouth see *Dartmouth MSS,* I, 337.

11. See Reed to DeBerdt, Dec. 24, 1773, Letterbook, p. 77.

12. Dennis DeBerdt to Reed, Oct. 8, 1774, Reed MSS, Vol. III.

13. Reed to DeBerdt, Dec. 24, 1774, Letterbook, p. 123.

14. Quincy corresponded with Reed after his return to Boston and also during a sojourn in England in late 1774 and early 1775. His death came aboard ship during his return to America. See Quincy to Reed, Aug. 20, 1774, Reed MSS, Vol. III, and *DAB,* XV, 307-8.

15. Reed to Thomas Cushing, 1773, Reed MSS, Vol. II.

16. *Pennsylvania Gazette,* Oct. 20, 1773.

17. Draft, Reed to Lord Dartmouth, Dec. 22, 1773, Reed Letterbook, pp. 295-96.

18. This committee had taken on new form early in December when it inventoried all the tea stocks in the city and set a ceiling price of six shillings, six pence per pound for tea. *Pennsylvania Gazette,* Dec. 8, 1773.

19. Reed to Dartmouth, Dec. 22, 1773, Letterbook, p. 295.

20. *Pennsylvania Gazette,* Dec. 29, 1773; Draft, Reed to Dartmouth, Dec. 27, 1773, Letterbook, p. 297; for the tea crisis see also Drake, *Tea Leaves,* and Stone, "How the Landing of Tea Was Opposed in Philadelphia," *Pennsylvania Magazine of History and Biography,* XV (1891), 385-93.

21. Draft, Reed to Dartmouth, Dec. 27, 1773, Letterbook, pp. 297-99.

22. Draft, Reed Letterbook, pp. 77-78.

23. Copy, Reed MSS, Vol. II.

24. See *Pennsylvania Gazette,* Dec. 29, 1773, and Schlesinger, *Colonial Merchants,* p. 291.

25. Draft, Reed Letterbook, p. 299.

26. See the quotation from the letter of Lord Shelburne to Lord Chatham concerning Dartmouth's stand, March 15, 1774, in W. B. Reed, *Reed,* I, 61n.

27. Draft, Letterbook, pp. 300-303.

28. Meigs, *The Violent Men,* p. 9.

29. *DAB,* XVII, 481.

30. This description of the meeting is based upon a "Narrative" written by Joseph Reed included among the Thompson Papers in the New-York Historical Society. Thomson's own version, given in a letter to William H. Drayton, differs in some details. Both are pub-

lished in the *Collections* of the New-York Historical Society, 1878, pp. 270-78.

31. *Pennsylvania Gazette*, May 25 and June 8, 1774.

32. *Pennsylvania Gazette*, June 8, 1774. Only thirteen of the nineteen members of the committee signed this reply and Reed was not among them. No importance is to be attributed to this, however, for the *Gazette* (*ibid.*) reported that the members who were unable due to business to attend the meeting at which the letter was written had subsequently fully approved of it.

33. *Dartmouth MSS*, I, 353. There is no draft of this letter in Reed's Letterbook.

34. *Pennsylvania Gazette*, June 1 and June 8, 1774.

35. *Ibid.*, June 15, 1774.

36. Charles Thomson's memorandum, dated June 11, 1774, on "A Meeting of a Number of Gentlemen," Thomson Memo Book, Gratz Collection, Historical Society of Pennsylvania.

37. Stille, *The Life and Times of John Dickinson*, p. 344.

38. Draft, Reed to Dartmouth, June 10 [11], 1774, Letterbook, pp. 304-6. An example of the misleading type of official report to Dartmouth which Reed was trying to offset is Gage's dispatch from Boston, June 26, 1774, in which he flatly predicts that neither Philadelphia nor New York would ever agree to non-importation. Quoted in W. B. Reed, *Reed*, I, 70n.

39. *Pennsylvania Gazette*, June 22, 1774. See also Hiltzheimer, *Extracts from the Diary of Jacob Hiltzheimer*, ed. by Parsons, p. 31.

40. *Pennsylvania Gazette*, June 29 and July 6, 1774.

41. "Minutes of the Provincial Deputies," *Pennsylvania Archives*, 2d series, III, 545-48.

42. *Ibid.*, p. 549.

43. Reed MSS, Vol. III.

44. *Pennsylvania Archives*, 2d series, III, 549-64; Schlesinger, *Colonial Merchants*, pp. 351-55.

45. Reed to Dartmouth, July 18, 1774, Letterbook, p. 306.

46. *Ibid.*, pp. 307-8.

47. Reed to Pettit, Jan. 31, 1775, Reed MSS, Vol. III.

48. Lord Dartmouth to Reed, July 11, 1774, *ibid.*

49. Draft, Letterbook, pp. 311-13.

50. Reed to Charles Pettit, Sept. 4, 1774, Reed MSS, Vol. III.

51. Esther Reed to Dennis DeBerdt, Nov. 2, 1774, W. B. Reed, *Esther*, p. 204.

52. J. Adams, *Works*, II, 357-402.

53. *Ibid.*, p. 378.

54. J. Adams, *Works*, II, 392, and Reed to DeBerdt, Sept. 26, 1774, Letterbook, p. 108.

55. Silas Deane to Mrs. Deane, Sept. 23, 1774, "Correspondence of Silas Deane," *Connecticut Historical Society, Collections*, II, 185.

56. Washington, *Diaries*, ed. by Fitzpatrick, II, 166.

57. Reed to Dartmouth, Sept. 25, 1774, Letterbook, pp. 311-20.

58. Draft, Sept. 26, 1774, Letterbook, pp. 107-10.

59. Reed to Dartmouth, Oct. 24, 1774, Letterbook, pp. 321-23. Reed's next letter to the Earl, Nov. 6, 1774, tried to impressed upon him the great dangers which would be involved if the petitions and addresses of the Congress were not received by the government or were treated with contempt. *Ibid.*, p. 324.

60. See *Pennsylvania Gazette*, Nov. 2 and 16, 1774, and Schlesinger, *Colonial Merchants*, pp. 457-58. Joseph Galloway thought the new membership "warm People of neither Property nor significance among us." Mrs. T. Etting, "Some Letters of Joseph Galloway," *Pennsylvania Magazine of History and Biography*, XXI (1898), 478.

61. Reed wrote to Pettit that a favorable aspect of his position as chairman was his ability to refrain from entering into personal debates. Feb. 2, 1775, Reed MSS, Vol. III.

62. Lincoln, *Revolutionary Movement in Pennsylvania*, p. 186.

63. Draft copy, Letterbook, p. 123.

64. See Reed to Pettit [Jan., 1776], Reed MSS, Vol. IV; Cushing and Sheppard, *History of the Counties of Gloucester, Salem and Cumberland*, pp. 536-37; and Fithian, *Journal*, ed. by Albion and Dodson, pp. 247-48. (Philip Fithian was a resident of Greenwich at the time.)

65. Jan. 31, 1775, Reed MSS, Vol. III.

66. Reed was particularly suspicious of Joseph Galloway, a power in the assembly. See Reed to Pettit, Jan. 14, 1775, *ibid.* Reed wrote even more bitterly of Galloway on Feb. 25, again to Pettit. He concluded that there was no hope of Galloway's reformation and stated, "His State of Health is so wretched that there may be hopes of his not existing to increase and continue public confusion much longer." *Ibid.*

67. *Pennsylvania Archives*, 2d series, III, 625-31.

68. Draft, Letterbook, pp. 282-84.

69. See Reed to Pettit, Jan. 31, 1775, Reed MSS, Vol. III, and Reed to Dartmouth, Feb. 10, 1775, Draft, Letterbook, pp. 285-89.

70. Reed to Pettit, Jan. 31, 1775, Reed MSS, Vol. III; DeBerdt to Reed, Oct. 8, 1774, *ibid.*

71. Draft, Letterbook, pp. 285-89.

72. Jan. 31, 1775, Reed MSS, Vol. III.

73. DeBerdt to Reed, Jan. 6, 1775, *ibid.*

74. June 1, 1775, *ibid.*

75. Aug. 10, 1775, *ibid.*

76. Bancroft, *History of the United States*, VIII, 73.
77. Feb. 13, 1775, Draft, Letterbook, pp. 127-29.
78. DeBerdt wrote Mrs. Reed on June 1, 1775, that Dartmouth "much wishes to hear from him [Joseph]." Reed MSS, Vol. III.
79. Aug. 20, 1775, *ibid.*
80. DeBerdt to Reed, Jan. 6, 1775, *ibid.*; see also Mrs. Reed's hopeful reaction to the first bit of news in her reply to her brother, March 14, 1775, W. B. Reed, *Esther*, p. 209.
81. Draft, Letterbook, p. 287.
82. See Alden, *General Gage in America*, pp. 239-41.
83. *Pennsylvania Magazine of History and Biography*, XXVII (1903), 257.

CHAPTER V: 1775: GENERAL WASHINGTON'S CONFIDANT

1. *Pennsylvania Gazette*, April 26, 1775.
2. *Ibid.*, May 3, 1775.
3. See Minutes of the Associators, Peters MSS, Vol. VIII, Historical Society of Pennsylvania.
4. Reed had known Roberdeau even before he moved to Philadelphia in 1770. See Roberdeau's Letterbook, pp. 217-19, Historical Society of Pennsylvania.
5. Cary to Reed, May 3, 1775, Reed MSS, Vol. III; Warren to Reed, May 15, 1775, *ibid.* Ironically enough, in this same letter, Warren referred Reed to his "very intimate friend," Dr. Benjamin Church, who was being sent by the provincial congress of Massachusetts to the Continental Congress, as "a Gentleman, a good Companion and a person of fine understanding."
6. Lincoln, *Revolutionary Movement in Pennsylvania*, pp. 196-209; Selsam, *Pennsylvania Constitution of 1776*, pp. 69-78.
7. Curwen, *Journal and Letters*, ed. by Ward, p. 28. Curwen, destined to remain loyal to Britain, was also present.
8. *Pennsylvania Gazette*, June 14 and June 21, 1775.
9. J. Adams, *Letters of John Adams Addressed to His Wife*, ed. by C. F. Adams, I, 41-42.
10. Washington, *Diaries*, II, 199.
11. Esther Reed wrote to Dennis DeBerdt the next day that her husband was "attending General Washington part of his way to Boston." W. B. Reed, *Esther*, p. 216.
12. Washington, *Writings*, ed. by Fitzpatrick, III, 301n.; *Pennsylvania Gazette*, June 28, 1775.
13. Pierson, *Narratives of Newark from the Days of Its Founding, 1666-1916*, pp. 191-92.

14. Pettit to Reed, July 22, 1775, Reed MSS, Vol. III.

15. Freeman, *Washington*, III, 464-70.

16. Boudinot lived in Princeton when Reed attended the College of New Jersey and both received their law training in Richard Stockton's office there.   See G. Boyd, *Elias Boudinot.*

17. Elias Boudinot to Reed, July 24, 1775, Reed MSS, Vol. III.

18. Esther Reed to Dennis DeBerdt, July 22, 1775, W. B. Reed, *Esther*, pp. 218-19.

19. July 22, 1775, Reed MSS, Vol. III.

20. July 26, 1775, *ibid.*

21. Pettit to Reed, July 22, 1775, *ibid.*

22. Cox to Reed, July 26, 1775, *ibid.*

23. Draft copy, Reed to a member of Congress, [May?], 1777, Reed MSS, Vol. IV.

24. Washington to Reed, Nov. 28, 1775, W. B. Reed, *Reed*, I, 132.

25. Washington to Reed, Jan. 23, 1776, *ibid.*, I, 146.

26. Aug. 13, 1775, Gratz Collection, IV, 14, Historical Society of Pennsylvania.

27. Reed MSS, Vol. III.

28. Freeman, *Washington*, III, 471-76.

29. Washington, *Writings,* III, 309.

30. Reed to Boudinot, Aug. 13, 1775, Gratz Collection, IV, 14, Historical Society of Pennsylvania.

31. See Freeman, *Washington*, III, 460, 528; IV, 18.

32. *Ibid.*, III, 535-37.   One of the youngest officers in Arnold's force was nineteen-year-old Aaron Burr, son of the Rev. Aaron Burr whom Reed had studied under at the College of New Jersey.   Young Burr had come to the camp at Cambridge with a letter of introduction to Reed from Elias Boudinot.   See Boudinot to Reed, July 24, 1775, Reed MSS, Vol. III.

33. Reed MSS, Vol. III.

34. Washington to Reed, Nov. 28, 1775, W. B. Reed, *Reed*, I, 130.

35. Reed MSS, Vol. III.

36. Esther Reed to Dennis DeBerdt, Sept. 8, 1775, *ibid.*

37. See Esther Reed to Dennis DeBerdt, June 24 and Oct. 28, 1775, W. B. Reed, *Esther*, pp. 216, 236; and Reed to Pettit, Aug. 20, 1775, Reed MSS, Vol. III.   David Ogden of Newark, N. J., later a Tory, probably took some of the credit for Reed's good health, having sent him a package of pills.   See Ogden to Reed, Aug. 8, 1775, Reed MSS, Vol. III.

38. See Reed to [Thomas Bradford?], Aug. 7, 1775, Reed MSS, Vol. III.

39. Reed to Pettit, Aug. 29, 1775, *ibid.*, and French, *The Siege of Boston*, p. 374.   The Vassall house, which is still standing (as is the

Wadsworth house), is better known today by the name of a later occupant and owner, Henry Wadsworth Longfellow.

40. Washington to Reed, Nov. 28, 1775, and Jan. 14, 1776, W. B. Reed, *Reed*, I, 130, 142. Washington later assured Reed he was grateful for reports of such criticism since "I know—but to declare it, unless to a friend, may be an argument of vanity—the integrity of my own heart." Feb. 10, 1776, *ibid.*, p. 157.

41. Jan. 23, 1776, *ibid.*, p. 146.

42. Freeman, *Washington*, IV, 72.

43. French, *The First Year of the American Revolution*, p. 500.

44. Dec. 30, 1775, Reed MSS, Vol. III.

45. Reed to Pettit, Sept. 11, 1775, *ibid.*

46. Reed to Thomas Bradford, Sept. 14, 1775, *ibid.*

47. Freeman, *Washington*, III, 544-51.

48. Benjamin Church to Reed, Oct. 8 and Oct. 10, 1775, Reed MSS, Vol. III.

49. Freeman, *Washington*, III, 551n.

50. Washington to Reed, Nov. 20, 1775, W. B. Reed, *Reed*, I, 127.

51. Washington to Reed, Jan. 23, 1776, *ibid.*, I, 146.

52. Washington to Broughton, Sept. 2, 1775, in Force, comp., *American Archives*, 4th series, III, 667.

53. See, e.g., Reed to Ephraim Bowen, Oct. 13, 1775, *ibid.*, p. 1056.

54. Reed to Bowen, Oct. 17, 1775, and Reed to Glover and Moylan, Oct. 20, 1775, *ibid.*, pp. 1125-26. Another problem which confronted Reed was how to deal with his old sea-captain friend, the effervescent John Macpherson. The latter came to Cambridge with a grandiose plan for what Washington described as nothing less than the "destruction of the naval force of Great Britain." Washington persuaded him to lay his plan before Congress. Washington to Reed, Nov. 8, 1775, W. B. Reed, *Reed*, I, 126.

55. Reed to Glover, Oct. 12, 1775, in Force, *American Archives*, 4th series, III, 1037.

56. Reed to Glover and Moylan, Oct. 25, 1775, *ibid.*, p. 1182.

57. Reed to Esther Reed, July 26, 1775, Reed MSS, Vol. III. Reed's law clerk, Andrew Hodge, wrote on August 28 that he would attend the Chester Court on the 30th "for fear your clients should go to some other attorney, thinking their business will be neglected if no one attends on your account." *Ibid.*

58. *Ibid.*

59. Washington to Lee, Oct. 29, 1775, Washington, *Writings*, IV, 52.

60. Nov. 20, 1775, W. B. Reed, *Reed*, I, 127.

61. See Reed to Glover and Moylan, Oct. 30, 1775, in Washington's Letter Book, 1775-76, p. 137, Library of Congress.

62. See Washington to Reed, Nov. 20, 1775, W. B. Reed, *Reed*, I, 127.

63. Reed MSS, Vol. III.

64. Aug. 29, 1775, *ibid.*

65. Reed to Pettit, Oct. 8, 1775, *ibid.*

66. W. B. Reed, *Reed*, I, 158.

67. *Ibid.*, p. 128. That Esther Reed also shared this viewpoint is evident from her letter of September 8, 1775, to her brother in London. She asked, "But where sleeps all our friends in England? . . . Will nothing rouse them or are they so few in number [that] . . . their voice cannot be heard for the Multitude of our Enemies?" Reed MSS, Vol. III.

68. Force, *American Archives*, 4th series, III, 145, 1823. The committee of safety had Reed draft plans for the joint Pennsylvania–New Jersey defense of the Delaware. See Draft, Reed to N. J. Provincial Congress, Feb. 2, 1776, Reed MSS, Vol. IV.

69. See Washington to Reed, Nov. 20 and Dec. 15, 1775, W. B. Reed, *Reed*, I, 128-29, 134.

70. *Ibid.*, pp. 127, 130, 135.

71. Dec. 30, 1775, Reed MSS, Vol. III.

72. W. B. Reed, *Reed*, I, 145-46.

73. Jan. 31, 1776, *ibid.*, p. 147.

74. Selsam, *Pennsylvania Constitution of 1776*, p. 91; Rossman, *Mifflin*, p. 43.

75. Feb. 10, 1776, W. B. Reed, *Reed*, I, 160.

76. *Votes and Proceedings of the House of Representatives of the Province of Pennsylvania 1767-1776*, VI, 662-76.

77. *Pennsylvania Gazette*, Feb. 21, 1776.

78. March 3, 1776, Reed MSS, Vol. IV.

79. *Votes and Proceedings*, VI, 688-93; Lincoln, *Revolutionary Movement in Pennsylvania*, pp. 241-48.

80. *Votes and Proceedings*, VI, 676, 686.

81. *Ibid.*, p. 641.

82. Reed MSS, Vol. IV.

83. *Votes and Proceedings*, VI, 725.

84. Ford, ed., *Journals of the Continental Congress, 1774-1789*, IV, 180.

85. Reed wrote to Dennis DeBerdt on Feb. 24: "If I remain here [in Philadelphia] I shall be employed in public concerns and living on my little capital. I therefore rather incline to accept some office or post where my services may perhaps be as useful, and receive some compensation which, considering the demands of a growing family, it is my duty to attend to." W. B. Reed, *Esther*, p. 243.

86. Reed to Washington, March 3 and 7, 1776, W. B. Reed, *Reed*, I, 163, 165; Reed to Pettit, March 3 and [17?], 1776, Reed MSS, Vol. IV. Franklin was now living at Perth Amboy. In June he was

taken into custody by order of the provincial congress of New Jersey, Bowes Reed carrying out the arrest. See Reed to Esther Reed, June 27, 1776, Reed MSS, Vol. IV. Reed moved his family from Philadelphia fearing British naval raids on the city. He also hoped to cut living expenses thereby. See Reed to DeBerdt, Feb. 24, 1776, W. B. Reed, *Esther*, p. 243.

87. Washington, *Writings*, V, 50.

88. Ford, *Journals of Continental Congress*, IV, 342.

89. *Pennsylvania Gazette*, May 22, 1776.

90. *Votes and Proceedings*, VI, 736-40; Lincoln, *Revolutionary Movement in Pennsylvania*, pp. 260-63.

91. Unable to secure a quorum thereafter, the assembly adjourned on the 14th until August 26. For lack of a quorum at that time another adjournment until September 23 resulted. On that date the proprietary assembly adjourned forever. See Bolles, *Pennsylvania, Province and State . . . 1609-1790*, I, 466.

92. Ford, *Journals of Continental Congress*, IV, 359, V, 448. Congress had voted Gates's promotion on May 16. He was given command of the army in Canada on June 17.

93. Freeman, *Washington*, IV, 106.

94. Ford, *Journals of Continental Congress*, V, 419; see also Reed to Esther Reed, [June 4], 1776, Reed MSS, Vol. IV, in which Reed indicates that the prospect of a regular salary was important in his decision, the more so since as he wrote steps were under way to force the closing of the law courts in Pennsylvania until a new government had been established.

95. Reed's account of his assets shows that most of his fortune was tied up in lands which were potentially valuable but which were not as yet productive of any appreciable income. The value of many of the tracts, spread from New York to Virginia, was uncertain and thus Reed did not attempt a final total of his estate. Aside from land acreage, other assets Reed listed included sixty-five shares in the West Jersey Society, a one-twelfth share in the East Jersey proprietary, a share in a privateer, the brig *Hancock*, and personal debts owed to him. The grand total of all these assets would appear to be about £6,000. Concerning his own debts, Reed merely stated that his account books (which have not been preserved) would show how much he owed the estates of Ezekeil Furman and John Rhea.

Reed's will, June 11, 1776, made as is stated therein due to his imminent departure in the defense of the liberties of his country, which he was "fully resolved never to survive," ordered that his estate be equally divided between Esther and the three children, with a share reserved for the child with whom Esther was pregnant. Reed named

Esther, Charles Pettit, and John Cox as the executors. "Sketch of my affairs," June, 1776, and Will, June 11, 1776, Reed MSS, Vol. IV.

96. Mrs. Reed was particularly loath to see her husband depart for an indefinite but undoubtedly long absence at this time since she was expecting their fourth child. Theodosia Reed, named for her paternal grandmother, was born October 2 while Reed was with the army at New York.

97. Reed to Esther Reed, June 16 and 21, 1776, Reed MSS, Vol. IV.

CHAPTER VI: 1776: THE BRINK OF DISASTER

1. Robinson, *An Account of the Organization of the Army of the United States*, I, 32-33. For the evolution of the duties of the adjutant general see Washington's general orders issued at Cambridge in 1775 in Washington, *Writings*, III, 306 ff.

2. Reed wrote Esther from Pettit's home: "My comfort depends so much on yours that if you cannot reconcile yourself to absence, I will . . . return to you. I know I shall be censured for want of steadiness, but I am resolved to sacrifice every other consideration to your peace of mind consistent with my reputation, which I am sure you would not wish me to sully." June 16, 1776, Reed MSS, Vol. IV.

3. See Reed to Mrs. Reed, June 27, July 26, Aug. 29, and Sept. 6, 1776, Reed MSS, Vol. IV.

4. Reed MSS, Vol. IV.

5. June 26, 1776, *ibid.* See also Freeman, *Washington*, IV, 635.

6. Reed to Mrs. Reed, June 30 and July 1, 1776, Reed MSS, Vol. IV.

7. Reed to Mrs. Reed, July 3, 1776, *ibid.* See also the letters of July 1 and 4, *ibid.*

8. W. B. Reed, *Esther*, p. 241.

9. Quoted by Burnett, *The Continental Congress*, p. 147.

10. Almon, comp., *Parliamentary Register . . . 1774-80*, IV, 128.

11. For a detailed analysis of the Howe commission see Brown, *Empire or Independence. A Study in the Failure of Reconciliation, 1774-1783.*

12. Freeman, *Washington*, IV, 133.

13. Reed to Charles Pettit, March 3, 1776, Reed MSS, Vol. IV.

14. Reed to Pettit, June 26, 1776, *ibid.*

15. Dennis DeBerdt to Reed "per favour of Lord Howe," May 3, 1776, *ibid.*

16. Reed to Robert Morris, July 18, 1776, W. B. Reed, *Reed*, I, 199-200. Reed's letter to Mrs. Reed of July 16 contains similar sentiments. There he stated that if "exemption from Parliamentary taxation, and regulation of our internal government" were obtained,

he would "with a safe conscience retire." He felt that military measures must be pressed but he did not see that a conference to learn
the extent of the commission's powers would inconvenience these or
be a source of any danger. Reed MSS, Vol. IV.

17. Robert Morris to Reed, July 20, 1776, Reed MSS, Vol. IV.
DeBerdt's link with Kinsey had flowed from the former's position
as last colonial agent of the province of New Jersey.

18. See Reed to Pettit, July 14-15, 1776, Dreer Collection, "Generals
of the Revolution," II, 58, Historical Society of Pennsylvania.

19. See Reed's "Notes of Conference with Col. Patterson," Reed
MSS, Vol. IV, and Webb, *Reminiscences of General Samuel Webb
of the Revolutionary Army*, p. 39.

20. Reed to Mrs. Reed, July 26, 1776, Reed MSS, Vol. IV.

21. Reed MSS, Vol. IV.

22. July 22, 1776, *ibid.*

23. Reed to Mrs. Reed, Aug. 1, 1776, *ibid.* See also Reed to Pettit,
July 22, 1776, *ibid.*

24. Freeman, *Washington*, IV, 153-68.

25. Reed to Mrs. Reed, Aug. 29, 1776, Reed MSS, Vol. IV.

26. William B. Reed's claims (see *Reed*, I, 225-26) that it was Joseph
Reed who personally urged Washington to convoke the council of
war after witnessing signs of British naval activity are discounted on
solid grounds in Freeman, *Washington*, IV, 173n.

27. Field, *The Battle of Long Island*, p. 397.

28. Freeman, *Washington*, IV, 182, quoting Reed's letter to Mrs.
Reed, Sept. 2, 1776 (Reed MSS, Vol. IV).

29. See Force, *American Archives*, 5th series, III, 1497-98, for the
letter from Joseph Trumbull of Connecticut to William Williams,
Nov. 18, 1776, a copy of which was sent to Congress by General
Philip Schuyler, which included a bitter attack on Reed. On discipline in the army see Chapter V in Bolton, *The Private Soldier
under Washington*, and Bowman, *The Morale of the American Revolutionary Army*.

30. See Reed to Mrs. Reed, Sept. 17 and Oct. 11, 1776, and Reed's
draft of a letter to a member of Congress, [June ?], 1777, Reed MSS,
Vol. IV; also, Freeman, *Washington*, IV, 180-82, 192-95.

31. This house, now known as the Jumel Mansion, has been
preserved. It is situated on 160th Street off Amsterdam Avenue,
Manhattan.

32. Liffenwell was court-martialed and condemned to death for mis-
behavior before the enemy and for his attempt on Reed's life, but
was given a last-minute reprieve at Reed's request. Freeman, *Washington*, IV, 204.

33. Reed's descriptions of the battle are in his letters of September

16 and 22 to his wife, Reed MSS, Vol. IV. For a detailed analysis of the engagement see Johnston, *The Battle of Harlem Heights*, which includes a letter of Nathanael Greene in which Reed's "spirited conduct" is praised (pp. 145-46).

34. Reed to Mrs. Reed, July 26, 1776, Reed MSS, Vol. IV.

35. See Brown, *Empire or Independence*, p. 116 *et seq.* for the Staten Island conference.

36. Oct. 11, 1776, Reed MSS, Vol. IV.

37. Theodosia Reed was born Oct. 2, 1776. She died May 11, 1778, of smallpox. Mary Reed, *A Family Record*, p. 10.

38. Reed to Mrs. Reed, Oct. 11, 1776, Reed MSS, Vol. IV.

39. Oct. 14, 1776, *ibid.*

40. *Ibid.*

41. Freeman, *Washington*, IV, 225.

42. *Ibid.*, pp. 227-31.

43. *Ibid.*, p. 236.

44. Washington to Reed, Aug. 22, 1779, *Writings*, XVI, 152.

45. Nov. 16, 1776, Reed MSS, Vol. IV.

46. Reed to Lee, Nov. 21, 1776, Misc. MSS (Reed), New-York Historical Society.

47. Misc. MSS (Reed), New-York Historical Society.

48. See Washington to Livingston, Nov. 23, 1776, *Writings*, VI, 304-5, and Samuel Webb to Joseph Trumbull, Nov. 24, 1776, in S. Webb, *Correspondence and Journals*, ed. by Ford, I, 173.

49. Washington to Reed, 30, 1776, W. B. Reed, *Reed*, I, 258-59; also Freeman, *Washington*, IV, 269-72.

50. Facsimile, Misc. MSS (Reed, Joseph), New York Public Library.

51. Reed to John Hancock, Dec. 2, 1776, *ibid.*

52. W. B. Reed, *Reed*, I, 268; Freeman, *Washington*, IV, 272n.

53. W. B. Reed, *Esther*, p. 254. The family left Burlington Dec. 10, one day before Hessian troops entered the town. See Stryker, *The Battles of Trenton and Princeton*, pp. 42-44.

54. W. B. Reed, *Reed*, I, 267-68.

55. General Lee, after belatedly bringing his troops across the Hudson and starting them toward Washington's army, was captured by a British cavalry patrol on December 13.

56. Reed to Washington, March 8, 1777, W. B. Reed, *Reed*, I, 259.

57. *Ibid.*, p. 260.

58. June 14, 1777, *ibid.*, pp. 260-61.

59. See, e.g., Washington to Reed, Dec. 2, 1777, Aug. 22, 1779, *ibid.*, pp. 348-49, 263-64: May 28, 1780, *ibid.*, II, 202-06; also Freeman, *Washington*, IV, 429n.

60. See Washington to the President of Congress, Washington, *Writings*, VI, 335-36.

61. W. B. Reed, *Reed*, I, 269.

62. Reed to Washington, Dec. 12, 1776, in Stryker, *Trenton and Princeton*, pp. 322-23.

63. *Ibid.*, pp. 316-17, 327-29, and 314-16.

64. Bancroft, *History of the U. S. of America*, IX, 299n.; Stryker, *The Reed Controversy*, pp. 3-11.

65. Stryker, *Trenton and Princeton*, pp. 42-47.

66. *Ibid.*, pp. 75-76; see also Joseph Reed's "Narrative," written in 1782, in William B. Reed, *A Rejoinder to Mr. Bancroft's Historical Essay on President Reed*, pp. 65-67.

67. Draft copy, Cadwalader to Donop, Dec. 25, 1776, Reed MSS, Vol. IV.

68. George Washington to John Augustine Washington, Dec. 13, 1776, Washington, *Writings*, VI, 398.

69. Reed to Washington, Dec. 22, 1776, W. B. Reed, *Reed*, I, 271-73.

70. *Ibid.*, p. 273; see also Benjamin Rush, *Autobiography*, ed. by Corner, p. 124. Rush accompanied Reed from Bristol to headquarters.

71. W. B. Reed, *Reed*, I, 273-74; Donop's report to Gen. Knyphausen, Dec. 27, 1776, in Stryker, *Trenton and Princeton*, pp. 398-400.

72. Washington to Reed "or in his absence to John Cadwalader only," Dec. 23, 1776, W. B. Reed, *Reed*, I, 274-75.

73. Reed to Cadwalader, Philadelphia, 11 A.M., Dec. 25, 1776, Cadwalader MSS, I, 12, Historical Society of Pennsylvania.

74. *Ibid.*, p. 13.

75. Copy, Cadwalader to Washington, Dec. 26, 1776, Reed MSS, Vol. IV.

76. W. B. Reed, *Reed*, I, 276.

77. Copy, Cadwalader to Washington, Dec. 26, 1776, Reed MSS, Vol. IV.

78. Cadwalader to Washington, Dec. 27, 1776, in Stryker, *Trenton and Princeton*, p. 241.

79. W. B. Reed, *Reed*, I, 281; Freeman, *Washington*, IV, 329-30.

80. Joseph Reed's "Narrative," W. B. Reed, *Reed*, I, 282-83; see also Reed to Philadelphia Council of Safety, Jan. 1, 1776[7], Misc. MSS (Reed, Joseph), New York Public Library.

81. W. B. Reed, *Reed*, I, 284-86.

82. Aug. 22, 1779, Washington, *Writings*, XXVI, 159-60; see also Freeman, *Washington*, IV, 375. According to Benjamin Rush, one of Reed's harshest critics in the political wars in Pennsylvania, it was Reed who suggested the route Washington followed to Princeton. See Rush to John Adams, Aug. 19, 1811, in Rush, *Letters*, ed. by Butterfield, II, 1094.

83. Washington, *Writings*, VII, 5. The post was filled on a tem-

porary basis until Timothy Pickering took office in June. *Ibid.*,
p. 336n.

84. See Washington to Reed, Jan. 14, 15, and 19, 1777, *ibid.*, pp.
14-18, 36-37.

85. Feb. 20, 1777, Reed MSS, Vol. IV. Mrs. Reed, writing her
brother in March, described her fears when the Hessians, after having
forced the flight of her family from Burlington, were "within a few
hours march" of its retreat at Evesham. *Ibid.*

86. Cf. this document in *The Patriotism of Joseph Reed*, p. 7, with
the official text to be followed, given in Hamilton Schuyler, "Trenton
and Trentonians in the Revolutionary Era," in Walker, *A History of
Trenton, 1679-1929*, I, 119.

87. Howe, *Narrative . . . in a Committee of the House of Commons,
April 29, 1779*, p. 51; *Pennsylvania Journal and Weekly Advertiser*,
Feb. 5, 1777, Historical Society of Pennsylvania.

88. Ford, comp., *British Officers Serving in the American Revolution*,
p. 72.

89. Cited by Anderson, *The Command of the Howe Brothers during the American Revolution*, p. 165.

90. The complete lack of information concerning the history of
the document unearthed by the late Dr. Eliot (this writer interviewed
on Dec. 6, 1949, the book dealer, David Kirschenbaum of New York
City, who sold the paper to him) and the many Joseph Reeds in
Revolutionary New York, New Jersey, and Pennsylvania has made a
conclusive identification of the one named therein impossible. Perhaps the best suspect is a Joseph Reed of Newton, Queens County,
New York, whose name appeared briefly on a patriot militia roll in
1776 (for which act of treason he would have been obliged to beg
pardon and swear allegiance under the Howe proclamation) but whose
family included notorious Tories and who is almost certainly the
"Mr. Reed" taken prisoner by an American raiding party on Long
Island in 1781. He was imprisoned in Connecticut and then released
on parole. See Henry Onderdonk, Jr., ed., *Revolutionary Incidents
of Queens County*, pp. 55-56, 135; Sabine, *Loyalists of the American
Revolution*, II, 570.

Chapter VII: Camp or Council?

1. Selsam, *The Pennsylvania Constitution of 1776*, pp. 145-46.
2. *Ibid.*, pp. 146-51.
3. *Ibid.*, p. 183.
4. For the text of the constitution see Morison, ed., *Sources and
Documents Illustrating the American Revolution*, pp. 162-76.

5. Selsam, *Pennsylvania Constitution*, p. 205.

6. See above, Chapter V.

7. Reed to Esther Reed, June 4, 1776, Reed MSS, Vol. IV.

8. Reed to Esther Reed, Oct. 11, 1776, *ibid.*

9. Brunhouse, *The Counter-Revolution in Pennsylvania, 1776-1790*, pp. 20-22.

10. "Minutes of the Supreme Executive Council," *Pennsylvania Colonial Records*, XI, 186; *Pennsylvania Archives*, 2d series, III, 687.

11. Morison, *Sources and Documents*, p. 174.

12. Selsam, *Pennsylvania Constitution*, pp. 221-22.

13. Reed described the collapse of the legal profession in his letter to Dennis DeBerdt, Feb. 20, 1777, Reed MSS, Vol. IV.

14. Washington, *Writings*, VII, 190-91. After returning to Philadelphia, Reed continued to serve Washington in various ways, including the direction of some counter-intelligence efforts. See Washington to Reed, Feb. 23 and April 7, 1777, *ibid.*, pp. 191-92, 368-69. Even as a young lawyer, Reed had the reputation of a hard rider.

15. Ford, *Journals of the Continental Congress*, VII, 141. John Cadwalader was one of those elected but he declined.

16. "Minutes of the Supreme Executive Council," *Pennsylvania Colonial Records*, XI, 202.

17. Draft copy, Reed to a member of Congress, 1777, Reed MSS, Vol. IV.

18. Ford, *Journals of Continental Congress*, VII, 347.

19. Washington, *Writings*, VIII, 121.

20. Ford, *Journals of Continential Congress*, VIII, 386; Washington to Reed, May 29, 1777, *Writings*, VIII, 141.

21. Ford, *Journal of Continental Congress*, VIII, 428.

22. May 24, 1778, Reed MSS, Vol. V.

23. Washington to Reed, June 23, 1777, *Writings*, VIII, 293-96.

24. Reed to Timothy Matlack, June 21, 1777, Reed MSS, Vol. IV.

25. See Washington, *Writings*, VIII, 372n., and, for the military movements, Freeman, *Washington*, IV, 427-35.

26. Reed MSS, Vol. IV.

27. Reed to Supreme Executive Council, July 22, 1777, Reed MSS, Vol. IV. In a letter written to John Dickenson on Jan. 4, 1783, Reed gave the text of a paragraph which he said he had omitted from his letter to the council at the advice of an unnamed friend. In this paragraph Reed attacked the lack of security for judges under the constitutional provision for terms of seven years only, remarking that those who took the risks of accepting office during the dangerous travail of revolution might be subsequently rejected, for "when the decision is once had the neutral trimming crowd will poor forth its Candidates for those offices and Posts which they now shun with the

most wary and timid caution." Logan Papers, VIII, 93, Historical Society of Pennsylvania. Reed was referring in particular here to the Tory-minded who had found in the anti-constitutionalist party a convenient cloak for their opposition to the Revolution.

28. See Freeman, *Washington*, IV, 446-49.

29. See Esther Reed to Joseph Reed, June 21, 1777, Reed MSS, Vol. IV. Norriton or Norrington is the present Norristown.

30. Ford, comp., *Defenses of Philadelphia in 1777*, pp. 21-28.

31. W. B. Reed, *Reed*, I, 307-10.

32. At one time Reed wrote to Charles Pettit for the latter's wagon to effect an evacuation of the family if necessary. The Reed family remained at Norriton through the winter, however, though their house was once plundered by the British. See Reed to Pettit, Sept. 14, 1777, Reed MSS, Vol. IV, and Reed to Dennis DeBerdt, May 24, 1778, W. B. Reed, *Esther*, p. 286.

33. Reed to Washington, Sept. 16 and 18, W. B. Reed, *Reed*, I, 311-12.

34. Reed to Washington, Sept. 21 [23], [1777], *ibid.*, p. 314.

35. Washington, *Writings*, IX, 279n.

36. See Washington to General Pulaski (who had been given the cavalry command), Sept. 30, 1777, *ibid.*, p. 288, and Pulaski to Col. T. Bland, Oct. 1, 1777, W. B. Reed, *Reed*, I, 318. During one scouting trip Reed and Cadwalader were mistaken for British officers by a miller who told them where the rebels Reed and Cadwalader might be captured! Marshall, *Extracts from the Diary of Christopher Marshall*, ed. by Duane, p. 132.

37. Reed to Dennis DeBerdt, May 24, 1778, Reed MSS, Vol. V.

38. Gordon, *The History of the Rise, Progress, and Establishment of the Independence of the United States*, II, 523.

39. Reed to Wharton, Oct. 30, 1777, Reed MSS, Vol. IV. See also Reed to Washington, Oct. 23 and 24, and Nov. 16 and 18, 1777, in W. B. Reed, *Reed*, I, 325-28, 335-37.

40. See, e.g., the "Anecdote" sent by James Lovell, member of Congress from Massachusetts, to Gen. Horatio Gates, Nov. 27, 1777, Gates MSS, Box 8, New-York Historical Society.

41. Cadwalader to Reed, Nov. 30, 1777, Reed MSS, Vol. IV; Washington to Reed, Dec. 2, 1777, W. B. Reed, *Reed*, I, 348; Reed to Washington, Dec. 4, 1777, Ford, *Defences of Philadelphia*, pp. 286-91.

42. Elias Boudinot to President Wharton, Dec. 9, 1777, Reed MSS, Vol. IV; Gen. John Armstrong to Wharton, Dec. 7, 1777, copy, *ibid.*

43. Ford, *Journal of Continental Congress*, VIII, 746.

44. *Ibid.*, IX, 1027-28; see also Reed to Wharton, Dec. 10, 1777, Reed MSS, Vol. IV.

45. Lee to Washington, Oct. 20, 1777, Washington, *Writings*, IX, 389n.

46. Ford, *Journals of Continental Congress*, IX, 943-45, 1001, 1018.

47. *Ibid.*, pp. 947, 975.

48. The recollections of Bayard's eldest daughter concerning this winter are given in Wilson, ed., *Memorials of Andrew Kirkpatrick and His Wife Jane Bayard*, pp. 62-63.

49. Ford, *Journals of Continental Congress*, X, 41, 67. Charles Carroll and Gouverneur Morris were added to the committee on January 20.

50. Washington, *Writings*, X, 362n.

51. Feb. 23, 1778, Reed MSS, Vol. V.

52. See the committee's letter to Washington signed by Reed as chairman, April 10, 1778, Washington MSS, Library of Congress.

53. W. B. Reed, *Reed*, I, 363n.

54. Greene to Reed, March 9 and Oct. 26, 1778, Reed MSS, Vol. V.

55. See Reed to Wadsworth, July 27, 1778, Gratz MSS, Historical Society of Pennsylvania.

56. Freeman, *Washington*, IV, 583-86, 618-20. See also Johnson, *The Administration of the American Commissariat during the Revolutionary War*.

57. Freeman, *Washington*, IV, 586-611.

58. Ford, *Journals of Continental Congress*, X, 310, 319, 322, 324, 326, 328, 335.

59. Pettit to Reed, March 5, 1778, Reed MSS, Vol. V.

60. Reed to Charles Pettit, May 13, 1778, and Reed to Dennis DeBerdt, May 24, 1778, Reed MSS, Vol. V. The boy, Reed's second son, was baptized Dennis DeBerdt Reed by the Rev. James Sproat in Philadelphia, March 10, 1779. In 1805, five years after graduating from Princeton, he died at sea. Journal of Rev. James Sproat, Historical Society of Pennsylvania; *General Catalogue of Princeton University, 1746-1906*, p. 111.

61. See resolution of Congress appointing Reed, June 4, 1778, Ford, *Journals of Continental Congress*, XI, 570, Reed to Henry Laurens, June 15, 1778, Emmet Collection, # 888, New York Public Library.

62. See below, Chapter VIII.

63. Reed to Mrs. Reed, June 20, 1778, Reed MSS, Vol. V.

64. See Moylan to Washington, June 23, 1778, W. B. Reed, *Reed*, I, 368.

65. Draft copy, Reed to Charles Lee, July, 1778, Reed MSS, Vol. V.

66. Esther Reed to Mrs. John Cox, July 6, 1778, *ibid.*

67. Washington to President of Congress, Aug. 3, 1778, Washington, *Writings*, XII, 276; Draft copy, Reed to President of Congress, Sept.

7, 1778, Reed MSS, Vol. V; Cadwalader to Congress, Sept. 19, 1778, Ford, *Journals of Continental Congress*, XII, 941.

68. Ford, *Journals of Continental Congress*, XI, 668, 677. Reed's signature is to be seen in the lower right-hand corner of the official engrossed copy, now on display at the National Archives in Washington.

69. See Reed to Mrs. Reed, July 21, 1778, Reed MSS, Vol. V.

70. Ford, *Journals of Continental Congress*, XI, 709-48.

71. Reed to Mrs. Reed, Aug. 16, 1778, Reed MSS, Vol. V. Reed was now renting the Philadelphia home of John Cox, a larger one than that previously occupied by his family. See Reed to Mrs. Reed, July 21, 1778, *ibid.*

72. Reed to Mrs. Reed, Aug. 26, 1778, and Reed to George Bryan, Sept. 2, 1778, *ibid.*

73. See the draft of a report by Reed as chairman, committee of arrangements, to Congress, Sept. 7, 1778, and General von Steuben to Reed, Oct. 5, 1778, Reed MSS, Vol. V; see also General Anthony Wayne to Reed, Oct. 6, 1778, Wayne MSS, V, 103, Historical Society of Pennsylvania. Washington later praised the "good work" of the committee in a letter to Reed of Nov. 27, 1778, Washington, *Writings*, XIII, 348.

74. See Reed to Mrs. Reed, Sept. 6, 1778, Reed MSS, Vol. V; Ford, *Journals of Continental Congress*, XII, 915-1003; and Reed's bill for his attendance at Congress, Gratz MSS, I, 10 (Reed), Historical Society of Pennsylvania.

75. Reed to Bryan, Oct. 12, 1778, Reed MSS, Vol. V.

CHAPTER VIII: INTEGRITY, SOFT WORDS, AND HARD CASH

1. William Eden's Memorandum in Carlisle, *The Manuscripts of the Earl of Carlisle*, pp. 322, 337. This volume will be cited hereafter as *Carlisle MSS*.

2. Stephen and Lee, eds., *The Dictionary of National Biography*, VI, 362-63; X, 14-15, 963-65.

3. See Eden Memorandum, *Carlisle MSS*, p. 322.

4. The text of the instructions is given in Morison, *Sources and Documents*, pp. 186-203. For a detailed analysis of the Carlisle commission see Brown, *Empire or Independence*.

5. See Lord Carlisle to Rev. Elkins, n.d., *Carlisle MSS*, p. 376; and Almon, *Parliamentary Register*, X, 153.

6. DeBerdt to James Kinsey, April 10, 1778, Reed MSS, Vol. V.

7. See Johnstone to DeBerdt, April 11, 1778, *ibid.*

8. DeBerdt to Reed, April 10, 1778, *ibid.*

9. George Johnstone to Reed, April 11, 1778, *ibid.*

10. Reed to Mrs. Reed, June 9 and 11, 1778, *ibid.*

11. See Reed to Mrs. Reed, July 21, 1778, *ibid.* Reed, looking ahead to the reopening of Anglo-American trade after the war, did not want to see DeBerdt, a merchant, forfeit opportunities in that trade by becoming branded as a tool of the war ministry. See Reed to DeBerdt, July 19, 1778, Cadwalader MSS, Box, Historical Society of Pennsylvania.

12. Reed to Henry Laurens, June 15, 1772, Emmet Collection, #888, New York Public Library. A later revelation of Reed's attitude is his letter of July 19 to DeBerdt. Reed opened this letter with the flat statement that the reconciliation DeBerdt sought was unattainable, for "America will endure the Extremity of human Woe before she will ever submit to the Sovereignty of that Power which has so oppressed, insulted and distressed her. My Opinion," Reed continued, "is with my Countrymen fully upon this Point and therefore I cannot give the Commission the smallest Encouragement." Reed stated that he had not and would not see Johnstone "in his publick Character." He told DeBerdt that "the Touch of Corruption has been tried under his Auspices, and to the eternal Honour of my Country as well as Reproach to the Seducers, without the least Success." Cadwalader MSS, Box, Historical Society of Pennsylvania.

13. Reed to Henry Laurens, June 15, 1778, Emmet Collection, # 888, New York Public Library.

14. Reed MSS, Vol. V.

15. Washington to Reed, June 15, 1778, Washington, *Writings*, XII, 59. Reed also showed Johnstone's letter and his proposed reply to Robert Morris. See Reed to Morris, June 15, 1778, Reed MSS, Vol. V.

16. Joseph Reed, *Remarks on Governor Johnstone's Speech in Parliament with a Collection of Letters and Authentic Papers Relative to His Proposition . . . to Promote the Views of the British Commissioners*, p. 13. (Hereafter cited as J. Reed, *Remarks*.) For a wild tale concerning Washington ordering the arrest of Reed for corresponding with Carlisle and Johnstone in cipher, a tale without the slightest basis in fact, see Smith, comp., *Nuts for Future Historians to Crack*, pp. 74-76.

17. In one of the drafts for this letter Reed had expressed his own opinions: "The Day of Reconciliation and Dependence is past and Sovereignty of Britain over this Country gone forever." There remained, he continued, "not the smallest point on which to raise the Superstructure of that Peace which is the Object of your Commission." Independence, Reed said, was "a Principle for which we are resolved to fight, bleed and die and transmit with our expiring Breath to our

Children after us. The Ground, Sir, is irrevocably changed from Taxation to Empire." June 13, 1778, Reed MSS, Vol. V.

18. Reed to Johnstone, June 14, 1778, W. B. Reed, *Reed*, I, 377-78.

19. Van Doren, *Secret History*, pp. 99-100.

20. Lord Carlisle to Lady Carlisle, June 14, 1778, *Carlisle MSS*, p. 341.

21. Van Doren, *Secret History*, pp. 94-96. Carlisle's letter reached Congress June 13 but the reply, signed by Henry Laurens, was not drawn up until the 17th. Congress's answer ended all hopes of reconciliation short of independence. It stated that Congress was not prepared to negotiate anything short of a treaty of peace and commerce and would do that only upon George III's "explicit acknowledgment of the independence of these states or the withdrawal of his fleets and armies." Ford, *Journal of Continental Congress*, XI, 615.

22. June 15, 1778, Reed MSS, Vol. V.

23. Johnstone to Morris, June 16, 1778, *Pennsylvania Packet*, July 21, 1778. Washington later commented that the point of this letter and also of Johnstone's to Reed was evident. "They are, if I may be allowed so to express myself, of a pulse feeling cast." Washington to Henry Laurens, Aug. 20, 1778, Morgan Library. A third letter of similar vein was written by Johnstone to Francis Dana.

24. *DAB*, VI, 331-32.

25. Mrs. Ferguson's sworn statement, Feb. 16, 1779, in J. Reed, *Remarks*, pp. 43-47.

26. Mrs. Ferguson to Reed, June 18[?], 1778, W. B. Reed, *Reed*, I, 385.

27. J. Reed, *Remarks*, pp. 16-17. See also Reed to Mrs. Reed, June 20, 1778, Reed MSS, Vol. V.

28. Mrs. Ferguson to Reed, July 26, 1778, Reed MSS, Vol. V.

29. Mrs. Ferguson's statement, dated Feb. 16, 1779, and Reed's statement are both found in J. Reed, *Remarks*, pp. 19-21, 48-52.

30. Washington to Henry Laurens, Aug. 20, 1778, Morgan Library.

31. J Reed, *Remarks*, pp. 21-22.

32. Ford, *Journals of Continental Congress*, XI, 678.

33. *Ibid.*, p. 694.

34. *Ibid.*, pp. 701-2.

35. J. Reed, *Remarks*, p. 22; *Pennsylvania Packet*, July 21, 1778. It was only "on the plea of personal Favour" that Reed prevented the extracts from DeBerdt's letter being published too. See Reed to Mrs. Reed, July 21, 1778, Reed MSS, Vol. V.

36. Ford, *Journals of Continental Congress*, XI, 770-73.

37. *New York Gazette*, Aug. 26, 1778.

38. *Carlisle MSS*, p. 361.

39. Morison, *Sources and Documents*, p. 189.

40. June 23, 1778, *Carlisle MSS*, p. 346. Carlisle drew up a rather suspicious "List of Governors & Leading Men in the Several American States." Robert Morris was on the list for Pennsylvania, but Reed was not, Stevens, comp., *Facsimiles of Manuscripts in European Archives Relating to America, 1773-1783*, # 71.

41. Peckham, "Dr. Berkenhout's Journal, 1778," *Pennsylvania Magazine of History and Biography*, LXV, No. 1 (Jan., 1941), 88.

42. *Carlisle MSS*, pp. 368, 390.

43. *New York Gazette*, Oct. 5, 1778.

44. *Pennsylvania Packet*, March 9, 1779. An interesting example of Johnstone's carelessness with the truth is found in Benjamin Franklin's letter of March 19, 1780, to Reed, in W. B. Reed, *Reed*, I, 396-98.

45. Reed himself had not revealed Mrs. Ferguson's identity despite orders from the executive council of Pennsylvania that he do so. See George Bryan to Reed, July 24, 1778, Reed MSS, Vol. V.

46. Tom Paine to Reed, Sept. 18, 1779, Reed MSS, Vol. VI.

47. Not all the publicity was laudatory. Joseph Stansbury, a Philadelphia Tory who accompanied the British army to New York City after Clinton evacuated Pennsylvania's capital, had this to say of Reed:

> Of deep resentments, wicked, bold,
> The lust of blood, of power, of gold,
> Possesses alternate sway.
> And Johnstone's bribe had surely won
> Rebellion's pale-faced, matchless son,
> Had Mammon ruled that day.

The admission here that Johnstone *had* offered a bribe is noteworthy. The poem was written in 1779. That same year Stansbury served as emissary to the British for Benedict Arnold. Quoted in Watson, *Annals of Philadelphia and Pennsylvania in the Olden Times*, II, 305.

CHAPTER IX: PRESIDENT OF PENNSYLVANIA

1. Cadwalader MSS, Box, Historical Society of Pennsylvania.

2. Reed to Bryan, Oct. 12, 1778, Reed MSS, Vol. V.

3. Nov. 5, 1778, *Lee Papers*, III, 250. In December, 1777, Cadwalader had written to Reed, in reference to the latter's decision to accept a place on the Pennsylvania delegation to Congress, that "I cannot think as you do with respect to the accepting an appointment in this state. I look upon the present powers established as a most daring and dangerous usurpation; and can never consent to support or even countenance it. . . . I conceive this government can never be changed without another Revolution." Dec. 10, 1777, Reed MSS, Vol. IV.

4. Reed to Greene, Nov. 5, 1778, *Lee Papers*, III, 248, 252. Writing to Anthony Wayne in a similar vein, Reed stated that the Tories "are yet unhumbled and the extraordinary attention paid them by some Gentlemen of Rank . . . has had a very mortifying effect upon the Minds of those who have partook of the public Danger and run all Hazards." Oct. 25, 1778, Wayne MSS, V, 106, Historical Society of Pennsylvania.

5. "Minutes of Supreme Executive Council," *Pennsylvania Colonial Records*, XI, 560.

6. Bryan to Reed, Aug. 21, 1778, and Reed to Bryan, Sept. 2, 1778, Copy, Reed MSS, Vol. V.

7. Dallas, comp., *Reports of Cases Ruled and Adjudged in the Courts of Pennsylvania before and since the Revolution*, pp. 37-44; Reed to George Bryan, Oct. 23, 1778, Reed MSS, Vol. V. See also Loyd, *The Early Courts of Pennsylvania*, p. 126.

8. See Reed to George Bryan, Oct. 23, 1778, Reed MSS, Vol. V.

9. Nov. 5, 1778, *Lee Papers*, III, 250.

10. *Pennsylvania Archives*, 1st series, VII, 21.

11. Reed to Bryan, Oct. 23, 1778, Reed MSS, Vol. V.

12. *Pennsylvania Archives*, 6th series, XI, 344-46.

13. *Pennsylvania Colonial Records*, XI, 535.

14. See Reed to General James Potter, Aug. 12, 1778, Dreer Collection, "Generals of the Revolution," II, 60, Historical Society of Pennsylvania.

15. Certificate # 1661 of Reed's oath and Reed to Bryan, Oct. 12, 1778, Reed MSS, Vol. V.

16. *Pennsylvania Colonial Records*, XI, 595. Brunhouse, *The Counter-Revolution in Pennsylvania*, pp. 56-57, raises the point that Reed delayed that resignation until November 25 in order to canvass which seat offered him the brightest political future. In a letter to General Greene written Nov. 5, however, Reed had stated flatly, "I am in the Council." *Lee Papers*, III, 252.

17. *Pennsylvania Colonial Records*, XI, 625.

18. Brunhouse, *Counter-Revolution*, pp. 54-56.

19. Boudinot, *Journal or Historical Recollections of American Events during the Revolutionary War*, p. 25.

20. Greene to Reed, Oct. 26, 1778, Reed MSS, Vol. V.

21. Reed to Greene, Nov. 5, 1778, *Lee Papers*, III, 248, 252.

22. Reed to Jared Ingersoll, Dec. 15, 1778, Reed MSS, Vol. V.

23. See Gouverneur Morris to Reed, April 9, 1779, Reed MSS, Vol. VI.

24. See Robert Morris to Reed, March 29, 1779, *ibid*.

25. *Pennsylvania Colonial Records*, XI, 633. The *Pennsylvania Packet* of Dec. 5 maintained that the vote for James Read "was prob-

ably a mistake of the writer rather than an intended vote." The vote
for Bryan was undoubtedly Reed's own. He subsequently spoke of
his election as unanimous. See Reed to Jared Ingersoll, Dec. 5, 1778,
Reed MSS, Vol. V.

26. *Pennsylvania Packet*, Dec. 5, 1778.

27. *Ibid.*

28. *Ibid.* See also Joyce, *Story of Philadelphia*, p. 171, and
Drinker, *Extracts from the Journal of Elizabeth Drinker*, ed. by
Biddle, pp. 112-13.

29. See Washington to Reed, Dec. 8, 1778, Washington, *Writings*,
XIII, 382; Greene to Pettit, Dec. 7, 1778, Reed MSS, Vol. V; Wayne
to Reed, Jan. 24, 1779, Wayne MSS, VI, 63, Historical Society of
Pennsylvania.

30. Reed to George Bryan, Oct. 23, 1778, Reed MSS, Vol. V.

31. Macmillan, *The War Governors in the American Revolution*,
p. 92.

32. See Articles 19-22 of the constitution's "Plan or Frame of Government," Morison, *Sources and Documents*, pp. 168-71.

33. May 17, 1781, W. B. Reed, *Reed*, II, 302.

34. Morison, *Sources and Documents*, pp. 165, 169. Three years
was the regular term of office for a councilor, though in the first
council, in order to establish a rotation by which one-third of the
seats would be newly filled each year, four members were given two-
year terms and four others a one-year term.

35. See Macmillan, *War Governors*, pp. 58, 99n., 227, 275.

36. Reed presided for the first time at the council meeting on Dec.
4. *Pennsylvania Colonial Records*, XI, 635.

37. Anthony Wayne wrote Reed, Jan. 24, 1779, that under Reed's
leadership he and his officers hoped to see "Pennsylvania resuming
that rank and Consequence which she is Entitled to hold." Wayne
MSS, VI, 63, Historical Society of Pennsylvania.

38. Konkle, *George Bryan and the Constitution of Pennsylvania,
1731-1791*, pp. 164-65.

39. *Pennsylvania Archives*, 4th series, III, 710-16.

40. *Ibid.*, p. 714.

41. Morison, *Sources and Documents*, p. 170.

42. Hillegas, ed., *Journals of the House of Representatives of the
Commonwealth of Pennsylvania, 1776-1781*, p. 314. Cited hereafter
as Hillegas, *Journals*.

43. *Ibid.*, pp. 354, 435; see also Konkle, *Bryan*, pp. 170, 182-83, 189-98.

44. Hillegas, *Journals*, pp. 339, 341-42, 407. Letters of Reed's
documenting his role in the disposition of another tangible reminder
of the days when Pennsylvania was a proprietary colony, the Great

Seal of the province, are in the Penn-Physick Papers, I, 111-35, Historical Society of Pennsylvania.

45. See Bryan to Reed, Aug. 31, 1779, Reed MSS, Vol. VI; also Konkle, *Bryan*, pp. 175-79.

46. See Richard Henry Lee to Reed, June 30, 1780, Reed MSS, Vol. VII; copies of Reed to Jefferson, Feb. 22, March 14, and May 6, 1781, Reed MSS, Vol. IX; and Jefferson to Reed, June 3, 1781, Emmet Collection, # 14573, New York Public Library.

47. Reed to Trumbull, Dec. 8, 1779, Misc. MSS (Reed), New York Public Library; Trumbull to Reed, March 6, 1780, Reed MSS, Vol. VII. The persistence of this dispute heightened the problem of frontier defense in the contested area: see Reed to the Board of War, Nov. 20, 1780, to Washington, Dec. 19, 1780, and to Col. S. Hunter, Jan. 26, 1781, Reed MSS, Vols. VIII, IX.

48. See Reed to Anthony Wayne, Jan. 23, 1779, Wayne MSS, VI, 61, Historical Society of Pennsylvania.

49. St. Clair to Reed, March 5 and 6, 1779, Reed MSS, Vol. VI.

50. Hillegas, *Journals*, pp. 336-37. These resolutions were enacted into statute law in 1780. See Reed to Gen. William Irvine, April 11, 1780, Irvine MSS, III, 7, Historical Society of Pennsylvania.

51. July 23, 1779, Reed MSS, Vol. VI.

52. Washington to Reed, Nov. 25, 1779, Washington, *Writings*, XVII, 180-84.

53. Reed to Washington, March 12, 1779, W. B. Reed, *Reed*, II, 69-70.

54. *Ibid.*; Reed to Wayne, [March 13], 1779, Wayne MSS, VI, 85, Historical Society of Pennsylvania.

55. See drafts of Reed to Washington, April 25, 1779, and Reed to Gen. Edward Hand, April 21, 1779, Reed MSS, Vol. VI; Reed to Capt. T. Cluggage, June 27, 1779, Provincial Delegates MSS, I, 8, Historical Society of Pennsylvania. See also Shimmell, *Border Warfare in Pennsylvania during the Revolution*.

56. Reed to Washington, draft, April 25, 1779, Reed MSS, Vol. VI. To counteract sentiment against sending troops away from the Pennsylvania frontier towns for Sullivan's expedition, Reed even resorted to publishing an article under the name "Pennsylvanian" in the *Pennsylvania Packet* of April 29, 1779. See Reed to Washington, May 1, 1779, W. B. Reed, *Reed*, II, 97.

57. Washington to Reed, Oct. 4, 1779, Reed MSS, Vol. VI; Hillegas, *Journals*, p. 387.

58. Washington to Reed, Oct. 22, 1779, Washington, *Writings*, XVII, 8. The general also expressed his "warmest thanks" for "your early attention and that of the Assembly to my requisitions."

59. Freeman, *Washington*, V, 138. The British had successfully inaugurated their Southern campaign by taking Savannah in December, 1778.

60. *Pennsylvania Archives*, 4th series, III, 724-25.

61. Brewington, "The State Ship *General Greene*," *Pennsylvania Magazine of History and Biography*, LX, No. 3 (July, 1936), 231.

62. *Ibid.*, pp. 232-41. For Reed's relations with the Continental Navy as president of Pennsylvania, see Lincoln, comp., *Naval Records of the American Revolution 1775-1788*, pp. 113, 147, 178; and p. 313 for data concerning a privateer brig named for Reed.

63. Rossman, *Thomas Mifflin and the Politics of the American Revolution*, p. 170. An earlier statement of the background of conflict is found in Stillé, *The Life and Times of John Dickinson*, p. 225: "To the public and private distress, caused by the scarcity of food and by the nominally high price it commanded, were to be attributed the disorders and disturbances of the public peace which marked the administration of President Reed."

64. Washington to Reed, Dec. 12, 1778, Washington, *Writings*, XII, 383.

65. April 2, 1779, W. B. Reed, *Reed*, II, 79. Washington had expressed his opinion of monopolists, with unusual vehemence, in his letter of Dec. 12, 1778, congratulating Reed on his election as president. "It is much to be lamented," he wrote, "that each state . . . has not hunted them down as pests of society, and the greatest enemies we have. . . . I would to God that one of the most atrocious in each state was hung in gibbets upon a gallows five times as high as the one prepared by Haman. No punishment is too great for the man who can build his greatness upon his country's ruin." Washington, *Writings*, XII, 383.

66. April 11, 1779, McDougall MSS, New-York Historical Society. See East, *Business Enterprise in the American Revolutionary Era*, Chapter VI, "Robert Morris and His Group."

67. April 11, 1779, McDougall MSS. Reed's desire for a sound currency is expressed in his message to the assembly, Nov. 13, 1779, *Pennsylvania Archives*, 4th series, III, 739-43, and in a draft of instructions for the state's delegates in Congress, Feb., 1780, Reed MSS, Vol. VII.

68. Ford, *Journals of Continental Congress*, XIV, 648-57.

69. *Pennsylvania Packet*, May 27, 1779.

70. Nevins, *The American States during and after the Revolution*, pp. 259-60; Oberholtzer, *Robert Morris*, pp. 54-55. See also Anne Bezanson, *Prices and Inflation during the American Revolution 1770-1790*.

71. *Pennsylvania Packet*, July 1, 1779.

72. See Cadwalader's open letter in the *Packet* of July 31, 1779.

73. W. B. Reed, *Reed*, II, 139.

74. Joseph Reed, *Remarks on a Late Publication in the Independent Gazetteer*, p. 41.

75. See e.g., James Thompson, Radical leader in York County, to Reed, June 16, 1779, Stauffer MSS, X, 676, Historical Society of Pennsylvania.

76. Brunhouse, *Counter-Revolution*, p. 75.

77. Philip Hagner's Narrative, copy, Reed MSS, Vol. VI; see also statement of Charles Willson Peale, copy, *ibid.*, and Brunhouse, *Counter-Revolution*, p. 75.

78. See the statement of Samuel Bayard concerning the recollections of his father, John Bayard, as to the "Fort Wilson Riot" made to W. B. Reed, Nov. 15, 1825, Reed MSS, Vol. XI.

79. Peale's statement, Reed MSS, Vol. VI. Esther Reed feared greatly for her husband's own safety at this time. In a letter of Oct. 5 to an unnamed addressee (probably John Cox) she wrote, "I conjure you by the friendship you have for Mr. Reed, don't leave him." *Ibid.*

80. Hillegas, *Journals*, pp. 384, 388.

81. Bernard Dougherty, assemblyman from Bedford County, to Reed, Jan. 27, 1781, Reed MSS, Vol. IX.

82. St. Clair to Reed, Oct. 20 and Dec. 3, 1779, Reed MSS, Vol. VI.

83. Brunhouse, *Counter-Revolution*, p. 77.

84. Hillegas, *Journals*, p. 319; Konkle, *Bryan*, pp. 179-80.

85. *Pennsylvania Archives*, 4th series, III, 735-36; George Bryan's biographer suggests that it was he who wrote the section of the message concerning the college. Konkle, *Bryan*, p. 183.

86. Hillegas, *Journals*, pp. 375, 378-83, 407. Interesting data concerning the action against the college are contained in notes made by Pettit during the debate in the Republican-dominated assembly in September, 1784, on the question of restoring the old charter. Reed MSS, Vol. XI.

87. Draft copy, July 14, 1780, Reed MSS, Vol. VII.

88. See Timothy Matlack to Reed, Jan. 20, 1780, and Jared Ingersoll to Reed, Feb. 1, 1780, *ibid.*

89. See John Cadwalader, *A Reply to Genl. Joseph Reed's Remarks on a Late Publication in the Independent Gazetteer*, p. 46.

90. Hillegas, *Journals*, pp. 246-47.

91. *Ibid.*, p. 234.

92. See draft, Reed to Robert Morris, [March 27], 1779, Reed MSS, Vol. VI.

93. Cadwalader subsequently claimed that Reed, at this meeting, threatened legal action and even the use of his military powers as

commander in chief of the state against those who were publishing attacks upon his character. See draft [April, 1779] of an address by Cadwalader, Cadwalader MSS, III, 21, Historical Society of Pennsylvania.

94. Morris to Reed, March 29, 1779, Reed MSS, Vol. VI.

95. Draft of an address by Cadwalader [March, 1779], Cadwalader MSS, III, 13, Historical Society of Pennsylvania.

96. *Pennsylvania Packet*, March 25, 1779.

97. See Reed's letter to Gen. Anthony Wayne, Jan. 23, 1779, pleading that the officers of the Pennsylvania line "do not suffer yourselves to be the Tools of any Party" and warning them against misrepresentations of the state's political affairs being made by Tories or "misjudging Whigs." Wayne MSS, VI, 61, Historical Society of Pennsylvania.

98. See, e.g., the resolution of the Whig Society of Chester County, March 5, 1779, Reed MSS, Vol. VI, and the letter from "An Impartial Enquirer" in the *Pennsylvania Packet*, March 30, 1779. A "Constitutional Society," formed to defend the government, published its manifesto in the *Packet* of April 1, 1779.

99. Hillegas, *Journals*, p. 396. Benjamin Franklin sent Reed his congratulations from France: "I am glad to see that you continue to preside in our new State, as it shows that your public conduct is approved by the people. You have had a difficult time, which required abundance of prudence, and you have been equal to the occasion." March 19, 1780, Reed MSS, Vol. VII.

100. Konkle, *Bryan*, pp. 186-89.

CHAPTER X: THE WAR ON THE HOME FRONT

1. Van Doren, *Secret History of American Revolution*, pp. 249-50.

2. *Ibid.*, p. 166.

3. *Ibid.*, pp.172-73; see also Bowes Reed to Joseph Reed, March 16, 1779, Bowes Reed to Timothy Mattack, March 27, 1779, and copy of letter from Arnold to Congress, March [17], 1779, Reed MSS, Vol. VI.

4. Van Doren, *Secret History*, p. 174.

5. See the depositions of Jesse Jordan, David Cochran, and John Boyd, Feb. 1, 1779, Reed MSS, Vol. VI.

6. For a copy of this agreement of June 23, 1778, see Reed MSS, Vol. V.

7. Van Doren, *Secret History*, pp. 175-76.

8. See Timothy Matlack to Arnold, October 5 and October [7?], 1778, and Arnold to Matlack, Oct. 6 and Oct. 11, 1778, Reed MSS, Vol. V.

9. See letter drafted by Reed for George Bryan to send to Arnold, Oct. 22, 1778, *ibid.*

10. Nov. 5, 1778, W. B. Reed, *Reed*, II, 39.

11. Van Doren, *Secret History*, pp. 176-77.

12. See Council Minutes, *Pennsylvania Continental Records*, XI, 672-74.

13. Benedict Arnold to the Council, Jan. 25, 1779, Reed MSS, Vol. VII.

14. Draft, Council to President of Congress, Jan. 25, 1779, *ibid.*

15. Ford, *Journals of Continental Congress*, XIII, 115.

16. *Pennsylvania Packet*, Feb. 9, 1779.

17. Brunhouse, *Counter-Revolution in Pennsylvania*, p. 66; Reed directly accused Gouverneur Morris of countenancing and encouraging Arnold, a charge Morris denied. See draft, Reed to Morris, April 16, 1779, and Morris to Reed, April 25, 1779, Reed MSS, Vol. VI, and also Reed to Alexander McDougall, April 11, 1779, McDougall MSS, New-York Historical Society. Outside Congress Arnold won support from the erratic Charles Lee. Writing to Horatio Gates on March 29, 1779, Lee said Arnold was "wickedly persecuted by the President of this abominable State and a Bandetti of ignorant, obsequious, mercenary Clowns, his Satellites, called the Council of State." *Lee Papers*, III, 319. Modern biographers of Arnold continue to reprobate the meanness displayed by the Pennsylvania authorities in their "persecution" of Arnold. See, e.g., Wallace, *Traitorous Hero: The Life and Fortunes of Benedict Arnold*, Chap. XVII. An extreme case of this is seen in the unwarranted statement by James Flexner that Joseph Reed "could have been one of the Jacobins who, during the French Revolution, gleefully counted the heads that rolled from the guillotine." *The Traitor and the Spy: Benedict Arnold and John Andre*, p. 227.

18. See, e.g., William Paca to Vice President Bryan, March 4, 1779, and draft copy, Bryan to Paca, March 5, 1779, Reed MSS, Vol. VI, and a statement, n. d., in Reed's hand of "The Points Stated by the Joint Committee of Council and Assembly . . . to the Hon. Continental Congress," Society Collection (Reed), Historical Society of Pennsylvania.

19. Ford, *Journals of Continental Congress*, XIII, 324, 379, 413-15.

20. See draft, Reed to Washington, April 25, 1779, Reed MSS, Vol. VI, and Washington to Reed, April 27, 1779, Washington, *Writings*, XIV, 448-51.

21. Van Doren, *Secret History*, pp. 192-93, 242; copy, Washington to Reed, June 4, 1779, Reed MSS, Vol. VI.

22. Van Doren, *Secret History*, p. 244.

23. *Ibid.*, pp. 248-49. This charge was cited by Reed's political enemies in Pennsylvania even after Arnold's treason. See John Cadwalader to Reed, Sept. 10, 1782, Reed MSS, Vol. X, and Reed to Cadwalader, Sept. 10, 1782, Cadwalader MSS, II, 34, Historical Society of Pennsylvania.

24. Van Doren, *Secret History*, pp. 249-50; Ford, *Journals of Continental Congress*, XVI, 161-62.

25. Washington, *Writings*, XVIII, 225. A corollary of the prosecution of Arnold by Pennsylvania was another launched, again through Congress, against Arnold's aide, Major Matthew Clarkson. Clarkson had written the council on Jan. 27, 1779, that anyone with the "smallest Ray of understanding" would know it had no right to call him to testify. Reed MSS, Vol. VI. On March 24, 1779, he received a formal reprimand before Congress. Ford, *Journals of Continental Congress*, XIII, 361, 363.

26. See Bernard Dougherty to Reed, Jan. 22, 1781, Reed MSS, Vol. IX.

27. Hillegas, *Journals*, p. 388; Reed's draft of memo on official salaries, [1779], Reed MSS, Vol. VIII. Reed wrote to Dennis DeBerdt, Sept. 16, 1779, of the melting away of his savings. Cadwalader MSS, Box, Historical Society of Pennsylvania.

28. Hillegas, *Journals*, p. 339. See also Reed to Gen. William Irvine, Aug. 8, 1779, Irvine MSS, II, 40, Historical Society of Pennsylvania.

29. Rawle, "Laurel Hill and Some Colonial Dames Who Once Lived There," *Pennsylvania Magazine of History and Biography*, XXXV (1911), 392-400.

30. Journal of Rev. James Sproat, p. 114, Historical Society of Pennsylvania. George Washington Reed, after graduating from Princeton in 1798, made the navy a career. He fought in the Barbary Wars and in the War of 1812. In the latter he was taken prisoner and died of fever in captivity in Jamaica on Jan. 4, 1813. See W. B. Reed, *Reed*, II, 230-33.

31. For embargo proclamations see *Pennsylvania Archives*, 4th series, III, 724, 727, 743. In September, 1780, Reed wrote bitterly of Congress's 1779 policy to Washington: "A few landed men, apprehensive of the taxes on their estates, poured out the public money with such profusion as to force the public bankruptcy, while they frustrated every measure for restoring public credit." W. B. Reed, *Reed*, II, 249. Yet he never lost sight of the primacy of Congress. To Nathanael Greene he wrote on Sept. 2, 1780, that "however Congress may be depreciated as well as their money, they are yet the supreme Power of the Country." Copy, Reed MSS, Vol. VIII.

32. *Pennsylvania Archives*, 4th series, III, 742.

33. Reed MSS, Vol. XI.

34. See Hillegas, *Journals,* pp. 401, 422.

35. *Ibid.,* pp. 450, 453-54, 456, 500-501.

36. See Reed to George Bryan, May 11 and 18, 1780, Reed MSS, Vol. VII, and copy of Reed to Anthony Wayne, Nov., 1780, Reed MSS, Vol. VIII.

37. Reed to Washington, July 15, 1780, W. B. Reed, *Reed,* II, 224. Reed expressed his feelings on this point most forcefully in a letter to Gen. Horatio Gates, May 30, 1780. The derangement of finances, he asserted, was due to "other Causes than Accident. God forgive me if I wrong any one by this opinion. But I am very sure there are some men in our publick Councils who do not regard a Return to Great Britain as the greatest possible evil." Gates MSS, Box 14, # 64, New-York Historical Society.

38. *Pennsylvania Archives,* 4th series, III, 767-74.

39. See Searle to Reed, Feb. 14, March 10 and 20, 1781, Reed MSS, Vol. IX, and Jan. 4, 1782, Reed MSS, Vol. X; also Searle to President William Moore (Reed's successor), July 23, 1782, W. B. Reed, *Reed,* II, 463-65, and Brunhouse, *Counter-Revolution,* pp. 97-98.

40. Hillegas, *Journals,* pp. 563, 613, 618. See Reed's message to the assembly in Feb., 1781, *ibid.,* pp. 567-68, and a draft of an address on the currency (April, 1781), Reed MSS, Vol. IX.

41. Hillegas, *Journals,* pp. 653, 677; Reed to William Moore, Aug. 18, 1780, Reed MSS, Vol. VIII.

42. Ford, *Journals of Continental Congress,* XV, 1371, and XVI, 196.

43. Reed to General Greene, copy, Sept. 2, 1780, Reed MSS, Vol. VIII.

44. Brunhouse, *Counter-Revolution,* p. 85. A different viewpoint is expressed in Macmillan, *War Governors,* p. 135, where Reed is included among the governors who "did everything within their power to satisfy the needs of the Continental forces."

45. See Reed to George Bryan, May 18, 1780, Reed MSS, Vol. VII.

46. Greene to Reed, June 29, 1780, *ibid.*

47. Washington, *Writings,* XVIII, 438-40. Lafayette sent a personal plea in a similar vein to Reed on May 31. Reed MSS, Vol. VII.

48. Hillegas, *Journals,* pp. 502-3; *Pennsylvania Archives,* 4th series, III, 764-65.

49. See *Pennsylvania Packet,* June 27, 1780, and Brunhouse, *Counter-Revolution,* p. 86. This bank was the forerunner of Morris's Bank of North America chartered in 1781 by Congress. See Janet Wilson, "The Bank of North America and Pennsylvania Politics," *Pennsylvania Magazine of History and Biography,* LXVI, No. 1 (Jan., 1942), 3-28.

50. June 22, 1780, W. B. Reed, *Reed,* II, 216.

51. June 29, 1780, Reed MSS, Vol. VII.

52. July 15, 1780, W. B. Reed, *Reed,* II, 227.

53. See, e.g., Reed to William Henry, July 19, 1780, Reed MSS, Vol. VII, and Reed to Mr. Wynkoop, Aug. 11, 1780, Reed MSS, Vol. VIII.

54. July 4, 1780, Washington, *Writings*, XIX, 113-17.

55. July 15, 1780, W. B. Reed, *Reed*, II, 223-24.

56. Irvine to Reed, June 15, 1780, Reed MSS, Vol. VII.

57. See Reed to Lacey, Aug. 1, 9, 11, 13, and 14, 1780, Reed MSS, Vol. VIII. For the council's advice that Reed take personal command see minutes for Aug. 13, 1780, *Pennsylvania Colonial Records*, XII, 452.

58. See Reed to Washington, Aug. 17, 1780, W. B. Reed, *Reed*, II, 238-39; Reed to Mrs. Reed, Aug. 18, 1780, Reed MSS, Vol. VIII; and Reed to Greene, copy, Aug. 19, 1780, *ibid.*

59. Thomas McKean to Reed, Aug. 29, 1780, Reed MSS, Vol. VIII.

60. Washington, *Writings*, XIX, 400.

61. See Reed to William Moore, Aug. 23 and 27, 1780, and Reed to Mrs. Reed, Aug. 26, 1780, Reed MSS, Vol. VIII.

62. Washington, *Writings*, XIX, 440-42; Reed to Washington, Sept. 2, 1780; W. B. Reed, *Reed*, II, 248-49. For an exchange of complimentary addresses between Reed and the militia officers upon their discharge at Trenton see *New Jersey Archives*, IV, 624-25.

63. Sept. 3, 1780, Reed MSS, Vol. VIII.

64. According to the letter of James Lovell, member of Congress from Massachusetts, to Samuel Holten, Sept. 19, 1780, Mrs. Reed died of acute dysentery. Lovell also mentioned that the musician James Bremner was "taken off by the dysentery." Emmet Collection, #528, New York Public Library.

65. See Reed to Washington, June 20 and 29, 1780, W. B. Reed, *Reed*, II, 214-16.

66. See Esther Reed to Washington, July 4 and 31 and Aug. 10, 1780, and Washington to Mrs. Reed, July 20 and Aug. 10, 1780, *ibid.*, pp. 262-65; also Lafayette to Mrs. Reed, June 25, 1780, Reed MSS, Vol. VII.

67. Aug. 22, 1780, W. B. Reed, *Reed*, II, 267.

68. Diary of George Nelson, 1780-81, Historical Society of Pennsylvania. See also Journal of Rev. James Sproat, pp. 141-42, Historical Society of Pennsylvania.

69. Reed to Dennis DeBerdt, Nov. 28, 1781, Reed MSS, Vol. IX.

70. *Ibid.*, Reed to Thomas McKean, Oct. 2, 1781, McKean MSS, II, 26, Historical Society of Pennsylvania.

71. Hillegas, *Journals*, pp. 516-17.

72. Reed to George Bryan, Oct. 5, 1780, Reed MSS, Vol. VIII.

73. Reed to George Bryan, Nov. 4, 1780, and Bryan to Reed, Nov. 7, 1780, *ibid.*

74. Hillegas, *Journals*, pp. 531, 606. A draft of the voluminous report is in Reed MSS, Vol. IX.

75. Konkle, *Bryan*, p. 221. Bryan also became one of the six judges of the High Court of Errors and Appeals, established that same April, with Reed, ex officio as president, the presiding judge. *Ibid.*, pp. 222-28.

76. Hillegas, *Journals*, p. 534.

77. See Reed's "Notes to Form a Report" on the mutiny, Reed MSS, Vol. XI. For graphic descriptions of the line's sufferings before the mutiny, see Wayne to Reed, Dec. 16, 1780, Reed MSS, Vol. VIII.

78. Gen. Wayne and Cols. Butler and Stewart to Reed, Jan. 4, 1781, Wayne MSS, XI, 104 and 111, Historical Society of Pennsylvania. For a thorough study of the mutiny see Carl Van Doren, *Mutiny in January*, especially pp. 78-79 for this development.

79. *Pennsylvania Colonial Records*, XII, 593; diary of George Nelson, Jan. 5, 1780, Historical Society of Pennsylvania.

80. Reed to [William Moore], Jan. 5, 1781, W. B. Reed, *Reed*, II, 310-11.

81. Draft of Reed's report to Washington, Feb. 19, 1781, Reed MSS, Vol. IX.

82. See Reed to [Thomas Barclay], Jan. 6, 1781, Dreer Collection, "Generals of the Revolution," I, 107, Historical Society of Pennsylvania. Collection cited hereafter as Dreer MSS.

83. Reed to [Thomas Barclay], Jan. 6, 1781, Dreer MSS, I, 107.

84. Reed to committee of Congress, Jan. 6, 1781, W. B. Reed, *Reed*, II, 320-21.

85. Reed to William Moore, Jan. 7, 1781, Dreer MSS, I, 108; Van Doren, *Mutiny*, pp. 113-19.

86. Reed to Moore, Jan. 8, 1781, Dreer MSS, II, 61; draft of Reed's report to Washington, Feb. 19, 1781, Reed MSS, Vol. IX.

87. John Witherspoon, Chairman, to Reed, Jan. 7, 1781, Dreer MSS, I, 109.

88. Washington, Wayne, Reed, and the Congress were all fearful that the mutineers might march to join the British at New York. Van Doren, *Mutiny*, pp. 127-28.

89. Reed to [William Moore], Jan. 8, 1781, Dreer MSS, II, 61.

90. Draft of Reed's report to Washington, Feb. 19, 1781, Reed MSS, Vol. IX; Reed to Committee of Congress, Jan. 8, 1781; W. B. Reed, *Reed*, II, 327-29. For the Reed proposals see a copy in the Wayne MSS, XI, 112.

91. See Reed to [William Moore], Jan. 8, 1781, Dreer MSS, II, 61.

92. Reed to Wayne, Jan. 8, 1781, Wayne MSS, XII, 10.

93. Mason told his captors of a plan to capture Washington. An echo of this appeared in a letter to Reed from Governor William Livingston of New Jersey, April 11, 1781. Livingston reported receiving word from Washington of a scheme to capture or assassinate the latter, himself, Reed, and some fourth American leader. Reed MSS, Vol. IX. No such plot materialized. For the trial and execution of Mason and Ogden see Van Doren, *Mutiny*, pp. 152-58.

94. Van Doren, *Mutiny*, pp. 195-98.

95. See *Pennsylvania Colonial Records*, XII, 602. A copy of Reed's broadside withdrawing the subscription is in Reed MSS, Vol. IX.

96. See Reed to the Auditors, Jan. 23 and Feb. 5, 1781, Reed MSS, Box 1.

97. Van Doren, *Mutiny*, pp. 201-2, 232-33. See also Samuel Atlee to Reed, Jan. 16, 1781, Reed MSS, Vol. IX.

98. Van Doren, *Mutiny*, pp. 196-99.

99. Writing to Reed and Potter on March 21, 1781, Washington thanked them for their report on the mutiny (draft copy, Feb. 19, 1781, Reed MSS, Vol. IX) and commented: "Sensible that circumstances was indeed critical, and that the greatest address and prudence were necessary on the occasion, I was happy to learn you were employed in settling those disturbances. I have now to thank you for the trouble you have taken in the affair; in the situation matters then were, I am persuaded what was then done was for the best and nothing now remains but to use every exertion to replace the Men who were discharged." Washington, *Writings*, XXI, 348.

100. See Reed to Gen. Irvine, Jan. 27, 1781, Irvine MSS, IV, 23, Historical Society of Pennsylvania; Reed's "Notes to Form a Report" on the army, n. d., Reed MSS, Vol. XI; and Reed to the Auditors, Feb. 5, 1781, Reed MSS, Box 1.

101. Draft, Reed to Wayne, June 13, 1781, Reed MSS, Vol. IX.

102. Thomas Moore to Reed, July 4, 1781, *ibid.*

103. Hillegas, *Journals*, pp. 580-81. The report was made on March 2.

104. *Ibid.*, pp. 657, 661-63; see also the draft of the protest of Reed and Potter, March 16, 1781, in the Reed MSS, Vol. IX.

105. Greene's letter was issued March 26, 1779. A copy is in Reed MSS, Vol. VI. Reed had complained to Greene about some deputies "openly hostile to the authority of the State" as early as November, 1778. See Reed to Greene, Nov. 5, 1778, *Lee Papers*, III, 247-49.

106. Pettit to Reed, Dec. 4, 1780, Reed to Pettit, Dec. 8, 1780, Reed MSS, Vol. VIII.

107. Pettit to Reed, Jan. 20, 1781, Reed to Pettit, Jan. 26, 1781, Reed MSS, Vol. IX.

108. See Washington to Reed, May 5 and 27, June 7 and 15, 1781, Washington, *Writings*, XXII, 45-50, 117-18, 171, 223-24.

109. Jefferson to Reed, April 10, 1781, Reed MSS, Vol. IX. See Greene to Reed, Nov. 1, 1780, Reed MSS, Vol. VIII, for an appeal for aid from the general.

110. Hillegas, *Journals*, pp. 654-55. See also Reed to Washington, May 17, 1781, W. B. Reed, *Reed*, II, 301, and a copy of Reed to Washington, June 6, 1781, Reed MSS, Vol. IX.

111. Hillegas, *Journals*, pp. 674-75. Reed may have been spurred on to send this sharp second message to the assembly by the receipt of a letter of June 15 from Washington: "From your Excellency's Zeal Inclination I have every Thing to expect and shall anxiously wait to hear how your Recommendations have been received and seconded by the legislature." Gratz MSS, I, 31, Historical Society of Pennsylvania. Reed voiced his thoughts on the legislature very bluntly to Greene in a letter written June 16. That body, he stated, "seduced from their duty by the vile popularity which every great and good mind must despise, dare not attempt anything vigorous, and where authority ought to supply the place of enthusiasm, and support private virtue, we behold it dwindled to a shadow." Copy, Reed MSS, Vol. IX.

112. June 26 and June 18, 1781, W. B. Reed, *Reed*, II, 354n.

113. Freeman, *Washington*, V, 301-2, 317-19. Reed, on Aug. 28, laid an embargo on all river craft of or under one hundred tons to permit their use in ferrying the armies and transporting supplies. *Pennsylvania Archives*, 4th series, III, 821. See also *Pennsylvania Packet*, Sept. 9, 1781.

114. Thomas McKean, President of Congress, to Reed, Sept. 11, 1781, McKean MSS, I, 106, Historical Society of Pensylvania.

115. *Pennsylvania Colonial Records*, XIII, 53; Reed to Col. J. Carpenter, Oct. 3, 1781, Society Collection (Reed), Historical Society of Pennsylvania; Reed to Gen. John Lacey, Oct. 8, 1781, Reed MSS, Vol. IX.

116. Brunhouse, *Counter-Revolution*, pp. 104-7.

117. *Pennsylvania Colonial Records*, XIII, 112.

118. He presided for the last time at the council meeting on October 8. *Ibid.*, p. 76.

CHAPTER XI: GREAT AND BITTER FRUITS

1. Aug. 14, 1780, Wayne MSS, X, 49, Historical Society of Pennsylvania.

2. June 16, 1781, copy, Reed MSS, Vol. IX.

3. Nov. 1, 1781, copy, *ibid.*

4. Brunhouse, *Counter-Revolution*, p. 338. Reed led the unsuc-

cessful Radical ticket, but the Republicans captured all Philadelphia's seats.

5. See copy of Reed to Greene, Nov. 1, 1781, in which Reed mentions Greene's letter to Pettit "of about two months ago, very expressive of your partiality to me on this subject." See also Greene to Pettit, Aug. 29, 1782, in which Greene "cannot help lamenting Mr. Reed's not getting the appointment." Reed MSS, Vols. IX, X.

6. Copy, Reed to Greene, Nov. 1, 1781, Reed MSS, Vol. IX.

7. Ford, *Journals of Continental Congress*, XXI, 1087. For the creation of the post by Congress see *ibid.*, XIX, 126.

8. Copy, Reed to Greene, Nov. 1, 1781, Reed MSS, Vol. IX.

9. Morris to Reed, July 4, 1781, Society Collection (Morris), Historical Society of Pennsylvania.

10. Copy, Reed to Greene, Nov. 1, 1781, Reed MSS, Vol. IX.

11. Reed to George Bryan, Dec. 25, 1782, Reed MSS, Vol. X.

12. Ford, *Journals of Continental Congress*, XXIII, 759, 819, 824, 869.

13. Reed to Bryan, Dec. 25, 1782, Reed MSS, Vol. X.

14. See Jared Ingersoll, Sr. to Reed asking Reed's advice on his son's studies, July 20, 1772, Reed MSS, Vol. II; Jared Ingersoll, Jr. to Reed from Paris, June 17, 1778; and Reed to Jared Ingersoll, Sr., Dec. 15, 1778, Reed MSS, Vol. V.

15. Binney, "The Leaders of the Old Bar of Philadelphia," *Pennsylvania Magazine of History and Biography*, XIV, No. 3 (1890), pp. 223-28. Ingersoll became one of Pennsylvania's delegates to the federal Constitutional Convention of 1787.

16. *Ibid.*, p. 228.

17. See Konkle, *Bryan*, pp. 240-41.

18. See Reed to George Bryan, May 23, 1782, Reed MSS, Vol. X.

19. Owen Biddle to Reed, Oct. 21, 1782, *ibid.* Reed had a law library numbering 227 volumes valued at £302 in March, 1785. Reed MSS, Vol. XI.

20. Nov. 28, 1781, Reed MSS, Vol. IX.

21. Joseph Reed's Will, Dec. 2, 1783, Reed MSS, Vol. X. Reed's elder sons reversed the careers set forth herein. Joseph became the attorney, and Dennis, in the brief five years he lived after graduating from college, the businessman.

22. See Charles Pettit to Reed, Feb. 13 and April 18, 1784, Reed MSS, Vol. XI.

23. Eberlein and Hubbard, *Portrait of a Colonial City, Philadelphia, 1670-1838*, pp. 493-94. The executors of Reed's estate sold the property to Edward Burd in 1793. Burd called the estate "Ormiston." The house, with changes made by him, is still standing in what is now Fairmount Park, Philadelphia.

24. Copy, Society Collection (Wilkinson), Historical Society of Pennsylvania.

25. Wilkinson to Reed, Jan. 15, 1783, *ibid.* See also Jacobs, *Tarnished Warrior: Major-General James Wilkinson*, pp. 59, 67-68.

26. Reed to Wilkinson, Jan. 16 and 18, 1783, Society Collection (Wilkinson), Historical Society of Pennsylvania.

27. Second Presbyterian Church, Minutes of the Corporation, 1772-1805, typed transcript, pp. 60, 64-67, Presbyterian Historical Society, Philadelphia.

28. Lesley, comp., *Early Proceedings of the American Philosophical Society*, pp. 101, 110, 114, 116, 129.

29. Copy, June 16, 1781, Reed MSS, Vol. IX.

30. Aug. 6, 1781, *ibid.*

31. Reed MSS, Vol. XI.

32. For this Radical strategy see the article by "An Enemy to Aristocracy" in *Pennsylvania Gazette*, Jan. 15, 1783. See also Benjamin Rush to John Montgomery, Oct. 15, 1782, Rush MSS, Library Company of Philadelphia.

33. See above, Chapter IX.

34. *Pennsylvania Colonial Records,* XIII, 79; *Pennsylvania Archives,* 1st series, IX, 434. For the text of Article IX see Morison, *Sources and Documents*, pp. 182-83.

39. Ford, *Journals of Continental Congress*, XIII, 528-29. The judges received their commissions from President John Hanson of Congress on Aug. 28, 1782. *Ibid.,* p. 533. Reed and the other agents for Pennsylvania had been appointed June 19. *Pennsylvania Colonial Records*, XIII, 310.

36. See the minutes of the court, incorporated in their final report to Congress, Jan. 3, 1783. Ford, *Journals of Continental Congress*, XXIV, 7-9.

37. *Ibid.,* pp. 11-23.

38. See Nevins, *American States during and after the American Revolution*, p. 586.

39. Reed MSS, Vol. X.

40. Reed to Bryan, Dec. 20, 1782, *ibid.*; Ford, *Journal of Continental Congress*, XXIV, 28-30.

41. Dec. 25, 1782, Reed MSS, Vol. X. Notes on Johnson's argument are in this volume of the Reed MSS.

42. Ford, *Journals of Continental Congress*, XXIV, 32.

43. *Pennsylvania Colonial Records*, XIII, 474-75. Connecticut accepted the decision, but mishandling of the Connecticut settlers already in the valley by Pennsylvania officials, as well as the recalcitrance of these settlers to accept the new status, prevented a peaceful and equitable solution of private titles to land there for five years.

44. The queries are reprinted in John Cadwalader, *A Reply to General Joseph Reed's Remarks on a Late Publication in the Independent Gazetteer*, pp. 9-10.

45. April 26, 1783, Cadwalader MSS, II, 67, Historical Society of Pennsylvania.

46. Washington to Reed, Sept. 15, 1782, Washington, *Writings*, XXV, 159-60.

47. April 3, 1783, Reed MSS, Vol. X.

48. April 23, 1783, *ibid.*

49. Brunhouse, *Counter-Revolution*, p. 123.

50. *Freeman's Journal*, Aug. 7 and 21, 1782.

51. Brunhouse, *Counter-Revolution*, pp. 124, 267.

52. "Brutus" in *Independent Gazetteer*, Sept. 7, 1782.

53. Draft copy, Sept. 11, 1782, Reed MSS, Vol. X.

54. Reed to Cadwalader, Sept. 11, 1782, Cadwalader MSS, II, 32.

55. Cadwalader to Reed, Sept. 10, 1782, Reed MSS, Vol. X.

56. Reed to Cadwalader, Sept. 10, 1782, Cadwalader MSS, II, 34.

57. See Cadwalader to Reed, Sept. 12, 1782, Reed MSS, Vol. X.

58. See *Freeman's Journal*, Sept. 11, 1782.

59. Reed to Cox, Sept. 9, 1782, Reed MSS, Vol. X.

60. Reed to Washington, draft copy, Sept. 11, 1782, *ibid.*

61. Shippen to Reed, Sept. 12, 1782, Smith to Reed, Sept. 13, 1782, *ibid.*

62. Washington to Reed, Sept. 15, 1782, Washington, *Writings*, XXV, 159-60.

63. Cadwalader to Reed, Sept. 12, 1782, Reed MSS, Vol. X.

64. Reed to Cadwalader, Sept. 14, 1782, draft copy, *ibid.*

65. Reed to Cadwalader, Sept. 23, 1782, Cadwalader MSS, II, 36.

66. Cadwalader to Reed, Sept. 30, 1782, Reed MSS, Vol. X.

67. Cadwalader to Clymer, Sept. 30, 1782, draft copy, Cadwalader MSS, II, 37.

68. Deposition of Hon. John Cox, Esquire, Vice President of New Jersey, Oct. 20, 1782, Reed MSS, Vol. X.

69. Deposition of Bowes Reed, Oct. 23, 1782, *ibid.*

70. Deposition of Daniel Ellis, Oct. 23, 1783, *ibid.* For the Donop-Reed episode, see above, Chapter VI.

71. Undated memorandum, Reed MSS, Vol. X.

72. Feb. 26, 178[3], *Pennsylvania Magazine of History and Biography*, V, 107.

73. Greene to Reed, April 23, 1783, Reed MSS, Vol. X.

74. Dickinson was chosen president on November 7, 1782, in the first contest for that position since the organization of the council in 1777. He won with 41 votes to 32 for the Radical candidate, General James Potter. *Pennsylvania Colonial Records*, XIII, 413.

75. See Brunhouse, *Counter-Revolution*, pp. 124-25, and Benjamin Rush to John Montgomery, Nov. 26, 1782, Rush MSS, Library Company of Philadelphia.

76. Reed to Bryan, Dec. 25, 1782, Reed MSS, Vol. X. Nothing among the Reed manuscripts sustains the suspicion that Reed was "Valerius."

77. Morison, *Sources and Documents*, pp. 175-76.

78. Brunhouse, *Counter-Revolution*, p. 125.

79. See *Pennsylvania Gazette*, Jan. 1, 1783; Reed's protest to Dickinson, Jan. 4, 1783, and the latter's reply promising rectification, Jan. 6, 1783, Logan Papers, VIII, 93, Historical Society of Pennsylvania; and *Pennsylvania Gazette*, Jan. 8, 1783.

80. Hamilton to Cadwalader, March 14, 1783, Cadwalader MSS, Box.

81. The originals of all these letters and statements (the Hamilton letter excepted) are in Vol. II of the Cadwalader MSS. An interesting contemporary diary notation indicating that Cadwalader too thought the situation "very gloomy" on Dec. 22, 1776, was made by a Delaware militia officer who spoke to the former that day. See T. Rodney, *Diary . . . 1776-77*, ed. by C. Rodney, p. 19.

82. Cadwalader, *Reply to General Joseph Reed*, p. 52.

83. See Morgan to Cadwalader, April 17, 1783, and draft copy, Cadwalader to Gen. Armand, April 18, 1783, Cadwalader MSS, II, 65, 66.

84. Draft copy of this article, Aug. 16, 1783, Reed MSS, Vol. X.

85. See, e.g., note 16, Chapter VIII above.

86. For the controversy in historiography see "The Valley Forge Letters" in the Philadelphia *Evening Journal*, Sept. 19, 23, and 25, and Oct. 1, 5, 24, and 31, 1842; H. Smith, comp., *Nuts for Future Historians to Crack*; Bancroft, *History of the U. S.*, IX, 299; W. B. Reed, *President Reed of Pennsylvania. A Reply to Mr. George Bancroft and Others*; Bancroft, *Joseph Reed: A Historical Essay*; W. B. Reed, *A Rejoinder to Mr. Bancroft's Historical Essay on President Reed*; B. Rush, *William B. Reed . . . Expert in the Art of Exhumation of the Dead*; [J. G. Johnson], *A Criticism of Mr. Wm. B. Reed's Aspersions on the Character of Dr. Benjamin Rush*; Stryker, *The Reed Controversy*; Eliot, *The Patriotism of Joseph Reed*; and this writer's "Was Joseph Reed Disloyal?," *William and Mary Quarterly*, VIII, No. 3 (July, 1951).

87. Copy, March 14, 1783, Reed MSS, Vol. X.

88. Undated and unaddressed draft, *ibid*. The Republicans won a majority in the council of censors but lacked the two-thirds majority necessary to call a constitutional convention. The Republican program for changes was so extreme that the second session of the council in 1784 saw the Radicals gain numerical superiority after winning

elections to fill vacancies. On Sept. 16, 1784, the censors voted down the call for a new convention. See Brunhouse, *Counter-Revolution*, pp. 156-63. Reed proved a correct prophet when he wrote William Bradford on May 2, 1784, that the Republicans "by aiming at too much . . . will probably lose the opportunity of doing anything." Reed MSS, Vol. XI.

89. See draft, Nov. 27, 1783, Reed to (Elias Boudinot), Reed MSS, Vol. X.

90. See Reed to Dennis DeBerdt, April 8, 1782, *ibid.*

91. *Ibid.*; see also DeBerdt to Reed, May 3, 1783, *ibid.*

92. See extract from trustee minutes in W. B. Reed, *Reed*, II, 398-99; see also Collins, *President Witherspoon*, II, 138-39.

93. See, as examples of Reed's letters warning trespassers, drafts of Reed to William Smith of Tuckaho Mills, Dec. 8, 1781, and Reed to John Woodruff, John Dean, and Philip Dean, sawmill operators, Dec. 8, 1781, Reed Letterbook, pp. 143-44, Reed MSS.

94. See draft of Reed to William Lane (Chairman of the West Jersey Society in England), March 1, 1782, Reed Letterbook, pp. 152-53, and Hillegas, *Journals*, pp. 683, 691-97.

95. See Reed to DeBerdt, April 2, 1782, Reed MSS, Vol. X.

96. See draft of notice by Reed, Nov. 26, 1783, and Reed's will, Dec. 2, 1783, *ibid.*

97. Greene to Rochambeau and Greene to D'Esting, Nov. 9, 1783, *ibid.*

98. See Adams to Reed, Feb. 11, 1784, and Jay to Reed, Feb. 20, 1784, Reed MSS, Vol. XI. Reed was also in contact with Franklin while in Europe. See Reed to Thomas Barclay, April 20, 1784, Society Collection (Reed), Historical Society of Pennsylvania.

99. Collins, *President Witherspoon*, II, 139-43. DeBerdt and others in London tried to carry on the campaign in England after Reed and Witherspoon returned to America, but with very little success. See DeBerdt to Reed, Feb. 7, 1785, Reed MSS, Vol. XI.

100. Reed to Nathanael Greene, Feb. 12, 1784, copy, and Reed to his son Joseph, May 2, 1784, Reed MSS, Vol. XI. See also Dr. James Hall to Benjamin Rush, London, April 5, 1784, Rush MSS, Library Company of Philadelphia.

101. Reed to R. Morris of New York, June 8, 1784, Reed MSS, Vol. XI.

102. *Ibid.* Morris was appointed the new agent for the society while Reed was in England.

103. See Reed to Jeremiah Wadsworth, March 15 and 17, 1784, and Reed to William Bingham, March 16 and 21, 1784, Reed Letterbook, pp. 174-181, Reed MSS.

104. Reed to Dennis DeBerdt, Oct. 30, 1784, Reed MSS, Vol. XI.

105. Feb. 12, 1784, copy, *ibid.*

106. Feb. 21, 1784, *ibid.*

107. May 2, 1784, *ibid.* See also Reed to William Bell of Philadelphia, Feb. 13, 1784, Princeton University MSS (General), Princeton University Library.

108. See Pettit to Reed, Feb. 13, April 23, and May 27, 1784, Reed MSS, Vol. XI.

109. May 2, 1784, *ibid.*

110. Reed to Bradford, May 2, 1784, *ibid.*

111. See Pettit to Reed, Feb. 13, April 18 and May 27, 1784, *ibid.*

112. Reed to DeBerdt, Oct. 2 and 8, 1784, *ibid.* Reed's sister died shortly after him in 1785. His eldest son Joseph was taken into Jared Ingersoll's family. Martha remained for a number of years in England with the DeBerdts. Esther, Dennis, and George were raised by Charles Pettit and Bowes Reed. See Reed's will, Dec. 2, 1783, Reed MSS, Vol. X, and the accounts, 1785-92, of his executors (Pettit, Ingersoll, and Bowes Reed), *ibid.*

113. Reed to DeBerdt, Oct. 8, 1784, Reed MSS, Vol. XI.

114. Brunhouse, *Counter-Revolution*, p. 164.

115. Reed to DeBerdt, Oct. 17, 1784, Reed MSS, Vol. XI.

116. See the official notification of Reed's election signed by John Bayard, the Speaker, Nov. 16, 1784, *ibid.*

117. Brunhouse, *Counter-Revolution*, p. 165.

118. W. B. Reed, *Reed*, II, 415.

119. Second Presbyterian Church Register Book, "Register of Burials in the Second Presbyterian Burial Ground," p. 171, Presbyterian Historical Society, Philadelphia. In 1868 the remains in the churchyard were disinterred. Those of the Reed family were moved to Laurel Hill Cemetery in northern Philadelphia. The new graves of Reed, his wife, and their daughter Esther were marked by a stone which includes this inscription: "Joseph Reed—Washington's First Secretary—President of Pennsylvania—Signer of the Articles of Confederation—Born 1741—Died 1785."

Bibliography

PRIMARY SOURCES

MANUSCRIPTS

Bradford, William, Jr. Papers. Wallace Collection, Volumes I and III. Historical Society of Pennsylvania, Philadelphia.

Burlington County, New Jersey. Minutes of the Court of Quarter Sessions of the Peace, 1764-1787. County Clerk's Office, Mount Holly.

Burr, Rev. Dr. Aaron. Account Book, 1752-1758. Library, Princeton University.

Cadwalader, John. Papers. Volumes I-III and Box. Historical Society of Pennsylvania. Volume II is devoted almost exclusively to manuscripts of the Cadwalader-Reed controversy.

Dreer Collection, "Generals of the Revolution," Volumes I and II. Historical Society of Pennsylvania.

Duane, James. Papers. New-York Historical Society.

Emmet Collection. New York Public Library.

Etting Collection, "Generals of the Revolution." Contains several Reed letters. Historical Society of Pennsylvania.

First Presbyterian Church, Trenton, New Jersey. Verbatim Copy of All Charters, Deeds, Records, and Manuscripts in the Archives. Verbatim Copy of the Minutes of the Trustees, 1757-1857.

Gates, Horatio. Papers. New-York Historical Society.

Gratz Collection, Volumes I and IV. Historical Society of Pennsylvania.

Historical Society of Pennsylvania. Society Collection (Morris), (Reed), (Wilkinson). Society Miscellaneous Papers.

Hunterdon County, New Jersey. Minutes of the Court of Common Pleas, Volumes IX-XI, 1762-1773. Hall of Records, Flemington.

—— Special Deeds, Volume I. Hall of Records, Flemington.

—— Wills, Folder 118J. Office of the Secretary of State, State House, Trenton.

Irvine, William. Papers, Volumes II and IV. Historical Society of Pennsylvania.

Jacobs Papers, Volume II. Historical Society of Pennsylvania.

Leaming, Aaron. Diary, Volumes III (1775) and IV (1777). Historical Society of Pennsylvania.

Logan Papers, Volume VIII.   Historical Society of Pennsylvania.

McDougall, Alexander.   Papers.   New-York Historical Society.

McKean, Thomas.   Papers, Volumes I and II.   Historical Society of Pennsylvania.

Nelson, George.   Diary, 1780-1781.   Historical Society of Pennsylvania.

New Jersey Deeds, Libers A-B and A-H.   Office of the Secretary of State, State House, Trenton.

New Jersey Supreme Court Minutes, 1765-1767, 1768-1769 volumes. Standard Master's Office, State House Annex, Trenton.

New York Public Library.   Miscellaneous Manuscripts (Reed, Joseph).

Penn-Physick Papers, Volume I.   Historical Society of Pennsylvania.

Philadelphia, Pennsylvania.   Court of Common Pleas Docket, 1761-1771, Ledger of Process Pendings, 1757-1771, Venire Docquet, 1774-1776.   Historical Society of Pennsylvania.

Princeton University Manuscripts (General).   Library, Princeton University.

Provincial Delegates Collection.   Historical Society of Pennsylvania.

Pyne-Henry Collection.   Library, Princeton University.

Reed, Joseph.   Eleven volumes of his papers, 1757-1785, arranged chronologically, with some additional documents and notes collected by his grandson, William B. Reed.   New-York Historical Society.

—— Two college notebooks, 1757, 1758.   New-York Historical Society.

—— Box of seventy-seven letters between Reed and Esther DeBerdt, 1764-1769, arranged chronologically.   The box also contains the inventory and accounts of Reed's estate, 1785-1786.   New-York Historical Society.

—— Copies of or extracts from twenty-eight letters to and from Reed, 1764-1775.   Bancroft Transcripts, New York Public Library.

—— Memorandum of an Agreement between Reed and Charles Read of Burlington, New Jersey, 1767.   East Jersey Manuscripts, # 98, New Jersey Historical Society, Newark.

—— Letterbook.   August 3, 1772-December 5, 1775, and November 19, 1781-November 9, 1784.   New-York Historical Society.

Roberdeau, Daniel.   Letterbook.   Historical Society of Pennsylvania.

Second Presbyterian Church, Philadelphia, Pennsylvania.   Transcript of Minutes of the Congregation, 1749-1772, 2 volumes, and Transcript of the Minutes of the Corporation, 1772-1805, 2 volumes, and Register Book, 1744-1833.   Presbyterian Historical Society, Philadelphia.

Sproat, Rev. James.   Journal.   Historical Society of Pennsylvania.

Stauffer Collection, Volume X.   Historical Society of Pennsylvania.

Thomson, Charles.   Memo Book, 1754-1774.   Gratz Collection, Historical Society of Pennsylvania.

Washington, George. Letter Book, 1775-1776. Library of Congress.
—— Letter to Henry Laurens, August 20, 1778. Morgan Library, New York.
Wayne, Anthony. Papers, Volumes V, VI, X, XI, XII. Historical Society of Pennsylvania.

PUBLISHED SOURCES

Adams, John. Familiar Letters of John Adams and His Wife Abigail Adams during the Revolution. Edited by Charles F. Adams. Boston, 1875.
—— Letters of John Adams Addressed to His Wife. Edited by Charles F. Adams. 2 vols. Boston, 1841.
—— The Works of John Adams. Edited by Charles F. Adams. 10 vols. Boston, 1850-1856.
Allinson, Samuel (comp.). Acts of the General Assembly of the Province of New-Jersey from the Surrender of the Government to Queen Anne . . . to the 14th day of January, 1776. Burlington, New Jersey, 1776.
Almon, J. (comp.). Parliamentary Register . . . 1774-1780. 17 vols. London, 1775-1780.
Annual Register, or a View of the History, Politics, and Literature, for the Year 1778. 3d ed. London, 1796.
Boudinot, Elias. Journal or Historical Recollections of American Events during the Revolutionary War. Trenton, 1894.
Boyd, Julian (ed.). The Susquehannah Company Papers. 4 vols. Wilkes-Barre, Pennsylvania, 1930-1933.
Burnett, Edmund (ed.). Letters of Members of the Continental Congress. 8 vols. Washington, D. C., 1921-1936.
Cadwalader, John. A Reply to General Joseph Reed's Remarks on a Late Publication in the Independent Gazetteer, with Some Observations on His Address to the People of Pennsylvania. Philadelphia, 1783.
Carlisle, the Earl of. The Manuscripts of the Earl of Carlisle Preserved at Castle Howard. Historical Manuscripts Commission, 15th Report, Appendix, Part VI. London, 1897.
Curwen, Samuel. The Journal and Letters of Samuel Curwen, an American in England, from 1775 to 1783. 4th ed. Boston, 1864.
Dallas, A. J. (comp.). Reports of Cases Ruled and Adjudged in the Courts of Pennsylvania before and since the Revolution. 3d ed. Philadelphia, 1830.
Dartmouth, the Earl of. Manuscripts of the Earl of Dartmouth. Historical Manuscripts Commission, 11th Report, Appendix, Part V. 3 vols. London, 1887, 1895, 1896.
Deane, Silas. "Correspondence of Silas Deane, Delegate to the First

and Second Congress at Philadelphia, 1774-1776," Connecticut Historical Society, *Collections*, II, 129-366. Hartford, 1870.

DeBerdt, Dennys. The Letters of Dennys DeBerdt, 1757-1770. Edited by Albert Matthews. Cambridge, 1911.

Drake, Francis. Tea Leaves: Being a Collection of Letters and Documents Relating to the Shipment of Tea to the American Colonies in the Year 1773 by the East India Tea Company. Boston, 1884.

Drinker, Elizabeth. Extracts from the Journal of Elizabeth Drinker, from 1759 to 1807. Edited by Henry Biddle. Philadelphia, 1889.

Durand, John (trans. and ed.). New Materials for the History of the American Revolution. New York, 1889.

Etting, Mrs. Theodore (comp.). "Some Letters of Joseph Galloway, 1774-1775," *Pennsylvania Magazine of History and Biography*, XXI, No. 4 (Jan., 1898), 477-84.

Fithian, Philip Vickers. Journal, 1775-1776. Edited by Robert Albion and Leonidas Dodson. Princeton, 1934.

Force, Peter (comp.). American Archives. 4th series, 6 vols., Washington, D. C., 1837-1846; 5th series, 3 vols., Washington, D. C., 1848-1853.

Ford, Worthington C. (comp.). British Officers Serving in the American Revolution, 1774-1783. Brooklyn, New York, 1897.

—— Defences of Philadelphia in 1777. Brooklyn, New York, 1897.

Ford, Worthington C., and Gaillard Hunt (eds.). Journals of the Continental Congress, 1774-1789. 34 vols. Washington, D. C., 1904-1937.

Franklin, Benjamin. Benjamin Franklin's Letters to the Press, 1758-1778. Edited by Verner Crane. Chapel Hill, North Carolina, 1950.

—— The Writings of Benjamin Franklin. Edited by Albert Smyth. 10 vols. New York, 1905-1907.

Franklin, William. "Letters from William Franklin to William Strahan," *Pennsylvania Magazine of History and Biography*, XXXV, No. 4 (1911), 415-62.

Freeman's Journal, The. Philadelphia, 1781-1783.

Furman, Moore. The Letters of Moore Furman, Deputy Quarter-Master General of New Jersey in the Revolution. New York, 1912.

Graydon, Alexander. Memoirs of His Own Times with Reminiscences of the Men and Events of the Revolution. Edited by John Littell. Philadelphia, 1846.

Hall, Charles. Life and Letters of Samuel Holden Parsons, Major General in the Continental Army and Chief Justice of the Northwestern Territory, 1737-1789. Binghamton, New York, 1905.

Hillegas, Michael (ed.). Journals of the House of Representatives of the Commonwealth of Pennsylvania, 1776-1781. Philadelphia, 1782.

Hiltzheimer, Jacob. Extracts from the Diary of Jacob Hiltzheimer of Philadelphia, 1765-1798. Edited by Jacob Parsons. Philadelphia, 1893.

Howe, Sir William. The Narrative of Lieut. Gen. Sir William Howe, in a Committee of the House of Commons, on the 29th Day of April, 1779. 3d ed. London, 1781.

Independent Gazetteer, The. Philadelphia, 1782-1783.

Kemble Papers, The. New-York Historical Society, *Collections*, 1883-1884. 2 vols. New York, 1884-1885.

Lee Papers, The. New-York Historical Society, *Collections*, 1871-1874. 4 vols. New York, 1872-1875.

Lee, Richard Henry. Life of Arthur Lee . . . with His Political and Literary Correspondence and His Papers on Diplomatic and Political Subjects. 2 vols. Boston, 1829.

—— Memoir of the Life of Richard Henry Lee and His Correspondence with the Most Distinguished Men in America and Europe. 2 vols. Philadelphia, 1825.

Lesley, J. P. (comp.). Early Proceedings of the American Philosophical Society for the Promotion of Useful Knowledge . . . from the Manuscript Minutes of Its Meetings from 1774 to 1838. Philadelphia, 1884.

Lincoln, Charles (comp.). Naval Records of the American Revolution, 1775-1788. Washington, D. C., 1906.

Lord, Clifford (ed.). The Atlas of Congressional Roll Calls for the Continental Congress, 1774-1781. Cooperstown, New York, 1943.

Lydenberg, Harry. Archibald Robertson, Lieutenant-General Royal Engineers. His Diaries and Sketches in America, 1762-1780. New York, 1930.

Marshall, Christopher. Extracts from the Diary of Christopher Marshall, Kept in Philadelphia and Lancaster during the American Revolution, 1774-1781. Edited by William Duane. Albany, 1877.

Mills, W. Jay (ed.). Glimpses of Colonial Society and the Life at Princeton College, 1766-1773, by One of the Class of 1763. Philadelphia, 1903.

Morison, Samuel (ed.). Sources and Documents Illustrating the American Revolution, 1764-1788, and the Formation of the Federal Constitution. 2d ed. Oxford, England, 1929.

New Jersey. Minutes of the Provincial Convention and the Council of Safety of the State of New Jersey. Trenton, 1879.

New Jersey Archives. Documents Relating to the Colonial, Revolutionary, and Post-Revolutionary History of the State of New Jersey. 41 vols. Newark, New Jersey, 1880-1949.

New York Royal Gazette, The. New York, 1778.

Onderdonk, Henry. Queens County in Olden Times. Jamaica, New York, 1865.

Onderdonk, Henry, Jr. (ed.). Documents and Letters Intended to Illustrate the Revolutionary Incidents of Queens County. 2d series. Hempstead, New York, 1884.

—— Revolutionary Incidents of Suffolk and Kings Counties; with an Account of the Battle of Long Island, and the British Prisons and Prison Ships at New-York. New York, 1849.

Paine, Thomas. The Writings of Thomas Paine. Edited by Moncure Conway. 4 vols. New York, 1894.

Peckham, Howard. "Dr. Berkenhout's Journal, 1778," *Pennsylvania Magazine of History and Biography*, LXV, No. 1 (1941), 79-92.

Pennsylvania. Votes and Proceedings of the House of Representatives of the Province of Pennsylvania. Vol. VI (1767-1776). Philadelphia, 1776.

Pennsylvania Archives. 9 series, 119 vols. Harrisburg, 1852-1835. Most useful were: 1st series, Pennsylvania Colonial Records, Vols. XI-XIII for Minutes of the Supreme Executive Council; 4th series, Vol. III, Papers of the Governors; and 6th series, Vol. XI, Election Returns.

Pennsylvania Gazette, The. Philadelphia, 1770-1785.

Pennsylvania Packet or General Advertiser. Philadelphia, 1770-1785.

Philadelphia. Minutes of the Common Council of the City of Philadelphia, 1704-1776. Philadelphia, 1847.

Pratt, Matthew. "Autobiographical Notes of Matthew Pratt, Painter." Edited by Charles Hart. *Pennsylvania Magazine of History and Biography*, XIX, No. 4 (1895), 460-67.

Princeton University. General Catalogue of Princeton University, 1746-1906. Princeton, 1908.

Reed, Joseph. "Narrative of the Movements of the American Army in the Neighborhood of Trenton in the Winter of 1776-77," *Pennsylvania Magazine of History and Biography*, VIII (1884), 391-402.

—— Remarks on a Late Publication in the Independent Gazetteer, with a Short Address to the People of Pennsylvania on the Many Libels and Slanders Which Have Lately Appeared Against the Author. Philadelphia, 1783.

—— Remarks on Governor Johnstone's Speech in Parliment with a Collection of all the Letters and Authentic Papers Relative to His Proposition . . . to Promote the Views of the British Commissioners. Philadelphia, 1779.

Reed, Joseph, and others. Four Dissertations on the Reciprocal Advantages of a Perpetual Union between Great-Britain and Her American Colonies. Written for Mr. Sargent's Prize-Medal. Philadelphia, 1766.

Reed, William B. Life and Correspondence of Joseph Reed. 2 vols. Philadelphia, 1847.

—— The Life of Esther DeBerdt, Afterwards Esther Reed, of Pennsylvania. Philadelphia, 1853.

—— Reprint of the Original Letters from Washington to Joseph Reed during the American Revolution. Referred to in the Pamphlets of Lord Mahon and Mr. Sparks. Philadelphia, 1852.

Rodney, Thomas. "Diary of Captain Thomas Rodney, 1776-77." Edited by Caesar A. Rodney. Delaware Historical Society, *Papers*. Wilmington, 1888.

Rush, Benjamin. Autobiography of Benjamin Rush. His "Travels through Life" together with his Commonplace Book for 1789-1813. Edited by George Corner. Princeton, 1948.

—— Letters of Benjamin Rush. Edited by L. H. Butterfield. 2 vols. Princeton, 1951.

Serle, Ambrose. The American Journal of Ambrose Serle, Secretary to Lord Howe, 1776-1778. Edited by Edward Tatum. San Marino, California, 1940.

Sherwood, Joseph. "Letters of Joseph Sherwood, Agent for the Province of New Jersey in Great Britain, from 1761 to 1766," New Jersey Historical Society, *Proceedings*, 1st series, V, No. 3 (Jan., 1851), 133-53. Newark, 1851.

Smith, Horace (comp.). Nuts for Future Historians to Crack. Philadelphia, 1856.

Sparks, Jared (ed.). Correspondence of the American Revolution; Being Letters of Eminent Men to George Washington, from the Time of His Taking Command of the Army to the End of His Presidency. 4 vols. Boston, 1853.

—— Life of Gouverneur Morris, with Selections from His Correspondence and Miscellaneous Papers. 3 vols. Boston, 1832.

Sproat, James. "Extracts from the Journal of Rev. James Sproat, Hospital Chaplain of the Middle Department, 1778." Edited by John Jordan. *Pennsylvania Magazine of History and Biography*, XXVII (1903), 441-45.

Stevens, B. F. (comp.). Facsimiles of Manuscripts in European Archives Relating to America, 1773-1783. 25 portfolios. London, 1889-1898.

Stryker, William (ed.). Documents Relating to the Revolutionary History of the State of New Jersey. 5 vols. Trenton, 1901-1917.

Sturgess, H. A. (comp.). Register of Admissions to the Honourable Society of the Middle Temple. 3 vols. London, 1949.

Thomson, Charles. "The Papers of Charles Thomson, Secretary of the Continental Congress," New-York Historical Society, *Collections,* 1878, pp. 1-286. New York, 1879.

University of Pennsylvania. Biographical Catalogue of the Matriculates of the College . . . 1749-1893. Philadelphia, 1894.

von Krafft, John C. The Journal of Lieutenant John Charles Philip von Krafft, of the Regiment Von Bose, 1776-1784. New-York Historical Society, *Collections,* 1882. New York, 1883.

Washington, George. The Diaries of George Washington, 1748-1799. Edited by John C. Fitzpatrick. 4 vols. Regent ed. Boston, 1925.

—— Writings of George Washington, 1745-1799. Edited by John C. Fitzpatrick. 39 vols. Washington, D. C., 1931-1944.

Watson, John. Annals of Philadelphia and Pennsylvania in the Olden Time. 2 vols. Philadelphia, 1845.

Webb, Samuel. Correspondence and Journals of Samuel Blachley Webb. Edited by Worthington C. Ford. 3 vols. New York, 1893-1894.

—— Reminiscences of Gen'l Samuel B. Webb of the Revolutionary Army. Edited by J. Watson Webb. New York, 1882.

Wilkinson, James. Memoirs of My Own Times. Vol. I. Philadelphia, 1816.

SECONDARY SOURCES

Alden, John R. General Gage in America. Being Principally a History of His Role in the American Revolution. Baton Rouge, Louisiana, 1948.

Alexander, Arthur. "Pennsylvania's Revolutionary Militia," *Pennsylvania Magazine of History and Biography,* LXIX, No. 1 (Jan., 1945), 15-25.

Alexander, Samuel. Princeton College during the Eighteenth Century. New York, 1872.

Anderson, Troyer. The Command of the Howe Brothers during the American Revolution. New York, 1936.

Appleton, Marguerite. "The Agents of the New England Colonies in the Revolutionary Period," *The New England Quarterly,* VI, No. 2 (June, 1933), 371-87.

Atkinson, Joseph. The History of Newark, New Jersey. Newark, 1878.

Bancroft, George. History of the United States of America, from the Discovery of the Continent. 9 vols. Boston, 1861-1866. Also, Centennial edition, 6 vols. Boston, 1876.

—— Joseph Reed: An Historical Essay. New York, 1867.

Banta, Theodore. Sayre Family. Lineage of Thomas Sayre, a Founder of Southampton. New York, 1901.

Bezanson, Alice. Prices and Inflation during the American Revolution: Pennsylvania, 1770-1790. Philadelphia, 1951.

Bill, Alfred. The Campaign of Princeton, 1776-1777. Princeton, 1948.

—— Valley Forge. New York, 1952.

Binney, Horace. "The Leaders of the Old Bar of Philadelphia," *Pennsylvania Magazine of History and Biography*, XIV, No. 3 (1890), 223-52.

Blackham, Robert. Wig and Gown; the Story of the Temple, Gray's and Lincoln's Inn. London, 1932.

Bolles, Albert. Pennsylvania, Province and State . . . 1609-1790. 2 vols. Philadelphia, 1899.

Bolton, Charles. The Private Soldier under Washington. New York, 1902.

Bowman, Allen. The Morale of the American Revolutionary Army. Washington, D. C., 1943.

Boyd, George. Elias Boudinot. Patriot and Statesman, 1740-1821. Princeton, 1952.

Boyer, Charles. Early Forges and Furnaces in New Jersey. Philadelphia, 1931.

Brewington, M. V. "The State Ship *General Greene*," *Pennsylvania Magazine of History and Biography*, LX, No. 3 (July, 1936), 229-41.

Brown, Weldon. Empire or Independence. A Study in the Failure of Reconciliation, 1774-1783. Baton Rouge, Louisiana, 1941.

Brunhouse, Robert. The Counter-Revolution in Pennsylvania, 1776-1790. Philadelphia, 1942.

Burnett, Edmund. The Continental Congress. New York, 1941.

Burns, James J. The Colonial Agents of New England. Washington, D. C., 1935.

Campbell, John P. "Nassau Hall," in The Princeton Book, pp. 239-45. Boston, 1879.

Cheyney, Edward. History of the University of Pennsylvania, 1740-1940. Philadelphia, 1940.

Clark, Dora Mae. British Opinion and the American Revolution. Yale Historical Publications, Miscellany, Vol. XX. New Haven, 1930.

Collins, Varnum. President Witherspoon; a Biography. 2 vols. Princeton, 1925.

—— Princeton. New York, 1914.

Corner, Betsy. "Day Book of an Education: William Shippen's Student Days in London (1759-1760) and His Subsequent Career,"

American Philosophical Society, *Proceedings*, XCIV, No. 2 (April, 1950), 132-36.

Cunningham, Timothy (ed.). The History and Antiquities of the Four Inns of Court . . . . London, 1780.

Cushing, Thomas, and Charles Sheppard. History of the Counties, Gloucester, Salem, and Cumberland, New Jersey, with Biographical Sketches of Their Prominent Citizens. Philadelphia, 1883.

Davis, William T. The Conference or Billopp House, Staten Island, New York. Staten Island, 1926.

DeWitt, Rev. John. "Historical Sketch of Princeton University," in Memorial Book of the Sesquicentennial Celebration of the Founding of the College of New Jersey, pp. 317-453. New York, 1898.

—— "Princeton College Administrations in the Eighteenth Century," *Presbyterian and Reformed Review*, VIII, No. 31 (July, 1897), 387-417.

Douglas, Elisha P. Rebels and Democrats. The Struggle for Equal Political Rights and Majority Rule during the American Revolution. Chapel Hill, North Carolina, 1955.

East, Robert. Business Enterprise in the American Revolutionary Era. New York, 1938.

Eastman, Frank. Courts and Lawyers of Pennsylvania. A History, 1623-1923. 3 vols. New York, 1922.

Eberlein, Harold, and Cortlandt Hubbard. Diary of Independence Hall. Philadelphia, 1948.

—— Portrait of a Colonial City, Philadelphia, 1670-1838. Philadelphia, 1939.

Egbert, Donald D. Princeton Portraits. Princeton, 1947.

Eliot, Ellsworth Jr. The Patriotism of Joseph Reed. New Haven, 1943.

Ellet, Elizabeth. The Women of the American Revolution. 2 vols. Philadelphia, 1900.

Field, Richard. The Provincial Courts of New Jersey. New York, 1849.

Field, Thomas. The Battle of Long Island. Memoirs of the Long Island Historical Society, Vol. II. Brooklyn, 1869.

Fisher, Edgar. New Jersey as a Royal Province, 1738 to 1776. New York, 1911.

Fisher, Sydney. Pennsylvania. Colony and Commonwealth. Philadelphia, 1897.

Ford, Paul L. "The Adoption of the Pennsylvania Constitution of 1776," *Political Science Quarterly*, Vol. X (Sept., 1895).

—— "Lord Howe's Commission to Pacify the Colonies," *Atlantic Monthly*, LXXVII, No. 464 (June, 1896), 758-62.

Freeman, Douglas S.   George Washington, A Biography.   5 vols. New York, 1949-1952.

French, Allen.   First Year of the American Revolution.   Boston, 1934.

Gordon, William.   The History of the Rise, Progress and Establishment of the Independence of the United States . . . . 4 vols. London, 1788.

Greene, Evarts, and Virginia Harrington.   American Population before the Federal Census of 1790.   New York, 1932.

Greene, LeRoy.   Shelter for His Excellency.   The Story of Pennsylvania's Executive Mansion and the One Hundred Governors of the Commonwealth.   Harrisburg, 1951.

Hageman, John F.   History of Princeton and Its Institutions.   2 vols. Philadelphia, 1879.

Hall, John.   History of the Presbyterian Church in Trenton, New Jersey from the First Settlement of the Town.   2d ed.   Trenton, 1912.

Hamlin, Paul.   Legal Education in Colonial New York.   New York, 1939.

Hartz, Louis.   Economic Policy and Democratic Thought: Pennsylvania, 1776-1860.   Cambridge, Mass., 1948.

Hatch, Louis.   The Administration of the American Revolutionary Army.   New York, 1904.

Hinkhouse, Fred.   The Preliminaries of the American Revolution as Seen in the English Press, 1763-1775.   New York, 1926.

Howard, George E.   Preliminaries of the Revolution, 1763-1775.   Vol. VIII of The American Nation: A History.   New York, 1905.

Ingpen, Arthur (ed.).   The Middle Temple Bench Book.   London, 1912.

Jackson, Joseph.   "A Philadelphia Schoolmaster of the Eighteenth Century," *Pennsylvania Magazine of History and Biography*, XXXV, No. 3 (1911), 315-32.

—— "Washington in Philadelphia," *Pennsylvania Magazine of History and Biography*, LVI, No. 2 (1932), 110-55.

Jacobs, James.   Tarnished Warrior: Major-General James Wilkinson. New York, 1938.

Johnson, John G.   A Criticism of Mr. Wm. B. Reed's Aspersions on the Character of Dr. Benjamin Rush, with an Incidental Consideration of General Joseph Reed's Character.   Philadelphia, 1867.

Johnson, Victor.   The Administration of the American Commissariat during the Revolutionary War.   Philadelphia, 1941.

Johnston, Henry.   The Battle of Harlem Heights.   New York, 1897.

Jones, Edward Alfred.   American Members of the Inns of Court. London, 1924.

——. The Loyalists of New Jersey. Newark, 1927.

Keasbey, Edward. The Courts and Lawyers of New Jersey, 1661-1912. Volumes I and II. New York, 1912.

Kemmerer, Donald. Path to Freedom; the Struggle for Self-Government in Colonial New Jersey, 1703-1776. Princeton, 1940.

Konkle, Burton. Benjamin Chew, 1722-1810. Head of the Pennsylvania Judiciary System under Colony and Commonwealth. Philadelphia, 1932.

—— George Bryan and the Constitution of Pennsylvania, 1731-1791. Philadelphia, 1922.

Lee, Francis B. History of Trenton, New Jersey. Trenton, 1895.

—— New Jersey as a Colony and as a State. 5 vols. New York, 1902.

Leigh, P. B. The Law Student's Guide; Containing an Historical Treatise on Each of the Inns of Court . . . London, 1827.

Lincoln, Charles H. The Revolutionary Movement in Pennsylvania, 1760-1776. Philadelphia, 1901.

Lippencott, Horace. The University of Pennsylvania, Franklin's College. Philadelphia, 1919.

Loyd, William. The Early Courts of Pennsylvania. Boston, 1910.

McAnear, Beverly. "The Selection of an Alma Mater by Pre-Revolutionary Students," Pennsylvania Magazine of History and Biography, LXXIII, No. 4 (1949), 429-40.

McCormick, Richard P. Experiment in Independence. New Jersey in the Critical Period, 1781-1789. New Brunswick, New Jersey, 1950.

Maclean, John. History of the College of New Jersey, from Its Origin in 1746 to the Commencement of 1854. 2 vols. Philadelphia, 1877.

Macmillan, Margaret. The War Governors in the American Revolution. New York, 1943.

Malone, Dumas, and Allen Johnson (eds.). Dictionary of American Biography. 21 vols. New York, 1928-1937.

Marks, Mary A. England and America, 1763 to 1783; the History of a Reaction. 2 vols. London, 1907.

Meigs, Cornelia. The Violent Men. A Study of Human Relations in the First American Congress. New York, 1949.

Montgomery, Thomas H. A History of the University of Pennsylvania from Its Foundation to A.D. 1770. Philadelphia, 1900.

Moore, George H. The Treason of Charles Lee, Major General, Second in Command in the American Army of the Revolution. New York, 1860.

Nelson, William. New Jersey Biographical and Genealogical Notes. Newark, New Jersey, 1916.

Nettels, Curtis. George Washington and American Independence. Boston, 1951.

Nevins, Allan. The American States during and after the Revolution. New York, 1924.

Perley, Sidney. The History of Salem, Massachusetts. Vol. III. Salem, 1928.

Pierson, David. Narratives of Newark (in New Jersey) from the Days of Its Founding, 1666-1916. Newark, 1917.

Raum, John. History of the City of Trenton, New Jersey. Trenton, 1871.

Rawle, William. "Laurel Hill and Some Colonial Dames Who Once Lived There," *Pennsylvania Magazine of History and Biography*, XXXV, No. 4 (1911), 385-414.

Reed, Henry. "Life of Joseph Reed." In Vol. VIII of The Library of American Biography, 2d series. Boston, 1855. This biography is an abridgment of the two-volume work written by this author's brother, William B. Reed.

Reed, Jacob W. History of the Reed Family in Europe and America. Boston, 1861.

Reed, Mary B. A Family Record. Philadelphia, n. d.

Reed, William B. President Joseph Reed of Pennsylvania. A Correspondence between Hon. William B. Reed and John C. Hamilton, Esq. Morrisania, New York, 1867.

—— President Reed of Pennsylvania. A Reply to Mr. George Bancroft and Others. Philadelphia, 1867.

—— A Rejoinder to Mr. Bancroft's Essay on President Reed. Philadelphia, 1867.

Robinson, Fayette. An Account of the Organization of the Army of the United States. 2 vols. Philadelphia, 1848.

Rossman, Kenneth. Thomas Mifflin and the Politics of the American Revolution. Chapel Hill, North Carolina, 1952.

Rush, Benjamin. William B. Reed . . . Expert in the Art of Exhumation of the Dead. Philadelphia, 1867.

Sabine, Lorenzo. Biographical Sketches of Loyalists of the American Revolution, with an Historical Essay. 2 vols. Boston, 1864.

Scharf, J. Thomas, and Thompson Wescott. History of Philadelphia, 1608-1884. 3 vols. Philadelphia, 1884.

Schlesinger, Arthur. The Colonial Merchants and the American Revolution, 1763-1776. New York, 1918.

Selsam, J. Paul. The Pennsylvania Constitution of 1776. A Study in Revolutionary Democracy. Philadelphia, 1936.

Sharpless, Isaac. Political Leaders of Provincial Pennsylvania. New York, 1919.

Shimmell, Louis. Border Warfare in Pennsylvania during the Revolution. Harrisburg, 1901.

Siebert, William. The Loyalists of Pennsylvania. Columbus, 1920.

Stephen, Sir Leslie, and Sir Sidney Lee (eds.). The Dictionary of National Biography; from Earliest Times to 1900. 22 vols. Reprint ed. London, 1921-1922.

Stillé, Charles. The Life and Times of John Dickinson, 1732-1808. Memoirs of the Historical Society of Pennsylvania, Vol. XIII. Philadelphia, 1891.

—— Major-General Anthony Wayne and the Pennsylvania Line in the Continental Army. Philadelphia, 1893.

Stone, Frederick. "How the Landing of the Tea Was Opposed in Philadelphia by Colonel William Bradford and Others in 1773," Pennsylvania Magazine of History and Biography, XV, No. 4 (1891), 385-93.

Stryker, William. The Battles of Trenton and Princeton. Boston, 1898.

—— The Reed Controversy. Further Facts with Reference to the Character of Joseph Reed. Trenton, 1876.

—— Trenton One Hundred Years Ago. Trenton, 1878.

Thomson, Mark. The Secretaries of State, 1681-1782. Oxford, 1932.

Todd, Charles. A General History of the Burr Family, with a Genealogical Record from 1193 to 1891. 4th ed. New York, 1902.

Van Doren, Carl. Mutiny in January. The Story of a Crisis in the Continental Army . . . . New York, 1943.

—— Secret History of the American Revolution. Garden City, New York, 1941.

Walker, Edwin, and others. A History of Trenton, 1679-1929. 2 vols. Princeton, 1929.

Wallace, Willard. Appeal to Arms. A Military History of the American Revolution. New York, 1951.

—— Traitorous Hero. The Life and Fortunes of Benedict Arnold. New York, 1954.

Wertenbaker, Thomas. Princeton, 1746-1896. Princeton, 1946.

Wescott, Thompson. Names of Persons Who Took the Oath of Allegiance to the State of Pennsylvania, between the Years 1777 and 1789, with a History of the "Test Laws" of Pennsylvania. Philadelphia, 1865.

Whitehead, William. Contributions to the Early History of Perth Amboy and Adjoining Country, with Sketches of Men and Events in New Jersey during the Provincial Era. New York, 1856.

Whiteley, Emily. Washington and His Aides-de-Camp. New York, 1936.

Wilson, James G.   Memorials of Andrew Kirkpatrick and His Wife
Jane Bayard.   New York, 1870.

Wilson, Janet.   "The Bank of North America in Pennsylvania
Politics," *Pennsylvania Magazine of History and Biography*, LXVI,
No. 1 (Jan., 1942), 3-28.

Woodward, Carl.   Ploughs and Politicks.   Charles Read of New
Jersey and His Notes on Agriculture, 1715-1774.   New Brunswick,
New Jersey, 1941.

Woodward, E. Morrison, and John Hageman.   History of Burlington
and Mercer Counties, New Jersey, with Biographical Sketches of
Many of Their Pioneers and Prominent Men.   Philadelphia, 1883.

Young, Eleanor.   Forgotten Patriot: Robert Morris.   New York, 1950.

Index

298 Index